Om Swami: As We Know Him

Ismita Tandon is an award-winning poet and author. She graduated from Sophia College, Ajmer and went on to pursue an MBA degree. Ismita has published three novels, one with Penguin and two with HarperCollins. She shares her poems regularly on her Facebook page, *A Lesser Known Poet*. She'd thought she was done writing books as her love for poetry far exceeded her desire to write. Her stint at the Om Swami ashram led her to lead a more spiritual life, compelling her to pen down this book. When not scribbling poems, she spends time with her black lab, Benoo, who much like Ismita, loves vegetarian food and a siesta.

Swami Vidyananda Om grew up in Bangalore. After spending time at an ashram in Bangalore and in Rishikesh, he found his guru in Om Swami. Swami Vidyananda is Om Swami's foremost disciple and was initiated in the tradition of Sri Vidya. An unusually talented singer, Swami Vidyananda is devoted to Swamiji. He lives in Sri Badrika ashram in Himachal in the service of Sri Hari. Swami Vidyananda enjoys singing for Bhagwan and loves eggless cakes.

OM SWAMI
As We Know Him

ISMITA TANDON
AND
SWAMI VIDYANANDA OM

First published in India by HarperCollins India

Worldwide publishing rights: Black Lotus Press

Copyright © Ismita Tandon & Swami Vidyananda Om 2016

P-ISBN: 978-93-5029-737-7
E-ISBN: 978-93-5029-738-4

Ismita Tandon and Swami Vidyananda assert the moral right to be
identified as authors of this work.

www.omswami.com

brahmānandaṃ paramasukhadaṃ kevalaṃ jñānamūrtiṃ
dvandvātītaṃ gaganasadṛiśhaṃ tattvamasyādilakṣhyam I
ekaṃ nityaṃ vimalamachalaṃ sarvadhīsākṣhibhūtaṃ
bhāvātītaṃ triguṇarahitaṃ sadguruṃ taṃ namāmi II

I bow down before my guru who is
Full of transcendental love, bliss and wisdom,
Vast as the sky, realized, beyond duality,
One and only, unmovable, the eternal witness,
And beyond the three modes of material nature.

Contents

BOOK ONE

If they could peep inside a moment of my life
They'd find only you
Flowing like water from one moment to another

Separate to the world
You are the beautiful Moon
I am a bird ordinary

In the dark you dazzle
The sky turns a midnight blue
Little more than a silhouette I call out to you

In grace you've bestowed
A magic so sweet
That a bird may bring the Moon to its knees

Such is your splendour
Your glory, your grace, O moon-faced Lord
May this bird remain forever bowed

Book One
____

THE LOTUS FEET

Ismita Tandon

Just as the lid of a kettle flutters when the warmth builds up inside, I cannot help but share with you that my whole being is bubbling with the life, love and happiness that is Swami's grace.

At one time, not too long ago, my belief in miracles, spiritual power and grace was limited to an acceptance that they may exist. My life was firmly rooted in the material world. After meeting Swami, everything I held to be true about life -- its very meaning -- was challenged, it was reduced to dust. Soon, I had to admit that the universe guarded many mysteries far beyond the scope of my rational mind.

Some of the events described in this book may challenge your own beliefs, and there may even be parts herein that seem quite unbelievable. That's fine. It is natural that you draw your own conclusions as you read. But once you experience His presence for yourself, your view will change forever. That I can promise you.

In any event, this book is not based on second-hand stories or hearsay. In these pages are first-hand accounts of Swami's miracles, the likes of which Swami Vidyananda and I have witnessed on countless occasions. My personal spiritual awakening under Swami's tutelage is detailed in the first half of the book, and I recount here whatever my limited awareness could capture of the time spent in His presence. The second half is Swami Vidyananda's account of his spiritual realization with Swami, after a lifetime of searching.

I hope that you may come to know Swami through our words. His greatness, you may discover here, lies in His simplicity, in not a word uttered in vain or an action performed without care. For Swami is beyond the labels of master or saint. He is the very embodiment of God's love.

If you think that my view is biased toward Swami, then let me confess: it is. Whatever Swami may be to others, He is my everything in the three worlds. He is the Divine that dwells in my heart. Perhaps if you were to witness the sheer power of His omniscience and His divine benevolence, you would feel likewise.

In Swami's Service Eternally,
Ismita

A Simple Monk – Or Is He?

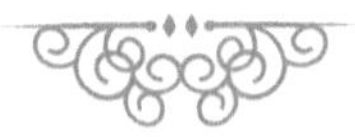

We mess up our lives, sometimes life messes it up for us, and the road home seems hazier than ever. You may even find, as I did, that you are not simply lost. You have been searching, craving direction for most of your life.

I had just walked out of a seven-year marriage. Outwardly, there seemed to be nothing greatly wrong with my life. My husband was a good man; I had known him since my teens and loved him very deeply. But try as I may, I felt little for him. As time passed, the empty space between us filled with an unutterable loneliness, a sadness that I could no longer contain.

Like most childhoods, mine was a mixed affair – a farrago of good and not-so-good memories. Growing up in the shadow of Papa's drinking problem was challenging, to say the very least. Our home was at turns filled with love and laughter and screaming and howling – and sometimes, all of these at once. He was a colonel in the army. Having served for long durations on the border combating terrorism, losing his own men and seeing innocent civilians die had affected him deeply. The worst part, he would sometimes say, was to put down young terrorists who were barely out of their teens.

For nights on end, he would keep tossing and turning in his bed recalling those encounters, calling out strange names and file numbers in the dark. Drinking was his way of coping in this world. And yet, he was as kind and loving as ever. His nation and his family — these were the only two things he cared about deeply. I grew to be a rebellious child; pampered and wilful. I thought it was my right to have everything that would make my life easy. The easier my life became, though, the unhappier I became.

As I was trying to settle down in my marriage, my father passed away. I had a deep but troubled bond with him; we were close, yet his battle with alcohol had scarred my heart irreversibly. In many ways, his struggles with alcoholism had rubbed off on everyone at home. I stifled my grief and pain at his death, and tried to move on.

If only it were so simple. Even though I went sailing with my husband a number of times, the emptiness of my life began to consume me from within. I tried to occupy myself: I wrote poetry, wrote fiction and got published; but the sense of purposelessness only grew more intense.

With time, the tiny chink in my heart became a deep gash. Unable to bear the pain, I separated from my husband and went to stay with my mother, who lived with my brother and his lovely wife. My marriage ended amicably.

Two years passed slowly – a turbulent two years in which I made more mistakes, some of which I could barely forgive. The more I tried to get a grip on life, the more I slithered on its roundabouts. And then the worst of my fears materialized. My mother was perfectly fine one day and then, almost suddenly, I was attending her cremation. I felt that it wasn't just my mother, but my whole world, on that pyre, burning.

Mamma had suffered a silent heart attack, and her kidneys had buckled. She had held us all together for so long and so bravely that her fall was inevitable. She was placed on dialysis and given six months to live. She only lived for six agonizing weeks. Many evenings I drove back from the hospital, crying out loud in the confines of my car, bawling like a mad woman as I rolled along the busy city streets. I had never been more afraid in my life. My mother had been my very strength, and now she would be no more.

There were countless days after her passing when I didn't feel like waking up. It was not just the pain of losing my mother that afflicted me – it was also fear: stark, naked fear of what was to become of me. I had no savings. I had a couple of books published in my name, but nothing more. I had come home to Mamma, thinking that, somehow, life would just work itself out. It didn't. I was more alone than ever. There were days my mind was darker than a dungeon and quieter than the silence death leaves behind. It thrived on darkness, shutting out every source of light, every switch, every comforting thought. It hibernated in nothingness, not always desolate, merely wanting to not want anything or anyone. It was content in its discontentment.

Even then it was not as if I was in any state to take charge of my life. Everything seemed to pile up, one thing on top of another. The loss of my mother, my failed marriage and words unspoken and feelings unexpressed for my father – it was simply too much for me to bear. I felt that my mind was beginning to disintegrate, and I struggled to piece together my thoughts. I would brush my teeth in the morning, and five minutes later I would have absolutely no recollection of it.

There were many mornings like this when I just didn't know where to begin or what to do with myself. I was truly lost. I felt like an explorer, aimlessly wandering over scorched dunes, up and down through the day; darkness falling like a curse at night, swallowing my cries. I tried getting drunk to forget everything. I tried overdosing to erase myself. I even thought of driving the car off a bridge. Every manner of grim imaginings haunted me: they would gather like storm clouds then dissipate, allowing mere glimpses of clarity before their return, darker and more foreboding than before. Only the fear that I might survive restrained me. I'd then have to live with that shame forever.

I missed Mamma; but more than that, I envied her for being free of this world, to be so fortunate as to be beyond the emptiness and loneliness that gripped my soul. I was happy for her. There were none of the usual stages of bereavement. It was, in this sense, much the same as my father's passing away. I don't remember mourning his loss, either – everyone at home was relieved in some way. He was in a better place – this, we truly believed. We had been mourning in silence for over a decade, throughout his slow demise.

Every day I prayed to God, not knowing if He was listening. I would wonder: why wasn't I born in the time of Krishna or Rama? Why was there no God to save me from my sorry life? Who was my saviour? Was it even possible for anyone to drag me out of my misery? I certainly couldn't seem to manage by myself. I would cry myself to exhaustion and try to hug the floor. My only companion at the time was Benoo, my black Labrador. She would sit by my side, and sometimes she would wrap herself around me to give comfort. But there was no respite.

That was when I came across Swami's blog by sheer chance. Or was it destined? His discourses, posts and emails relieved my pain like it had never existed. I wrote to Him and He replied. And in the following months, every time I wrote to Him, He replied. Those were the good early days, when Swami actually had time to read emails and reply to them. Sometimes, a question would play on my mind, but I would not write to Him for fear of bothering Him. But much to my amazement, He would then promptly send me an email addressing the very same question. He wrote as if He was privy to my innermost thoughts.

He would check up on me every now and then to ensure I was okay, too. No one had ever shown me such kindness. Without explanation, He knew I needed support, a pillar for a loose tendril. His emails showed He understood how eagerly I awaited them. No matter how terrible I was feeling, just a one-liner from him and I would be back on my feet, playing with Benoo or going for a run. He had become my reason to breathe.

Needless to say, Swami's entry into my life marked the beginning of my recovery. Soon, I offered to assist in editing His memoir. He didn't need me, but I needed to feel useful, to have a purpose. He gave me that purpose. Working on His memoir was a life-changing event. The mere thought of Him would make me feel like a child, as if I were five and not thirty-five. I felt He was my father, mother, brother – everything.

If His writings and discourses could erase my pain – if the thought of Him alone could bring peace to my heart – what would the real Swami be like, I wondered. I must admit that even though Swami had been a miracle in my life, I still only saw Him as a very intelligent and kind person. Words like sainthood and divinity didn't even occur to me.

Words, anyway, are mere representations of the sadness or happiness you have felt – they can never truly embody those feelings. Neither grief has a face, nor happiness an address, both cut from the same cloth. God's grace, however, is as unmistakeable as it is infinite: it is the warm, sheltering abode that you stumble upon most unexpectedly, and once you step inside, it leads you right to Him. This is how I found my way to Swami's ashram in Himachal.

I finally mustered the courage to thank Him in person, to meet the noble person behind the divine name. That He was a great saint was beyond my knowing. It had not entered my mind that devotees queued up and bowed their heads in reverence at His beautiful feet. This was all new to me -- totally unexpected even.

As children, we went to my grandfather's home in Lucknow for our summer holidays. While our cousins would bow, touch the feet of our elders and do pranams, my brother and I mostly confined ourselves to wishing them good morning and good evening. I may have been polite, but owing to my rebelliousness and shyness, touching feet or doing pranams wasn't really my way.

Now, here in this unfamiliar territory, I saw people crowding in great anticipation outside the humble pravachan (discourse) room, waiting for Swami to arrive. Today was His birthday. As soon as Swami approached, the sea of people parted. Many bowed at His feet, placed flowers at His padukas or touched their foreheads to them, while some simply took his charan-dhooli, dust from His feet, and smeared it on their foreheads. Imbued with his or her own unique sentiment, each devotee offered love and devotion by surrendering at His feet. I just sat with my hands in my lap. I was wearing gloves.

I seemed to have entered an unfamiliar world, but one that was full of love and reverence. It was so different from that which I knew -- an indifferent and often callous world. I didn't know what to expect from Him, for He seemed to be just like you and me in His emails. Well, not exactly like you and me; but a simple, truthful and compassionate person, who had given up a life of luxury for the welfare of mankind. Such a person is rare, though not unheard of, in these times. So while I had great regard and gratitude for Him in my heart, mine was a burning curiosity. I felt inexorably drawn to him; I yearned to see how this young, enigmatic monk really was in person.

The first time I saw Swami, I could barely look at Him. I lowered my eyes. I looked away. His aura was too powerful, too overwhelming for my comfort. Although He exuded love, there was a strange magnetic charge around Him, an attraction that all there in the small, quaint discourse room seemed to feel. In His ochre robe, He was as glorious as the rising sun hovering above the horizon. His dark smiling eyes were like little magnets that wouldn't let you turn your gaze away from. His deep, sonorous voice sang a touching eulogy to Mother Divine. I felt shy. I stole glances; but for the better part of the morning, I just stared bashfully at my palms resting in my lap. It was as if my eyes couldn't absorb His radiance, His tejas. I felt like a child in His presence – a feeling that I experience to this very day when I am with Swami. That is, a much-loved and pampered child.

In the months to come, I had the honour and the privilege to work with Swami on His memoir. The first time I read it, I was continually moved to tears by the simplicity and sincerity of the boy He once was, and the tenacity, rather the divinity of the Man He grew to be. I was so touched that I rushed to a tattoo parlour, and got a truly inspirational line from His memoir, 'Live. Love. Laugh. Give.' tattooed on my forearm. I had embraced this concise, profound revelation; I now had to live it. It is perhaps the simplest credo in the world, and yet how I failed at it miserably and repeatedly, I can scarcely bring myself to say.

I also felt angry at Swami as I read the memoir, for subjecting himself to such unwarranted hardship. I questioned Him a few times, 'What was the need to be at Naga Baba's place, to starve yourself almost to death? Why didn't you just walk away?'

I don't remember His answer. Or maybe there wasn't any -- He would just smile that beautiful, benevolent smile. Time and again, His composure and equanimity -- His understanding of human nature -- would amaze me.

The more I observed Swami, the more mystical He appeared to me. I thought that as I spent time with Him, I would know more about Him and understand Him better, but each day in His presence held surprises. Sometimes, I had the opportunity to sit with Him as He gave a personal audience to a devotee. His uncanny ability to see through people was downright intimidating at times. From accurately telling the location of a mole on a person's clothed body, to misdeeds that they hadn't confessed -- and even significant events of their past and future -- nothing, it seemed, could remain hidden from Swami.

His graceful fingers would entwine in the most secret and sacred mudras (ritual gestures), as He would consecrate a flower or a rudrakhsa (a prayer bead), and hand it to a wailing mother whose child had been sick for days, or an ill person -- or anyone who came with hope.

People would come to Him seeking all kinds of answers, and with all manner of prayers and pleas. These would concern matters as trivial as misplaced car keys to more serious issues, such as life-threatening ailments, tumours, accidents, broken relationships or even the loss of a child.

One incident during my first trip to the ashram left a particularly strong impression on me. It was a Saturday, the day Swami gave audience to the villagers. Two men sat in front of

Swami, their hands pressed together in supplication, requesting Him to end a sudden string of bad luck that seemed to have descended upon them. Ill health, monetary losses and even prison sentences loomed large for them.

The men had been involved in erecting a fence around the ashram premises while Swami was away in solitude. The fencing was stolen by miscreants the same night it was installed. Of their own accord, the men raised the fencing issue.

'The ashram fence was stolen, Swamiji. Some village folk cannot be trusted.'

'And you know nothing of it?'

They shook their heads in unison.

Swami chuckled.

'Since when do you think you can lie to me,' He said gravely. 'You are the ones who stole the fence.'

'No Swamiji, we have no idea ...'

'I'm not asking you, I'm telling you,' Swami said, even more seriously. 'I see you, I see you cutting the wire with your own hands in the night.' Swami's intense and usually mischievous eyes suddenly darkened, and He looked piercingly into the culprits' eyes.

A shadow of fright and disbelief crossed their faces even as their heads hung low.

'I can forgive anything but a lie,' Swami added.

They pressed their palms together and then lay flat on the ground, prostrating themselves before Swami, seeking His forgiveness. I could not read what Swami was thinking at the time. He is inscrutable if He wants to be. His expression was impassive.

'Let Nature take its own course,' He said to them. No one in the room could discern whether or not Swami accepted their apology. He sat there still as a rock, immovable, indecipherable.

The two men left soon afterward, vexed and shaken. A couple who had lost their baby girl to a kitchen fire entered next. He continued meeting people over the next few hours – patiently, and with His usual smiling countenance. Almost all the visitors – rich or poor – brought flowers, sweetmeats, gifts and money. He would return everything, only accepting a flower. Swami wasn't just another renunciant sitting high up in the Himalayas hoping to increase His following or expand His ashram. Nor was Swami explicitly offering hope or remedies to people. He didn't preach about a certain way of life or His own way of life either.

His conduct, I discovered, was His greatest teaching. Unlike many gurus, Swami wouldn't accept material or other offerings from those who visited the ashram. In the last four years, hundreds of people have stayed at the ashram and partaken of the food there, and not once has Swami sought any monetary contribution or assistance. Only in recent times, as large numbers of devotees have descended on the ashram, have Swami's most devoted followers suggested that visiting devotees contribute a small daily fee for their upkeep.

Swami's conduct was universally even-handed too. Whether it was a high-ranking government official or a politician seeking His darshan, or a simple villager, or a businessman with grand ideas about himself, Swami was just the same. I was to learn that, on principle, Swami never asks anyone their profession or status. I noted that many influential people seemed unnerved that their rank and prestige had little meaning in the presence of this unassuming saint.

His Energy

On the third day of my stay, Swami gave me an audience for a few minutes during the afternoon. I remember my elation and that I spoke incessantly to tell him as much as I could in that limited time – so much so, that when I later tried to recall Swami's responses, nothing came to mind. In my excitement, I had barely given Him a chance to utter a word. He might even have been intrigued at the rate at which I could speak, without any commas or full stops. This was the subject of quite some mirth later.

The evening discourse was particularly engrossing that day. A couple of hours passed by in the blink of an eye. It was 9.30 p.m. Swami addressed the crowd and said, 'If you have any questions, I'm happy to answer them, and then we'll call it a night.' The visiting devotees didn't want Him to leave, even after the discourse and the bhajans were over. Someone asked a question and Swami answered him.

All were experiencing the bliss of Swami's presence, and my chattering mind was still. Five minutes later, everyone had fallen silent. Not wanting Him to leave just yet, I asked, 'Swami, I've been reading *Autobiography of a Yogi* and it talks about extraordinary yogic feats. Do they really happen?'

Swami simply answered, 'It's a book that misleads seekers and meditators.'

I was taken aback. Here was a monk whose manuscript I had finished reading not days ago, and it was patently clear to me that He not only believed in supernatural phenomenon, but was capable of performing miraculous yogic feats Himself. Baffled and dissatisfied with His answer, I retorted almost immediately: 'But the instances seem so real. I'm midway through the book. The way Yogananda Paramahansa has described the manifestations of His guru, the simple instances in the book make one believe in the existence of the supernatural. It can't be all untrue.'

Swami appeared a little drawn and tired now. He had been sitting the whole day in the same place, meeting people and speaking for hours. He rose from His asana, and as He slipped His sculpted feet into His padukas, He gave a short reply: 'You are entitled to an opinion, Dolly.'

I felt snubbed. I wasn't trying to make a point, I was merely expressing my view. My mistake was that I had conveniently forgotten that I was in the presence of a saint -- one didn't quiz or debate a person of His stature. It was neither an exchange of ideas, nor was I in the living room of a friend discussing literature. Swami was the source of knowledge there, and His words were chosen most carefully, mindfully at all times. But I didn't know this at that time. Like the Buddha, He would never argue with anyone or try to prove a point.

He stood up and took His leave. 'I'll see you all tomorrow. All of you, please rest. It's been a long day.' Everyone did their pranams and Swami walked out of the room in His usual brisk manner. Though I was disheartened by His answer, it didn't break my heart. What did I care about *Autobiography of a Yogi*, anyway? I was lodged in the small mud cottage with ten to fifteen other devotees. It was the same cottage in which Swami had stayed for three months when He first moved to the ashram.

It was a magnificent night, dark and dazzling with stars; the universe articulate above the mountains. It was freezing, but I braved the cold, and stayed outside to savour the glorious spectacle above. Soon I was alone, and all the lights in the ashram had been extinguished. I felt a little scared to be outside sitting all by myself, so I decided to go back to the cottage.

I had just pushed open the door when I heard voices, travelling clearly through the thin mud walls. 'Why do they ask Swamiji such meaningless questions? It's His time to rest, and they won't even allow Him that.' The other replied, 'Where does this kind come from? Why do they even come?'

They were talking about me. I even recognized their voices, and their faces flashed before my mind's eye. I quietly stepped outside again into the frigid valley air. I stood out on the concreted terrace, looking up at the sky for a long time, crying softly at first and then angrily.

Had I felt strong, I would likely have shrugged off these devotees' indiscreet murmurings. But in my raw, damaged state of those times, their critical words were clubs and knives, and I felt wounded. I had come here with the best of intentions. I had come here to thank Swami for His kindness, for steering me away from a life I had come to hate. In those moments, I couldn't understand where I had gone wrong.

Even as my roiling emotions got the better of me, I understood that these devotees didn't have a problem with me per se — they just wanted their Swami to get rest. Swami had little time to spare: His workload was immense, with so many people lining up outside to meet Him; and try as I might, I couldn't find fault with it. But I was hurt all the same. First, He had snubbed me, and now I could see that the devotees perceived me as little more than a nuisance. I felt that discomforting ache of being the unwanted, unwelcome person in someone else's home.

I remember asking God, 'Why did you call me here? There's enough difficulty in my life, why did you have to put me through this? Have I not seen enough?' I cried out in sheer pain.

I was angry with God, I was angry with Swami. The night was cold, but my heart was colder. Even if I had wanted to I couldn't go inside, because the tears just wouldn't stop. 'I'll never come back here, never, never again,' I said to the expanse of twinkling lights above. If there was a God listening, I made sure that my cries reached His ears. Swami had said repeatedly in His discourses that this was sacred ground and that the Divine Mother dwelled here. I was past caring. I just wanted to go home.

Before I knew it, my four-day stay was over. It was time for a proper private audience with Swami – not just the five short minutes He had given me earlier. I felt anxious, as it was time to leave the ashram, to leave Swami. My ego had taken a blow too, because He hadn't given me any private audience for the first four days of my stay there. I knew He was incredibly busy, and I could see for myself His commitment to His devotees. Yet it was hard for me to accept that I, who had travelled so far, had been treated just as any other devotee at the ashram. I didn't know then that the first thing Swami breaks is ego.

It was ego that distanced me from Him, that made me doubt Him. And though I had witnessed Him foretelling the past, present and future of strangers as if He were reading their book of life, I was still apprehensive and sceptical, even afraid. He seemed too great to approach. He was beyond my reach, out of my league. I wasn't anyone special here. Could He possibly put my mind to rest? I pondered over this while I was sitting quietly during my last private audience with him.

As if sensing my inner turmoil, Swami asked me to come closer. I didn't think much of it. I hate to admit it, but I didn't set much store by his request. I just sat on the floor near to him. He was seated on the cot in front of me. Outwardly, I was quiet and seemingly composed -- or so I thought -- but my mind was churning over, a million things spinning in its space. I was upset because I was to leave soon, and the incident with the devotees also played intermittently in my mind.

I felt like shouting -- wanting, desperately hoping for the crowd to disappear. 'If you are really who everyone thinks you are then why don't you show me a glimpse,' I cried out in my mind. Just then He quietly placed His hand on my head. My eyes closed spontaneously. I wanted to open them, but I couldn't. It was as if the crowd outside had fallen into oblivion. My mind and its myriad voices were engulfed in silence. And the next instant, heat was surging through my scalp and rushing through my entire body like a streak of lightning.

Just as a pot placed on fire experiences its warmth and it continues to build up, my head was experiencing a flow of energy from Swami's hand. It was intense, warm and calming at once. Though the exchange lasted no more than half a minute, it was an experience of a lifetime. I had never experienced such tranquillity. I felt like I was a feather floating freely in the air, carried on musical winds. A tremendous feeling of relief washed over me, releasing the anxiety and disquiet I had contained within for decades.

His powerful energy wasn't merely a vague feeling or a feel-good experience. It was real and palpable. It had its own presence. Just like you and I have a body and a consciousness that holds its reins, Swami's body is the abode of several mysterious energies. It was one among the nine companion energies I encountered that day. From my highly strung, unstable and disturbed state, I had been elevated to quietude and gentleness in a matter of seconds.

The change in my mental outlook was dramatic. I experienced it in the way my breathing changed, my body relaxed and my mind felt no worry or anxiety. I was free of the shackles of my relentless fears and guilt. I would leave the ashram even more in awe of Him than when I had arrived.

'So you said to Mother Divine that you are never coming back here?' Swami chuckled. 'In anger, out of ego, you lashed out, Dolly.' His twinkling eyes sought mine. 'You can't be stubborn with Nature,' He continued. 'Her scale is too big. She'll take from you what she needs from you. I'll see you here again very soon.'

I had never told Him what I had silently cried out to the Divine in the cold night. But at that time, of course, I hadn't known He was the Divine I had been cursing. He had heard my inner ranting and raving, though he had been sitting far away in His cottage. I wasn't going to give up so easily, however.

'Really?' I exclaimed. 'I just came here to thank you and have done that. I'm not coming back.'

'March 2014.'

The firmness in his voice rendered me speechless. If He could hear my tub-thumping thoughts for Mother Divine, He probably could see the future too. At any rate, I couldn't find my voice to answer Him. I looked at him and He was smiling.

Like me, you too may find it hard to believe, but let me tell you in no unclear terms that Swami hears you, He reads your thoughts. He sees yours intentions, your fears, your worries; and then one by one, like thorns He plucks them from you. His magnanimity is such that you aren't even aware of the kindness He has bestowed on you. The pain He takes away as quietly as the cooling breeze that gently fans you to sleep on a hot summer night. This is my experience of Swami.

The Healer

After I returned home from the ashram, there seemed to be a subtle change in my behaviour. I couldn't be sure of this, though. But I was absolutely certain that the severe dermatitis in my hands, a condition I had suffered since childhood, had completely and inexplicably vanished.

Since I was twelve, I had suffered from a form of eczema, a type of skin infection that led to deep fissures forming on my hands and feet. These cuts usually appeared along the faint lines on my fingers, toes and the sides of the soles of my feet. Dry weather, humidity, rains and cold would trigger a bout of eczema, and over two long decades, for a better part of each year, I battled this affliction. The fissures would often be so deep it was as if I had cut myself with a sharp kitchen knife.

A simple act of eating my meal with my hands, using a detergent or touching a dusty surface would be rewarded with a shooting, stinging pain on the cuts in my hands. These cuts weren't merely dry or dead skin. At the peak of the infection season, I would wake to find that the cuts had not only deepened but were bleeding too. It was painful to hold a toothbrush in the morning. If something brushed against my hands accidentally, I would suffer excruciating pain. Immersing my hand in cold water during winters was a task I dreaded. Contact with anything at all would sting, for I didn't just have one or two or three cuts but a dozen, and sometimes even more.

It crossed my mind many times while growing up that my problem was not too different from the beggars, lepers on the street who had gauze or shabby cloth wrapped around the stumps of their fingers. I felt that perhaps I had been a leper in my previous life. I would joke about this with my mother, although she didn't find it quite as amusing as I did. There were plenty of skin specialists she consulted for me, and none could really help.

One good doctor recommended an ointment, a mix of three – four generic fungal infection medicines that helped control, if not completely eradicate the infection. And the medicine became the one cream that I would smear on my fingers day and night.

In the early years of my marriage, my mother-in-law would taunt me, though not unkindly, saying that it was most convenient for me to have a disease that required me to avoid cutting vegetables or touching dusty surfaces. The juice from the fruit and vegetables would aggravate the cuts, as would the use of detergents for cleaning utensils or washing clothes. Effectively, the new bride was excused from kitchen work. It didn't bode well to be perceived a shirker so early in my marriage.

In the extremely cold November 2013 weather at the ashram, my cuts had flared up once again. And it didn't help that we bathed and did our dishes with freezing water, too. In my first brief meeting with Swami, I sat on the floor, with my palms pressed together, waiting for Him to say something.

'Did you hurt yourself? Is that blood on your hand, Dolly?' This was His question in the first audience of five minutes He had given me.

Instead of answering, I jumped like a baby monkey and put my hand right in front of Him. 'I get these cuts, a sort of fungal infection ...' Swami winced as He saw the deep cuts and the dried blood caked around my fingers. He turned His face away and said in a pained voice, 'This is terrible, Dolly. It must really hurt.'

'Oh no, Swami, it isn't as bad as it looks. I'm used to them. I've had them all my life.'

'Not anymore,' He murmured.

I didn't think much of this conversation. It wasn't the first time someone had asked me about my cuts. After I returned from the ashram, my cuts healed rapidly. Still, I didn't think it had anything to do with what Swami had said. The condition was like that: almost with a mind of its own, it came and went at will -- or so I thought.

Six weeks passed, and soon it was time for Swami to visit my city. He had been travelling for discourses to Delhi, Mumbai, Bangalore, Chennai and Pune. I was most excited and attended His discourses both in Mumbai and Pune.

During my private audience with Him in Pune, I came to realize what He had done. After a lovely half hour of discussing the memoir manuscript I had sent to HarperCollins, I took His leave. As I got up, He picked up a tiny glass bottle from the side table and began applying a dark liquid to His fingers on both hands. The way He was applying the liquid on His fingers stopped me in my tracks. It was exactly as I had done for most of my life -- delicately applying ointment on each finger, dabbing it till it became dry -- so I could use my hands and carry on with my daily chores. The very mannerisms of his activity were identical to my own.

Taken aback, I couldn't help but ask, 'What are you doing, Swami?'

'I'm applying some tincture. Doctor Renu Madan gave this for a blister on my finger. I need to apply it a few times in the day.'

He showed me His hands and sure enough, just as the faint creases on my fingers had deepened into cuts, skin was peeling off His fingers, and on their tips were lines where the skin had broken. These fissures were not as severe as those I suffered, but they were there nonetheless.

Seeing my concerned expression, He said, 'It's just dryness and nothing more. The next person must be waiting.' He put the bottle down and gestured toward the door, smiling.

'But Swami, they look just like mine.'

He continued smiling, and sent me off. Outside, Ganesh Om, a zealous devotee of Swami who had been looking after Swami on the trip, stood waiting. We exchanged a few words, and I was on my way.

While I was driving back home, the penny finally dropped. My cuts had healed so quickly, because Swami had somehow taken my condition upon Himself. I had not suffered any episode of dermatitis for almost two months -- the longest period I had ever gone without applying my medicine. There appeared to be no other explanation.

Surprisingly, the cuts did not reappear in the terrible summer months that followed; nor in the monsoon, the breeding season of all fungal infections. They returned the next winter, but by that time I would be in the ashram again. Swami took one look at the painful cuts on my hands and within a week they were gone – just like that. I asked Him if He had taken my eczema on Himself. His response was an adorable smile and a witty riposte, 'Eat the mangoes, don't count the trees.'

The Divine Play

I experienced many a strange phenomenon in the ashram. There, in Swami's presence, my rational beliefs would be sorely tried. Sometimes when Swami entered the discourse room, an enchanting fragrance would flood the room, as if He was cloaked in the scent of an exotic flower, a flower whose fragrance I didn't know. Rose, jasmine, lotus – all crossed my mind – but this fragrance was nothing like any I had inhaled. It was not of this world.

Once, the scent overwhelmed me, and like a bloodhound on the hunt, I was gripped with an overpowering urge to locate its source. As I approached Swami, I blurted out feverishly, 'There's this fragrance coming from you, Swami! It's overpowering.' There were other people in the discourse room. They looked at me and each other blankly – they detected nothing.

'What's this fragrance?' I persisted. 'It's intoxicating.'

'I'll turn it off, if it's too much.' Swami spoke in His quiet manner.

And then, the fragrance was gone – just like that. How could it be? Of all the things in the world, how can you make a fragrance disappear in a fraction of a second? I was intrigued beyond words.

'The energy that was outside a moment ago,' He said reading my mind, 'is now inside me.'

I fell quiet, for what more was there to know? In my heart, I knew it was a divine fragrance. It was a miracle, a boon granted to inhale the very air that this holy saint breathed.

I noticed that the fragrance wasn't always the same. It remained strong and almost overpowering for me, but changed at times, as if tempered with some different exotic scent. Swami's response to my observation wasn't discouraging. The fragrance depended on which bhava, sentiment, He was in, He told me. If He were being a child in Mother Divine's creation, or worshipping Her as His feminine principle, it would be quite different to that if He were calling upon the fierce Kali, which is when the fragrance of roses would appear. This is not a sweet fragrance of the usual red rose, but a rose-like fragrance that would evoke a wondering and fear in you.

Other phenomena were equally baffling. Sometimes when Swami would eulogize Mother Divine, I would experience a slight pain, like a fine needle penetrating through my head from ear to ear. The deep baritone from His throat deepened even more when He lost Himself to the glory of the Goddess. It was a distinctive sound, intense like the thundering clouds, and seemingly capable of shattering window panes. As the tempo of the mantras would build, the sensation in my ears would intensify. I experienced a sort of semi-trance, as my eyelids felt heavy and closed of their own accord. My only focus would be the sound, the sweet music coming from Swami's throat. Its hypnotic quality filled me with bliss.

The first few times this occurred, I dismissed it as nothing. But it is hard to ignore the sensation of any kind of pain in the body, no matter how mild it is. As the frequency of these experiences increased, curiosity nagged at me. I wanted to ask Swami about it, but was also reluctant to pose the question. It seemed silly to say that His singing left me dizzy and made my ears ache, and it would feel especially so in the company of other devotees, for no one else had uttered a word about it. It was too powerful a sensation to leave unexplained, though. It felt like a sonic beam cast in the air, and not everyone could hear it; but those who did would just fall to their knees.

Finally, I mustered the courage and asked Swami why I felt this pain in my ears along with that overwhelming feeling. And why didn't everyone feel it?

Swami didn't dismiss my question as silly. 'When the Goddess sings, the soul recognizes Her energy. The human body, unable to take in Her power, experiences discomfort or pain. The purer the soul, the more it yearns for the Divine.'

It's not that you would experience this regularly. It happens when Swami is most enraptured in His devotions. It is then that the deep vibration from His throat resonates beyond the physical plane, and this connection with Mother Divine excites a tingling sensation in your ears. This is just one of the many mysterious aspects of Swami in a human form.

My acceptance of the Divine in a human body didn't come overnight, though. Back then, while I was baffled and completely in awe of Him, I wasn't an ardent devotee. I was not even a devotee, for that matter. My progress was laborious, even painful. It was as if at some point in my life, I had blithely led myself into a quagmire, miles of unending mud and stench, and I was now slogging my way through it. Daily I clambered through the muddle of worldly desires. I could see that I had been living in a wasteland.

The most difficult thing in the world is to give up your flawed existence -- to admit that your mode of living and belief systems are built on false premises, and you hadn't known any better. Although I was beginning to sense a change within myself, I remained tied to my old, aggressive ways. The same desire for control that prevailed within me as a child and helped me weather life's difficulties, now held me from declaring myself a devotee, a follower.

But even as my struggles raged within, Swami's grace was perplexing and becalming me in equal measure. The more I wanted to see a normal person I could relate to, however, the more I had to concede that He was anything but ordinary. Many times, I could feel that He was not alone, as if there were mysterious energies that surrounded Him at all times.

As if my being in awe of Him wasn't enough -- feeling powerful energies around Him and inhaling His unearthly, holy scent -- Swami began to delight in reading my mind. There was a spate of incidents where He would reveal, with the innocence of a child, everything from my most mundane thoughts to my deepest musings. Even before a thought was formed in my mind, He could articulate it for me. To say I was shocked would be an understatement. He almost always knew what I was going to say next. And there were countless times when even I didn't know what I was about to say. But He did.

Many times I would be eager to share an incident with Him, or something that had transpired which involved only me and someone else, and He would already be privy to it. It was as if He could step through time, strip away its mystery, learn its secrets and follow a chain of events in moments.

A few times, I even tested him by asking him what I was thinking. 'A test is never out of reverence,' He would reply. 'I no longer take any test.' And when I would go quiet, a few seconds later, He would tell me exactly what I was thinking. Exactly. Word for word. 'I won't do it next time,' He would say with a soft laugh. Yet, holding onto my own ego, I would soon forget about these instances. They were beyond rationalizing, so I dismissed them as coincidences; clever guesswork on His part or random intuitiveness.

In March 2014, exactly as Swami had predicted, I was travelling to the ashram again. HarperCollins had just bought the rights to Swami's memoir. Swami was already in the midst of writing His Ayurveda book *The Wellness Sense,* and I was to spend the better part of my ten days' stay editing the manuscript.

The night before boarding the flight from Mumbai, I received an email from Swami saying that there was some urgent work that needed His attention elsewhere, as the consecration ceremony of Sri Hari was fast approaching in April. He would return to the ashram the day after my arrival.

I was upset at the thought of Swami being absent from the ashram. It reminded me of returning to an empty home; my mother had gone, and I was abandoned in its empty shell. An aching, empty feeling overtook me. Just as a flower trembles in the storm, I couldn't help my reaction, and I let my displeasure be known. At my worst, I was still the aggressive, rebellious child who wanted things to go her way; and I was yet piecing my life together after it had fallen apart.

I was also apprehensive about coping on my own in the ashram surroundings, amongst virtual strangers. A strange melancholy would come over me from time to time, and it had been this way since my childhood. I would refuse to speak to people, be rude, alienate others and be alienated. If I was hurting, I would inflict hurt wantonly, mostly on those who loved and cared about me. And as my life progressed, it only worsened. My temper tantrums at these times, I am ashamed to say, spared no one.

Mentally and emotionally, I wasn't as vulnerable as I had been three months earlier, but inside I still felt wobbly; the slightest hitch could derail me completely and push me over the edge. Swami's absence was one such event. I boarded the plane with a heavy heart, unsure of where I was headed and why. It was as if I had been promised the world and it had all slipped out of my grasp.

Once we were airborne, as is my habit I pulled out my little notebook to pen my thoughts. A poem was brewing inside. I don't remember being sad, or overly troubled at that moment; in fact, I felt quite detached. In our quietest moments, we sometimes stumble upon truth, ideas that have long evaded us.

> Come like the promise of rain,
> On a sultry summer night,
> Seamless like the countless threads,
> Woven into a beautiful bedspread of blue and white.
>
> Mirthful like a wild elephant,
> Tramping through an endless trek.
> Swift as the morning sun,
> Rising over my balcony, blinding me.
>
> Certain like the dewdrops,
> Laying face down on moist leaves.

Blow in like the unexpected draft that
Gently tugs at the hall curtains.

Come like a poem, sweet and urgent,
Fall from that higher realm of consciousness.

I remember feeling both content and amazed at the way the verses had arranged themselves. I had been crying out to be saved for a long time; but no one had ever come. And yet each time I wrote a poem, I felt that I had been saved – that the answers were already there.

I emailed the poem to Swami as soon as I landed. The euphoria of the poem's creation had subsided, and I sent it more out of habit – perhaps even flippantly. I was at the time under the illusion that Swami was an ordinary man with extraordinary abilities. I may have been on my way to see a great saint, but He was a man; a mortal like the rest of us, of human emotions and flaws – subject to the laws of nature. How wrong I was.

A three-hour-long road journey lay ahead of me. The drive from Chandigarh airport to the ashram was breezy, comfortable and filled with thoughts of what lay ahead of me. It was like hurtling down a mountain slope, unconcerned as to where I might end up. I felt numbed somehow that Swami wouldn't be there at the ashram. In the past few months, He had become my anchor; I looked up to Him far more than I had realized.

The driver was a local and quite chatty. We stopped for lunch. I was no longer in any rush to reach the ashram, and so we lingered for a while over our food. As the soft evening light descended on the mountains, we reached the point from where I had to proceed on foot. A villager was there to carry my backpack, and we descended on an old country lane. After picking our way down a narrow pathway, I found myself in an open valley flanked by tall trees, both green and golden, gracing hills as they ran high and low.

And there, cooling a bed of white pebbles, flowed the river Giri. The meandering riverbed was articulate under its pristine waters, inviting and invigorating. Rocks of various sizes, emerald green with algae, sat at its bottom like giant, uncut gems. The air was chilly -- and so was the water. I let out a laugh as I dipped my foot into the flow. Even at the ford, it ran up to my calves.

I crossed the river holding my companion's hand; the current was powerful, and it took an effort to keep my balance. It was a good twenty-minute trek to the ashram, through stones and sand, dried congress grass and a small herd of wary cattle returning home. I increased my stride, eager to catch a glimpse of the little hut perched precariously on the edge of a cliff.

The hut was Swami's dwelling, a lone cottage that stood proudly against the backdrop of the mountain and a quiet evening sky. Its tin roof stood in the middle, seemingly dividing the earth from the ether, marking the beginning of another time and space. I remember waving gleefully like a child at the window veiled by dark maroon curtains, as if Swami was inside and He could see me.

In time, it would become my regular practice to wave to the window as I walked toward the ashram. It felt good, even though the curtains were almost always drawn. There is a quiet loveliness about the ashram and its surroundings. Tucked away at the foothill of two gigantic mountains that seem to be the still and mighty form of Lord Narayana and Mother Divine, it offers their protection to those who have come seeking refuge.

A deep sense of tranquillity and innocence thus wells inside you as you take each step toward the ashram. That the earth beneath our feet is special — the wind and the sky, mountains and trees, have ears and eyes, is an experience many devotees would share with me later. In the midst of the ashram compound, I saw the painted temple nearing completion, and there was evidence of new construction, with rocks and debris piled high in places. Swami Raghavananda and Swami Vidyananda showed me to the little mud cottage where I was to sleep. They had had it cleaned by some village ladies.

It was the same tiny room where I had stayed during my first visit. It had a window shielded by dusty brown curtains in one of the mud walls, a wooden plank in the other, and that is all there was to it. A mattress and a quilt were laid on the floor for me, and a cot in the corner was piled with more quilts and mattresses. Both the Swamijis told me to help myself to another quilt if I felt cold in the night. Theirs was a thoughtful suggestion. It was early March and quite chilly for me, unaccustomed to the bracing, cool mountain air as I was.

After dinner, I snuggled under a pair of quilts and settled in my makeshift bed to read before going to sleep. There was a forty-volt bulb in the cosy room, and a little family of ants and some unknown insects seemed keen on sharing my bed. Soon fatigue had me curled in a deep slumber under the quilt. It was 9 p.m.

Sometime during the night, I woke up. There, just inches away from where I lay, was a benign form looming over me. Startled, I murmured, my eyes still half-closed, 'It's you! You've come.'

I sat up in attention. Rays of piercing white light were illuminating the space. The tiny room was alive, the dark night driven out by the beautiful white light emanating from Swami's body. He was cloaked in a halo from head to toe, like the aura that surrounds a brilliant full moon; tangible and visible to the naked eye. Just as none can doubt the exquisite brightness that lights up the sky on a full moon night, He was here, clothed in that brightness – larger than before, exalted by the luminescence around Him. He floated above the ground effulgent, cocooned in a silvery consciousness. That soft soothing light wasn't just coming from Swami: He was that light.

I was stunned. He had appeared out of nowhere. But He wasn't merely a construct of my imagination. He was real. He was there, right in front of me, gazing down upon me with those compassionate, benevolent eyes. More astounding still was that despite the familiarity of His form, I instinctively knew that this manifestation wasn't human. All the mythology, the story books I had read as a child, couldn't have prepared me for this vision.

A burning desire to touch the Divine's holy feet entered my mind. This was strange for me, as I mostly greeted Swami with a warm good morning or good evening, and I only touched His feet occasionally – if I felt like it – and now, my whole being ached with surrender, with devotion. Compelled by forces beyond my knowing, I reached out to touch His feet.

To my amazement, the foot I had reached out to bent completely backward and it pulled away. The soft, bright light around it receded. This was the first instant that I realized something was not normal. I looked back to see my body still lying on the floor, in the sleeping position, while I, a peach-coloured form, was sitting upright, gazing at myself. I was gripped by acute fear; disbelief at this experience I didn't understand.

To see your body both sleeping and sitting at the same time, at the same place – like a mirror image split in two – is not an everyday occurrence. I looked at Swami's radiant form, His face bearing the most loving smile, like a parent encouraging a child to believe what she saw.

The next thing I knew my body was waking up. It was like coming out of a dream; except this was no dream. That which they call the elusive soul had come out of hiding for those precious minutes. The immortal essence had stared upon its mortal form. I was too scared to delve into what had happened, and burying myself under the quilts again, I drifted back into slumber.

The next morning Swami arrived. He sat cross-legged on an ordinary cot. The simple surroundings: the gentle whirring of the table fan; a faint crack running in the wall; the grey cemented floor -- it was all too simple. There wasn't one sign of the great wealth I had read about in His memoir. His ochre robe consisted of three pieces of unstitched cloth, wrapped around the lower body, draped across the shoulders, and the angavastram, a piece of ochre cloth around his neck. He sported a vermillion mark on his glabella, and a full-moon like sandalwood tilak sat high on his forehead. He looked glorious.

I squealed in delight as soon as I got an audience.

'Who visited me last night, Swami?' I said. 'It was so real.'

'My astral body,' He replied in a matter-of-fact tone, a faint smile emerging on his lips. He didn't ask me when, who, where or what. There was no denying or pretence as to what I was referring to. He knew.

'Oh really, Swami? How can it be?' I asked most excitedly. I didn't know how to talk to saints or how to express myself in their presence. I wasn't brought up in such an environment. I just talked to Him as I would talk to my next-door neighbour or a friend.

'Somethings are better not said twice, Dolly,' he said. He extended his long arm to reach a glass that was lying on a small side table, and took a sip of water.

'Swami, what about me? There were two of me. I was coloured ochre, the colour of your robe. Is that how our auras look?'

'No, they really have no colour.'

'Then why did I look all ochre?'

'It's the colour of devotion, of surrender, just like Mira loved Girdhar Gopal ...'

'You saw two of you,' He continued. 'One is who you are currently. And the second is who you will be in the future. This is the path of transformation. Only the dye of devotion will wash off the various colours of grief, desires and pain I see in you. Ochre is the colour of surrender, of devotion. It's the colour of the rising sun, of the setting sun; it's the colour of fire. All your afflictions will burn and the real you will shine forth. It'll take time, but it'll happen, Dolly.'

This was where our conversation ended, but my mind wasn't yet ready to grasp the significance of what He had said. I was no Mira. I had lived far too recklessly and selfishly to devote myself to a person, to a cause. I craved devotion; having it or giving it had never occurred to me. It would take a whole year before devotion's sweet hue would slowly unveil itself.

In retrospect, I did realize one thing, though: my soul had sight, it had eyes. And those eyes had recognized Swami's presence, for the first words I had uttered were, 'It's you.' The Dolly of this world may not know or revere Him, but in my purest state I knew Him like a wave knows the ocean, like pebbles know the riverbed, and the sun knows its trajectory.

The Playful Swami

Eight days passed as swiftly as a tiny bird hopping from boulder to boulder as she crosses the river. Less than seventy-two hours remained until my departure, and I was already beginning to feel the pangs of separation. Only one who has been in Swami's presence can understand the tightness in the chest I feel when I was to leave Swami and the ashram behind.

That evening we were sitting in the discourse room along with Swami Paramananda and Swami Vidyananda. Suddenly Swami said, 'Let's have a bonfire, shall we?'

'Really, Swami, we can have a bonfire here!' I was excited at the very thought of it.

Swami nodded, and both the other Swamijis rushed out to bring wood from the backyard. In front of the discourse room is a large cemented space, where they placed the logs on a small, improvised platform of bricks. Before I knew it, they had kindled the fire. We spread a couple of mats on the ground and placed a chair close by for Swami. It was a windy evening, and moonbeams seemed to fall right where we sat.

Soon we were all settled by the fire, listening to Swami talking about the fifteen companion energies or devis that accompany the Adya Shakti, the Divine Mother. Swami Paramananda was yet to be initiated by Swami. At one time he had worked for big companies like IBM as a consultant and had travelled abroad on foreign assignments frequently. He had been spellbound with Swami at their very first meeting in Bangalore. A week later, he had dropped everything and come to the ashram to be in Swami's service. In his white robes, Swami Paramananda appeared to be a gentle soul, whose eyes would moisten the moment Swami began speaking of the Divine Mother. He would then wipe his tears unobtrusively with his angavastram. He had many questions regarding Devi worship, which Swami answered in His kind-hearted, patient way under the beautiful awning of stars. Swami had a long stick in His hand with which He prodded and flipped the logs every now and then, to entice the flames.

I was too much in awe of Swami and the talk regarding Devi sadhana (Goddess worship) to open my mouth. What did I know of such things? It was a strange little group, and I was the stranger in it. There was Swami and His loving disciples, who were clearly devoted to the divine in Him. And then there was me, who mentally dissected every word that fell from Swami's mouth and wondered if such a world really existed, where the Goddess bathed in milk and honey, while Her beast guarded the door. A place where the Divine Mother ate food in crockery studded with gems, and appeared at the behest of the young saint in front of me.

It was too much for my mind to absorb. Suddenly Swami began singing a eulogy to Mother Divine and my thinking mind was laid to rest. More singing followed, and I couldn't have felt happier. When Swami sings, even a sceptic will believe in those moments that he or she is indeed in the presence of divinity. As the singing picked up its tempo, so did the wind. I pulled my woolly cap nicely over my ears. Quite a few logs had burnt to glowing coals, except a thick, long stump that flickering tongues of flame steadily consumed.

The bonfire embers had been flying at us all this time but with the wind picking up, they swirled crazily in the air around us. Swami cautioned us all to sit farther from the flames. Swami Paramananda stoked the fire with more wood, before he and Swami Vidyananda took Swami's permission to finish their dinner and return in twenty minutes time. The old kitchen was a hop, skip and jump away, and they soon got busy with heating their dinner.

The wind was whipping gusts all over the place now, almost overwhelming the fire. The temperature dropped all of a sudden. I shivered in the cold and inched a little closer to the dying embers of the bonfire. Swami's chair was right next to me. He noticed my rubbing my hands together and leaned forward to stoke the fire, prodding the big lumpy log in my direction. But it wouldn't budge. Suddenly Swami got up from His chair, came to my side and, with His bare hands, pushed the big burning log into the centre of the glowing, vermillion coals. Flames sprang forth, engulfing the log and bringing our bonfire back to life. And He burnt His index finger.

'There was no need to touch the burning log,' I said in a voice that betrayed my confusion and anger. For the life of me, I couldn't understand why He had touched the log with His hand when He obviously knew it was hot.

What He said next melted my heart and my head hung in shame. 'I wanted to start the fire because you were cold, Dolly.'

I didn't know what to say. It was downright foolish to do something like that, but maybe that's what saints did: care for other people — or at least this one did, I concluded. Swami was keenly looking at the area where He was burnt, and sure enough, a blister was beginning to form.

'What can I get you, Swami? There's Burnol in the kitchen. I used it for a little girl the other day.'

'No, it's all right, let Swamijis finish their dinner. They may get upset if they hear about it while they are eating.'

I could barely believe someone would be so considerate. But what was I thinking? He had just picked up a burning log to keep me warm. I don't know what I felt — perhaps I was equally shocked and perplexed — but whatever that feeling was, it wasn't any good. Swami dipped His finger in a glass of water that was sitting nearby. My mind was still trying to fathom Swami's stoking the fire with His bare hand. It made little sense. Had I known at that point that He was privy to all my thoughts, I would have screened them. Or perhaps used gentler words than 'foolish' or 'why the hell would you do that?'

The wind was absolutely wild now, and the fire became frenzied, raining embers on us, crackling and hissing like a woman gone mad. We were both quiet. Swami's face wore a sombre look.

'What are you thinking, Swami? Is it hurting too much?'

It was a moment before He replied, 'No, it isn't ... I was just thinking how painful it must be for burn victims with second and third degree burns.'

He leaned forward, staring right into the centre of the fire and lapsed into silence. I was too frivolous and self-centred back then to feel anyone's pain, except my own. But I knew it was time to give Him space and bask in His gentle presence, and so I sat quietly by His side. The fire kept lunging at us, filling my eyes with smoke and my clothes with soot, making me cough. Swami still had His finger in the glass when the wild flames raged high toward His chin. Without raising His eyes, Swami took His finger out of the glass and flicked a drop of water on the fire. The gesture was made with such finality that without His having uttered a word, I somehow knew He had ordered it to fall back.

Just as a snapping stray dog yelps, at being kicked, curls up and runs away into a dark alley, the flames instantly cowered, and to my astonishment, leapt into the direction of the wind. The change in the movement of the fire was as swift as the flick of a switch.

The Swamijis returned that very moment and I blurted out, 'Swami just made the fire fall back! It was amazing. I don't know how He did that.'

Looking at the Swamijis' puzzled expressions, Swami just laughed.

'One should not play with the forces of nature. There's always a price to pay,' He said.

Another fine evening came to an end, but the real show was yet to come.

The next evening, also my second-last evening at the ashram, we once again settled by the bonfire. Swami shared much about His stay at Naga Baba's. Each time He added a new detail, a hilarious anecdote, I would exclaim, 'Oh, why didn't we put this in the memoir?' He regaled us with stories of His time at Rudranath, and while some were heart-warming, most were more poignant than those I had read in the manuscript.

A couple of hours passed, yet it felt like minutes. Swami had His dinner quite early in the evening, and since He had been speaking non-stop for some time now, hunger was gnawing at

His tummy. Not wanting to trouble Swami Vidyananda so late in the night, He asked for a snack — anything light, a piece of sweetmeat or a bar of chocolate. Swami Vidyananda went to His cottage and came back with a bar of milk chocolate and handed it to Swami.

Swami gently tore the wrapper, broke a small piece of chocolate and offered it to Mother Divine in His customary fashion: closing His eyes and holding the food to His lips as He murmured a prayer. He then broke rows of chocolate and gave one to each of us. Swami Paramananda was speaking to Swami now.

I was hungry and quickly peeled the golden wrapper. Before biting into the chocolate, I thought, maybe I should throw the wrapper into the fire. As I was still processing this thought, Swami turned to face me and said, 'You may throw the wrapper in the fire, Dolly.'

'Oh, I was thinking the same thing.' I looked up at Him and smiled.

Today the fire was at its best behaviour: it burnt slowly and steadily, the meek flames neither casting embers nor soot. Yesterday's raging fire was now as soft as a street lamp on a lonely road. The faint orange glow from the fire matched Swami's ochre robe, creating a mysterious, mischievous aura around Him. If the fire was different, Swami was different too; His sombre mood of yesterday was replaced with dimpled cheeks and a twinkle in His eye.

'This was my first thought when you gave me the chocolate.' I said to Him.

'That's not true, your first thought was whether it'd be appropriate to throw the wrapper in the fire, to throw something like that in my presence.'

I was flabbergasted. 'How did you know?'

He was absolutely right. This was my first thought, but it was so faint that it had barely registered in my mind. Stuttering, I asked Him how He could have possibly known a thought even I was hardly aware of. Swami just smiled and resumed His discussion with Swami Paramananda, who had asked Him a question about Shiva and Shakti. Swami responded by saying how Ma Parvati's extreme penance had brought Shiva to her. She survived on one bilwa leaf a day till it melted Shiva's heart.

I was only somewhat paying attention to what was being said, as my mind was a little shaken by Swami knowing my thoughts. A parallel commentary was running in my mind: 'Who has ever heard of meditating and getting Shiva as their groom? I can't even think of doing such penance. It's beyond me.'

'You can, Dolly.' Swami interrupted my contemplation. 'Can what?' I knew exactly what He was saying, but I was jittery and too embarrassed to admit it. 'It's possible through sadhana to meditate on Shiva's form.'

Oh God! I thought. He has been reading my mind all this while. What about the not-so-pious thoughts I have had about Him, about how attractive He looks?

The moment I had that thought, Swami said playfully, 'Yes, those ones too.'

I jumped from my seat and started walking away from Him.

'Swami, don't read my mind, please. Don't.'

I was so embarrassed. The Swamijis sat there smiling, and Swami continued to rattle every thought that came to my mind.

'Please stay out of my mind.' By now I was shrieking like a five year old, stamping my foot, begging Him to stop.

I was scared to think any thought, because most of my thoughts were about Him. Hell, almost all my thoughts were about Him!

God, I'm a terrible person, I thought, for thinking such things in the presence of a saint.

'Dolly, come and sit down. I won't do that anymore.' He coaxed me back to my place.

Just as I settled down, He said, 'No Dolly, I don't think you are a terrible person. I think you are very sweet.'

'You are doing it again, Swami!' I was overcome with shyness. I didn't know want to do -- to laugh or to cry. He was reading my innermost thoughts. It was as if He was picking them even before they were formed. He somehow had this ability to sieve through thoughts, to isolate a single thought from those entangled like serpents in a dark pit.

Perhaps it was more that Swami was pulling out thoughts from my head like a child who dips his fingers in a cookie jar to pick out a favourite cookie and bite on it. Swami was pulling out one cookie after another out of my head. I was petrified of what He might find next. My mind was the one place where I could be the person I really was. This was scary. Again reading -- or should I say raiding -- my mind, He explained, 'It's not like I'm reading your mind, Dolly, you are just transparent to me. I see through you. I just know your thoughts.'

If only I had known this earlier, I might have chosen different thoughts in His company. I sighed as I pondered this.

'No, you wouldn't have.' He smiled that beautiful smile. I knew exactly what He was referring to. This time, I neither shrieked nor shouted, and had the decency to mentally admit that He was right. It was quite an experience to have my mind, my innermost desires taken apart in a matter of seconds. It was one memorable evening in Swami's presence, the beginning of many more to come.

The next morning, the most amazing thing happened. Well, at least, those who know me would think it was amazing. I became quiet. The previous night's episode had left me tongue-tied in Swami's presence. I was over-cautious in my speech and considered my every thought, mentally guarding my mind like a fortress. I was determined to keep it free of unwanted, unwelcome musings. For me, this was like torture: my mind is always bubbling like a cauldron with thoughts, images and dialogue. The notion that my mind was transparent to Him was acutely unsettling; so, for a change, I stilled the inner chattering and my voice. In the past, Swami had marvelled at my capacity to speak at such an alarming rate which barely allowed another person to speak at all. Today, I would appear the very model of the meditating, quiescent devotee.

Swami seemed even more intimidating than ever. I acutely felt the daylight streaming in through the insipid curtains of the discourse room. It was brighter than usual. It almost felt that warmth and light was shining through Him, and not just from the fierce winter sun outside. The crimson tilak on His forehead flashed like a warning in front of my eyes. Did He look even more powerful, invincible this morning? Was it real, the slight fear that I experienced in His presence, His might?

The subtlest things in the world are thought waves, drifting in and out of consciousness like silent rainclouds, condensing into great or mediocre ideas, or simply dissipating within a moment. And here I sat, in front of someone with the power to pick those thought waves; to play with them at will, like one browses the Internet: opening new tabs, accessing old ones.

My mind didn't possess the capability to process or accept such a phenomenon -- not yet, anyway. And what the mind doesn't understand, it brushes aside to deal with later. In due course, I would also learn that not only could Swami read minds, He could suggest a thought in the mind of another. The power of such a person seemed unimaginable to me.

I had seen so much in the preceding few days that I couldn't have imagined existed in this day and age. I felt exposed. But somewhere, a tiny seed of hope had sprouted: with this miracle Swami in my life, I was going to be all right.

Suddenly, Swami picked up an unusually thick, heavy book that was lying nearby. It was the Ramcharitmanas, the epic poem of the deeds of Rama. On the cover was an exquisite, colourful picture of Lord Rama, Ma Sita and Laxmana.

'Think of a question, any question in your mind,' He said, leafing through the book.

'And not tell you, you'll just read my mind?'

He nodded like a child with that mischievous smile that tells you he is up to something.

I composed myself to frame a question, to think of something of great relevance, but like a coiled spring releasing, my mind had already sprung the question. A little embarrassed, I looked at Him and said, 'Did you get my question?' The corners of His lips curled into a smile and a faint 'hmm' came from His throat in response.

He then asked me to choose any letter from the Hindi alphabet. Once again, I didn't have to say it out loud. Like a loose petal on the ground He had picked it from my mind. He then opened the last few pages of the book, and did some calculation on His fingertips. He put a finger on the letter I had chosen in my head to show me that He had indeed got it right.

It wasn't just the letter -- the very letter -- but the answer to the question itself that had me squirming in my place. I was overcome with a sudden urge to bite my nails. I was definitely nervous now, for it was such a silly question to ask – sheer foolishness, I thought. I could have chosen to ask anything but that.

Once again, He was turning the pages. He soon found what He was looking for. Raising His arched eyebrows ever so slightly, He said, 'Ma has blessed you.'

He then read out the particular chaupai (quatrain verse) in Sanskrit. I could make out parts of it, but no more. I was so curious, I didn't want to miss a word. Sensing my curiosity and excitement, Swami read the verse and then explained the meaning.

Sunu siya satya asis hamari | poojahi mana kamana tumhari ||

'Sita is praying to the Goddess Parvati during the Swayamwar (ceremony for choosing a husband), pleading that only the young prince Rama lift the bow. The Goddess Parvati blesses Sita, that she'll have her heart's desire.'

Swami sat smiling, immovable as a rock, while I was as fidgety as a bird in a cage. Suddenly, His recitations continued, cutting through the sweet noise in my head. In a playful voice tinged with laughter, He was reciting Kabir's doha:

Dhīrē-dhīrē rē manā, dhīrē saba kucha hōya.
Mālī sīncē sau gharā, ṛtu ā'ē phala hōya.

'Slowly, slowly O mind, everything happens at its own pace. Though the gardener may water with a hundred buckets, the fruit arrives only in its season.'

The Seer

On my last evening at the ashram, Swami Vidyananda and I took a stroll with Swami on the long terrace nestled between the majestic twin mountains. While we walked, I kept up a constant chatter. I was leaving the next day, and with all the recent mystical happenings, my head was filled with questions.

The walk had almost come to an end when Swami Raghavananda came to ask if the driver needed to pick me up in the morning from the ashram or from across the river. The newly built muddy road on which the idol of Sri Hari had travelled a fortnight earlier was once again rendered broken and boggy by the rains. I would be the second person to travel on it. The driver felt it unwise to undertake that journey. It was far too risky, he said. This meant I had to cross the river before 6 a.m.

Despite my protesting that I didn't mind the cold, Swami forbade me from crossing the river, as it would not only still be dark then, but the water would be absolutely freezing. His gentle heart just couldn't bear the thought of my stumbling over rocks as I braved the Giri's chilled currents, in the half light of the morning. He asked me to tell the driver to come all the way to the ashram; that nothing would happen to him or his car: 'Tell him, I'll be watching over him.'

I finished speaking to the driver, and looked at Swami. He was looking past me, as if peering far into the distance. He suddenly seemed serious. With a faraway look in His eyes, He said to me, 'Tomorrow is a very hectic day for you.'

'Well, all I have to do is catch my flight to Mumbai, get a cab to the CST station in Fort, and from there catch a super-fast train to Pune and I'll be home.' I smiled at Him, but He didn't smile back.

'It'll be a tiring day, Dolly.'

The evening passed, and soon Swami was bidding us all goodnight. I thanked Him for my stay at the ashram.

'I'll see you soon, Dolly,' He said, and started walking away.

Every fibre of my being was urging me to get down on my knees and touch my forehead to His feet. My impulse to call out to Him was so strong, I had to bite down on my lip to contain it. I had seen an extraordinary side of this kind, young monk in the past few days, and in the short time I had known Him my life's course had profoundly altered for the better. He had shown me love and a rare consideration, unattached to any material wish. And in leading me from an empty existence of shattered desires and wounded pride, He rekindled in me a long-dormant yearning for a life beyond all I had known. Hope now reigned where there had been none; and Swami was the source of my hope. But I still wasn't ready to bow to Him.

And yet, a part of me was running after Him, crying out to Him; something beyond my control was pushing me to offer my obeisance. I even called out to Him in my head to turn back or ask me to bow to Him. But this isn't Swami's way. In the end my ego won, and I stayed rooted to the spot till His fiery robe disappeared in the dark of the night.

The next morning, Swami Vidyananda bade me farewell before the dawn. As the small car laboured on the steep and treacherous inclines, it seemed like a joke to call this muddy track a road. The eleven-kilometre stretch, though uneventful, had my heart coming to my mouth on several occasions. The four-hour drive from the ashram to the airport was spent thinking of all the exciting stories I had to tell my brother, Om, and my sister-in-law, Pavitra. I couldn't wait to share the events of the past ten days.

By noon we were at Chandigarh Airport, and the day seemed to be proceeding well. But it would soon turn into a veritable living nightmare. My flight landed at Mumbai Chhatrapati Shivaji Airport forty minutes late, leaving me with a little over an hour to make it to Victoria Terminus or CST, as it's known in South Colaba, at the other end of Mumbai. I took a cab from Santacruz Airport but changed my mind halfway through the trip, as the only way to beat Mumbai traffic is to take the local train.

At the local train station in Andheri, I stood in a queue and spent ten precious minutes waiting to buy a ticket. I was getting frantic, and in my rush to board the local train, I boarded a general, unreserved carriage packed with men. These weren't your average, decent men; they were the kind of crowd a lone woman dreads. Rowdy, lecherous rogues breathed down my neck, leering at me, taking advantage of the rush by pressing themselves obscenely against my legs and back, and smirking at their opposites. Space was so limited that at times, I couldn't even put both my feet on the ground. I had to keep one atop the other while my hand tightly gripped a pole for support. There was nothing I could do but endure the situation.

The awful stench of the carriage, too, was overpowering. It reeked of tobacco (beedi, not cigarettes), dried fish and, the worst of them all, the odour of sweaty bodies. I had crash landed back into a dirty reality -- physically and psychically. After the salutary mountain air and the clean, wholesome sojourn at the ashram, it was all too much to take. I was ready to burst into tears, but that would have been a mistake because countless pairs of eyes were watching my every move. The next forty-five minutes felt like a lifetime as the train halted every few minutes and a fresh wave of heat, sweat and warm bodies got out and got in. I was sick and tired of fending men off. I couldn't wait to get home. I stood right near the door, thinking that when my stop comes, I'll move out quickly. Mine was the last stop.

I wasn't wearing a watch and my phone was in a tiny bag on my back. In that crush there was no way I could get my bag off and pull out my phone. Luckily, there was an old Muslim gentleman who seemed to be watching out for me, asking me to move to the side a little as a fresh avalanche of men would rush in at every station. He had an old rusty wristwatch on, and I kept asking him the time every few minutes, worrying all the while that I had missed the train, and thinking of how I would manage being stranded in Mumbai.

I made it to the train station precisely four minutes before the train's scheduled departure. I was now faced with the difficult task of making it to the last platform. Running wasn't an option, as my rucksack was twice my weight; and with each step forward it pulled me back just a little. I felt extremely tired, dehydrated and unable to walk. Since morning, I had travelled through three states -- by car, plane and a local train. I had no strength left to make a dash for it.

The clock was ticking and I had a sinking feeling in my stomach that the train would leave right before my eyes. Until this time, I had never been so tired in my life that I could barely carry my own weight. And now, as I walked and tried to run, sweating both inside and outside, I remembered what Swami had said about this being a tiring day.

He could only have been peering into the future when He cautioned me the day before. Thinking of Swami gave me strength, and I managed to walk steadily toward the train. The notion of throwing my rucksack down and dragging it was tempting, but time was running short -- it was down to seconds now. Panting like a dog, I had barely set foot on the train before it pulled out of the station.

It may seem to be just bad luck that my day turned out the way it did, but the finality and conviction with which Swami had warned me haunted my mind. I also realized that without His divine grace, it would not have been possible to make it this far. I would learn that nothing Swami says is without reason. It always comes to pass. He could see the future as clearly as I could see my own face in the mirror. Countless incidents would later reinforce my belief that He could not only see my future but see me too, no matter where I was.

In time, I would become absolutely comfortable with His knowing things that I hadn't told Him -- or was about to tell Him or wanted Him to know -- without my having to state them. He knew me inside out. That Swami has many facets was beginning to dawn on me. He appears to you in the sentiment in which you most revere Him. And my journey to discover Him and myself in the process had just begun.

My good karma from some life must have borne fruit — or maybe it was simply His grace — that I would soon find myself spending six months in the serene ashram environment, surrounded by hills, quietude — and the source of that quietude: Swami. It turned out to be the perfect opportunity to observe Swami from close quarters — to see a flower unfold, reveal some of its mystery, its seasons, its magic.

Sri Hari Darshan

I was back in the ashram in June 2014. The glorious idol of Sri Hari had been consecrated and stood majestically in the simple mandir.

I found it difficult to look at the idol. I would catch a glimpse and then lower my eyes or look away completely, just as a woman feels shy and self-conscious in the presence of an admirer, a lover. The ever-smiling face of the Lord was welcoming, but knowing. The beautiful lotus eyes seemed to look right through me. I felt desire stir inside. I had never felt even the likes of this on my innumerable visits to temples. It was the strangest thing, my reaction to the idol. I clearly remember thinking, during my first meeting with Sri Hari's idol, that no such ardour had ever flowed through my veins.

An idol was to be revered from a distance. One certainly didn't covet an idol; definitely not the way my heart was yearning for it, at least. Swami was travelling for discourses to Canada and the US for the following one month. I had arrived in His absence. And yet, was He really absent, I wondered?

Sri Hari had arrived few days prior to my March visit. The consecration ceremony was to be held in twenty days. The idol had travelled all the way from the south packed in a sturdy wooden crate. The crate lay in the temple. The villagers, labourers and I were all curious to see what the idol looked like. I wasn't going to be there for the consecration ceremony, hence the desire to see Sri Hari was even stronger.

My unspoken wish was granted, as Swami had ordered that the idol be placed in the sanctum sanctorum, just a few days before I was to leave the ashram. All the three Swamijis – Vidyananda, Paramananda and Raghavananda – along with some villagers, pried open the crate. Inside, the black stone idol was ensconced in a bed of shredded paper, thermocol and bubble wrap, all of which had been obviously laid with the utmost care. The idol was exceptionally heavy, and it took all the strength of six or seven villagers and the Swamijis to move the crate to the sanctum. Even Swami lent a hand.

With a pair of scissors, Swami began cutting through the bubble wrap. We had all gathered around the crate excitedly, and the Swamijis joined Swami and started removing the packaging at the waist, working their way down to the legs, and then on to the chest. Addressing the small group that was gathered there, Swami said, 'No one is supposed to see the idol before Prana pratishtha (a ceremony of infusing the idol with life). But since we have to place the idol in its rightful place, you are the lucky few who'll have His darshan.'

The packing had been meticulous, and revealing the Lord from its layers was not an easy job at all. Slowly, the Lord's hands with the conch and the lotus were unveiled. We were all fascinated by how lifelike He looked. Even in stone, He had that power upon us to treat Him with deference. We all felt it strongly. Suddenly Swami looked up and said to me, 'You can join in too, Dolly.' I gave Him my most dazzling grateful smile and quickly jumped in to help. While the Swamijis slaved at the idol's hands, feet, and chest, I went straight for the Lord's face, tugging at the bubble wrap with frenzied fingers. I was so curious to see His face. 'Very clever of you, Dolly.' Swami smiled knowingly. It was hard for me to hide my triumphant expression.

Soon the idol's long, pointed nose and delicately sculpted lips revealed themselves. Next, very gently, I touched the idol's cheeks, removing the shredded bits and thermocol particles from the face. I tenderly stroked the high cheekbones, feeling a surge of great love and awe for the black stone idol.

As the face fully revealed itself, I couldn't help but notice the striking resemblance between Swami and the idol. They both had a full face, round and wholesome. And those exquisite lotus eyes, that cleft in the chin and the benign smile. I noticed a mark on the idol's left cheek, a tiny scratch. I pointed it out to Swami, and squealed, 'Swami, the idol has a scratch on the left cheek, just like the pimple on your left cheek! Exactly at the same spot.'

Swami, who was busy with the idol, turned to face me, and spoke plainly, 'When this heals, that shall heal too.'

The disbelief in my eyes made Him say, 'When they will unwrap the idol before the Prana pratishtha ceremony, they won't find a mark on its cheek.' I thought, maybe He is teasing me again. How could a stone idol heal itself? After a strenuous thirty minutes of heaving and manoeuvring, the idol stood proud in its place, commanding us all to fold our hands in reverence.

As Swami stepped on the platform, clearing some thermocol from the crown of the idol, I noticed something rather incredible.

The height of the idol was exactly the same as Swami's. I was intrigued. I wondered if the sculptor had carved it thus, to match Swami's height.

'It's five feet nine inches,' Swami said smilingly, as He stepped off the platform. 'We never gave the sculptor a definite height for the idol.' A white cloth was tied, covering the Lord's limbs and face. It would be removed, to reveal the Lord in His glory, on 4 April, the day of the consecration.

But today, when I laid eyes on the Lord again, it was 8 June 2014. I realized that I felt differently towards the idol now compared to how I had felt at our first meeting. The gleaming black idol with the smiling face and mischievous eyes evoked a sea of emotions in me. I was attracted to it. Its powerful presence and graceful limbs evoked desire in me. It was such a strange thing to feel for an idol, to be sitting in the temple and be suddenly overcome with the awkward coyness of a teenager. I had walked into the temple accompanied by my younger brother Om, with the utmost devotion for the Lord. But while he admired the idol, I was stealing glances at it -- just as I did during my first meeting with Swami in November.

I was almost at my wits' end in the temple, wondering what was wrong with me -- and trying to make sense of my feelings. If this were an attractive, living man, no matter how far out of my reach, it may be quite natural to desire him. But who has ever heard of anyone being attracted to an idol?

That was my dilemma. I knew what I was feeling; in my heart, there was no denying it. I told Suvinder Gargas (husband of Swami's quiet, kind, radiant-faced sister, Upasana) and Om the very same evening that I felt so passionately about the idol that I was almost embarrassed to say it. Could this be how Radha or Mirabai felt for Krishna? Suvi Bhaiya, as I fondly call Him, teased me. He went on to narrate how Swami was only sixteen years old when He chanted Vedic mantras at Bhaiya's wedding. From his very first meeting with Swami all those years ago, Suvi Bhaiya had never once uttered His name. Swami's radiance and His divinity was evident to him even when Swami was just a teenager. Hearing such reverence in Bhaiya's voice, I marvelled at the charisma of such a person.

It took me a few days to be able to completely behold Sri Hari, to come to terms with the attraction that had unsettled me. Deep inside, I still felt the same enchantment that had gripped me at my first glance of His sculpted countenance, but the notion of it no longer made me feel uncomfortable. It was easy to love Him once I accepted that in flesh and in stone, they were the same.

I specially went to the side of the garbhagriha (sanctum sanctorum), for I was no longer allowed entry there now that the consecrated idol of the Lord was in place. I gazed at His left cheek. There was no sign of any mark on Sri Hari's face. Or on Swami's.

The Lotus Feet

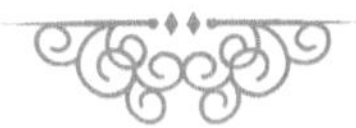

In the early days of my move to the ashram I was both wary and fascinated by Swami Raghavananda, the second disciple to be initiated by Swami. He had served Swami selflessly in the Himalayas for six months during the most crucial phase of His sadhana. A man of lean frame and small stature but by no means weak or frail, Swami Ragahavananda displayed none of the polish and gentleness that the other Swamis possessed. On the contrary his manner was loud.

I would see him moving about the ashram, keeping the sanctum-sanctorum clean, serving Sri Hari and chanting the Lord's name. Most nights he would just sleep in the temple. His laughter would ring in the temple hall many times a day as he conversed with villagers queueing for Sri Hari's darshan.

I wasn't sure what to make of him. His light-brown eyes at times made me unsure.

After all, it was a new place, miles away from civilization. It was natural for my conditioned human mind to be wary of its new strange surroundings and the only other three inhabitants. More so in the absence of Swami in the ashram, as He disappeared in solitude for weeks.

Eventually I let my guard down as I realized Swami Raghavananda's heart was as pure and clean as a child to whom everything is a play. He was kind and gentle too, just not in the accepted way.

The simple ashram life led by Swami's three disciples was a far cry from the buzzing activity I had heard ashrams were associated with.

Swami treated Swami Raghavananda with the utmost love and tolerance. Villagers and greedy construction workers would often approach Swami with make-believe statements about Swami Raghavananda's dealings in order to get more money out of the ashram.

To everyone, Swami would say one thing, 'Swami Raghavanda is forgiven a hundred crimes in lieu of the devotion with which he served me in the woods.' He then bestowed a loving parental smile on Swami Raghavananda. 'Nothing He says or does can ever make me distance myself from him. His devotion to me and the ashram is unparalleled.'

Swami had just returned to the ashram after a fortnight in solitude. Two months had passed since I had moved to the ashram. That morning Swami Raghavananda came in to discuss maintenance and other pressing ashram issues, such as acute water shortage, solar heaters malfunctioning, the JCB operator demanding exorbitant amounts to clear the ashram road damaged by the recent landslide, our neighbours encroaching on our land, letting their cattle loose and destroying our property.

Twenty minutes later when the meeting ended Swami Raghavananda bowed His head at Swami's feet, kissed the ground and in a swift movement leaned forward to run his palm under the sole of Swami's delicately dangling foot.

He then touched the palm to his forehead most reverentially, cast a shy smile in Swami's direction and in one hop skip and jump he was out of the room.

I had seen people bow and do pranams in many different ways with utmost reverence to Swami, but this was by far the most endearing and intriguing way.

I immediately thought of my own hesitation in bowing to Swami. It's easy to raise a person to a divine status and put him on a pedestal; what's difficult is to find that love growing every day. In this day and age where people are quick to flock to a guru, based on his persona, discourses, teachings and charisma and equally quick to spit and hurl abuses at him, I could only marvel at Swami Raghavananada's love and devotion for his Swami. I wondered if such a time would come for me.

⌇⌇⌇

In the months of August and September, we would all sit outside after dinner, enjoying the balmy evenings, basking in Swami's presence. The lovely evening breeze would sometimes blow in an enchanting fragrance. I would immediately speak up, like the overly smart child in the class who knows the answers already.

'It's that fragrance again!'

Swami would smile and in the dark of the night, His smile would seem more mysterious than ever. His striking eyes shone most beautifully, casting a spell on everything animate and inanimate.

One summer evening, Swami Paramananda was in the kitchen making a mango shake for us. The one fruit that Swami loves is mango. While we sat outside the temple waiting for our mango shake, Swami Vidyananda lightly massaged Swami's feet, adoringly playing at times with His toe. Swami sat on a chair, and we sat on the ground on either side of Him. Swami would tell Swami Vidyananda not to press his feet.

'I feel shy,' Swami would say. 'I don't like to take any seva (selfless service) when it is not absolutely needed.'

Swami Vidyananda would stop momentarily, start playing with Swami's toe and then resume.

Swami Paramananda had been gone twenty minutes, when Swami said to Swami Vidyananda, 'Swamiji, please go and see what's taking him so long, maybe he needs help in carrying the glasses.'

Swami Vidyananda got up and went to check on Swamiji. It was the perfect opportunity for me to ask Swami all the mystical questions that I had saved for Him. I started talking, my thoughts pouring out of me in a rush. As always, He heard me out most patiently.

I must have been speaking for a few minutes when He interrupted, 'It doesn't feel like you are doing it for the first time, does it?'

I was about to ask what He was referring to when I realized that I had taken up where Swami Vidyananda had left off -- I was pressing Swami's feet without even realizing it.

'Oh you are right, Swami, it doesn't feel awkward at all. It's the first time I'm pressing your feet, yet, it almost seems familiar. Why's that?' Again, the famous smile and no response.

Only on the previous day had Swami shared a little of Swami Vidyananda's several past-life connections with Him. Both Swami Paramananda and I had begged, cajoled and implored Swami to tell us how we were connected to Him. He had calmed us down by saying, 'What's the fun in telling you when you can actually see it for yourself? All in good time,' He had assured us.

My mind put two and two together. 'I've done this before, haven't I, pressed your feet in some life? I must have been in your service too!' Swami just laughed. 'Tell me, please, Swami.' If it were possible to shake an answer out of Swami I would have done so, but it is not possible to shake a mountain from its place. Instead, I waited for Him to speak.

'One day when you are ready, I'll show it to you, Dolly.'

'When will I be ready, Swami, I'm so unhappy and confused all the time ...' I thought of all the anger, ego and greed I had stored inside me. I was never going to be ready. Suddenly, I felt really sad. I would never achieve the things that I heard Swami talk about. I wasn't cut out for that sort of thing. I was weak and brittle. All my life I had given up on things and people too easily, too quickly. Putting His hand gently on my head He said, 'Think of a very fine needle. The thread has to be absolutely straight, free of knots and lint to pass through the needle. It'll happen.'

The conviction in His voice and its loving inflection had me struggling to keep the tears welling in my eyes from falling in earnest. I was nobody. I was unimportant. He didn't have to bother with me. However little my happiness mattered in the overall scheme of things, it still mattered to Him. I mattered. I felt like crying at His feet, emptying my heart out. He was my everything. Luckily, both the Swamijis returned just in time and saved me from ruining a perfectly pleasant evening.

I was still too warm inside to take a sip from my glass. I massaged Swami's feet, and this time not only mindfully, but with the utmost devotion. After a couple of minutes, I couldn't help but exclaim, 'Swami, your left foot is very soft and cushy compared to your right, which is as hard as a mountain. How is that possible?' Swami was about to take a sip. He paused before the glass touched his lips. 'You think so?'

'It's true. Feel for yourself.' I looked at Swami Paramananda and Swami Vidyananda. 'The left foot is like a soft, comfy mattress – it's fleshier – while the right one feels all bone and sinew.'

Swami Paramananda was the first to agree. 'Yes, Swamiji, she's right, the difference is definitely noticeable. How's it possible, Swamiji, for your feet to be so different?'

Swami's response left us dumbfounded. 'In my devotional sentiment, I seat Devi in my left. She is soft and feminine. So, the left side of my body is all her, whereas in the right sits Lord Narayana, hence it's all masculine and hard.'

There was no doubt in our minds that we were in the presence of divinity. Though we were all in such awe of Swami – the fragrant, beautiful, mysterious Swami – in some sense, at least, we were still discovering Him, catching glimpses here and there of unrevealed numinous dimensions of His being.

We were, however, quite used to Swami's ascetic side. Massaging His feet assumed even greater significance for us because Swami rarely allowed anyone to press his feet. He just wouldn't take physical seva. He would just let us touch His feet. So after that day, each time we would sit outside, the Swamijis and I would squabble over who would press Swami's feet.

Swami told us a joke: 'Two disciples were pressing their master's feet after dinner. Soon the master was fast asleep. In his sleep, the master turned to one side, burying one leg under the other. Neither of the disciples wanted to share this leg, and they soon started fighting over who would massage the master's leg. With neither ready to give in, the argument became heated and a fight erupted. Suddenly, the master woke to find one of the disciples holding a sword over his legs. "What's going on? Why are you holding a sword over me?" asked the perplexed master.

'Both the disciples replied in unison, "Master, please go back to sleep. The matter is just between us, and we'll settle it – even if we have to cut your leg off to settle it."'

We laughed heartily and Swami laughed too, as if He hadn't heard the joke before. That childlike simplicity, that innocence would wash away anyone's clever plans and thoughts in a second. His presence has that effect.

For all the pettiness we displayed around Him and manifested in our lives, He only ever bestowed love and compassion on us. I have come to believe that pettiness has steered all of us precisely where we now find ourselves. It is by Swami's grace that we can be free from the smallness that inhabits our confined hearts. If there is only one boon that we would ask Him, may it be that we become more like Him.

The Universal Consciousness

Men, women, children; young and old – people of all walks of life flocked to the ashram to see Swami, pulled by His magnetism and attracted to Him like bees to a flower. There was this strange longing that anyone who came in contact with Him experienced in their heart. A definitive void appeared like a sudden whirlpool in water as devotees left their Swami to get back to their lives, homes, husbands, wives, children, jobs.

The whole world seemed to be a sea of desires, and Swami, the one eternal answer to all those that were unfulfilled. And yet, in the eyes of the one desired by all, I never saw the faintest hint of desire. Never, not once. As women bent to touch His feet, Swami would quietly look away. Public expressions of devotion by both men and women were received with acceptance and grace. Everything He said and did was laced with love and care, and He always showed an acute understanding of the pain of those who sought his comfort.

There was no discrimination in His presence. He looked upon men and women as souls, and anyone seeking His refuge with sincerity and faith was granted His time and attention. If someone were to raise His voice in anger, utter words of hatred or argue, Swami would simply go quiet. Insolence and scepticism was met with composure and misdeeds with compassion. He would only say one thing: 'If I'm real fire then you'll melt one day.'

And I saw many melt and dissolve in His presence, including myself.

His heart would be moved by the smallest gesture, touched by the slightest sign of discomfort of those whom had travelled far to seek His blessings. Like a young, radiant Buddha, He would meet people throughout the whole day, and fill their cup with His grace.

I realized He was a guru unlike any other. I was witness to manifestations of many of His great powers and siddhis (abilities); but He would make no mention of them. Instead, He had the most practical approach to life. He would ask questions, answer questions and address us with a childlike simplicity. In fact, He had been insistent that His memoir be only an account of His journey, and not His siddhis. He didn't wish to mislead anyone, He said, as He had been greatly misled Himself by books written by masters glamorizing spirituality. He expressed great regard, though, for the account of the life of Sri Ramakrishna Paramahansa. Swami believes Him to be one of the greatest saints of our time. It is Sri Ramakrishna's simplicity that He admires most. Swami, I discovered, was not too different from the great Bengali saint.

Mother Divine spoke through Swami and healed through Him, yet He remained wholly unaffected by the adoration, adulation and wealth people were willing to lay at His feet. Offers of donation – cheques worth lakhs of rupees – were declined, simply because He saw no real devotion for the Divine in the hearts of men. For all those months in His company, I never saw Him take any gift or any money from anyone. He'd always say that whatever devotees would offer here, the Divine would have to return many times over. 'I don't stop people from doing good karma and do whatever they want for the ashram,' He said once, 'but all of that must go towards the ashram and social causes alone and none towards my personal needs.'

Swami would sometimes spend a week or fortnight in the ashram, and then either travel for discourses or briefly retire in solitude. While He was away, I realized the many challenges that living in an ashram entails. The middle of nowhere is exactly how a city person would describe the ashram's location. It was not only far from the hustle and bustle of regional cities, it was deprived of even a tea shop or a small rundown store from where you could buy a cheap packet of biscuits or bathing soap.

To purchase vegetables, groceries or other necessary items, we had to cross the river and travel forty minutes by road to the nearest town, Giripul. I could count Giripul's shops on my fingers. Built in a higgledy-piggledy manner, they crowded together on each side of the town's dusty main road. It is here that the villagers bought medicines after a quick consultation and prescription from the Doctor Sahib-cum-shopkeeper. The knowledgeable Doctor was actually no more than a certified compounder, a glorified pharmacist; at least, that is what his certificate on the wall indicated.

I would not have believed such primitive places still existed had I not seen this place for myself. It had its blessings, the least of which was the goodwill of the people of the district. Village folk had great veneration for Swami, and would occasionally bring fresh beans, peas, capsicum and ripe tomatoes from their fields for the ashram kitchen. This was a godsend, especially during the monsoon, when the ashram was virtually cut off from the town. The river Giri would rise up to our chins, all muddy and out for blood. Its swift current made it dangerous and at times impossible to cross to reach Giripul.

The only other means of reaching the town was via an eleven-kilometre stretch of road, running from the main highway to the ashram that had been carved into the landscape by JCB. It was not much more than a primitive, hilly track: narrow, unstable, prone to landslides and ridden with rocks, it was, in short, a very poor substitute for a road. But it was the best that could be managed. And with its completion, we were most grateful that we would no longer be completely stranded by the river Giri in spate.

The road ran through countless fields belonging to villagers, many of whom didn't always look kindly upon their neighbours. The biggest causes of friction there were generations-long feuds, based almost entirely on casteism. That such discrimination should persist in this day and age is as much a surprise as it is a matter of great sadness. Some villagers would engage in violence in its many forms, launching verbal assaults or outright physical attacks on their neighbours with monotonous regularity. Clashes seemed to erupt over the most trivial of issues.

On several occasions while I was there, Swami sat patiently with feuding parties and resolved their issues. Swami's humility was like no other. One time, to my utmost astonishment, He folded His hands in front of some of the more uncouth villagers whose dispute He was mediating. His unerring ability to see the goodness in people, and understand their concern and pain, gave Him unearthly skill in conciliation.

As the monsoon descended upon the region, it became as good as impossible to travel on the muddy road. It would melt away under the onslaught of the season's drenching rains, leaving little hope even for a small car to pass. A vehicle could easily become bogged, and if it slid off the track, its fate would likely rest at the bottom of the valley, several hundred feet below.

The rains were almost incessant once they started. For three to four days at a stretch, it would rain as if the sky had a grudge to settle. We would be holed up in the ashram till the rains stopped and the sun dried up the puddles enough for a car to find its way in. This was also a time when there was much construction happening at the ashram. Residences, guesthouses and separate washrooms for the hundreds of visitors that congregated to meet Swami were steadily forming before our eyes.

The hiring of labour, transportation of construction material, the JCB – all of these required the weather to be amicable. The sun needed to shine bright and clear, so the narrow road could allow the building materials to be ferried from the city. Most city drivers were afraid to drive in these parts and only the locals dared to do so, out of devotion for Swami.

The construction work was managed by Swami Paramananda, who liaised with the locals and meticulously oversaw its progress. The project, as most are, was time-sensitive; and with limited finances, the construction schedule could scarce afford to be interrupted by the weather and road conditions. Yet how could one even hope to stop the relentless rain from causing landslides that blocked the only road to the ashram?

It was while pondering this that I heard Swami say that we needn't worry, as the rains wouldn't bother us over the ensuing few days. I had read in the first draft of His memoir how He had performed yajnas (ritual of making offerings to the fire) out in the open in the Himalayas for holding the rain at bay. This He chose to redact, and it would not appear in the version of the memoir which went to the press. Now, it was absolutely critical that offerings be made for His sadhana's completion. But just as the occasion arose where I might be able to witness this feat, my sceptical mind questioned if shifting the very forces of nature was even possible. Needless to say, Swami was right: the rains didn't bother us, and construction work continued unabated.

Time and again, I saw ample evidence of divine intervention in the heavens above the ashram. Just as it would seem that a monsoonal downpour was imminent, Swami would quietly assure us that the weather would remain clement. The gloomy sky would inexplicably transform, the sun would shine, our trucks would move and the work would be completed with Swami's grace. He would then cheerfully warn us to brace ourselves, for the fury that He had been holding back would now be unleashed. And it would rain till we were thoroughly tired of seeing water.

It was hard to believe, but the rain would cease as He predicted -- even though the weather forecast indicated otherwise. And one doesn't need a weather forecast in this part of the country. The skies above the ashram relay their own telecast: one look at the dark, foreboding clouds covering miles of space above, and you knew it was going to rain. And yet, over the next six months, I saw the dark, sullen, gloomy sky shine bright like a summer day, and a scorching, blazing sky be run over by a herd of dark clouds raining with wild abandon when He so wished.

The weather would hold out at critical junctures for two or three days till a particular task had been completed on the ashram premises, or to allow someone to reach the town for a medical emergency or some absolutely vital official business.

I could only conclude, despite my hesitation in believing such phenomena even existed, it was happening in front of my eyes. It all seemed surreal at first, but the mind that questions will, as it bears witness, gradually bow with acceptance. I began to realize that manifesting His thoughts was child's play to Swami; He commanded the forces of Nature with His intent. It allowed Him to heal sickness and foster miracles as people came to Him with love and hope. I came to see Him as the very embodiment of the cosmic consciousness that pervades creation. And like creation, His word, His every action held purpose and meaning. There was no other explanation that would allow a mere human being, even a saint or a siddha to subject the gigantic, indestructible forces of Nature at His will.

In the month of February 2015, a college friend, Swati Vashishtha, the bureau chief for CNN IBN, Rajasthan, visited me in the ashram. She had planned a short three-day trip. Swati is a keen photographer with an eye for beauty in the most mundane of things. I was thrilled about her arrival, and eager to show her around the ashram. Swami was very happy that finally someone I knew and cared for was coming to visit me.

Swati arrived laden with gifts and vegetables, the latter being essential for me to properly feed my lovely guest. The evening before her arrival, I asked Swami if we could have a bonfire when Swati came. I cherished my memories of the previous bonfires with Him, and it would be simply wonderful to share this experience with Swati.

It had been pouring the preceding few days. Grey, sombre clouds had been building and angrily dumping their waters on the earth, and gathering again like a flock of ravens storming the sky. We built a bonfire near the hawan-kund next to the temple under a dark sullen sky. It was the new moon.

One of the joys of living in the ashram is gazing at the night sky. The vast expanse dazzles with stars, major and minor constellations trailing the midnight-blue sky. On a clear night, it seems that one can almost peer into eternity itself, into the space flecked with millions of galaxies. But not a single star was visible that night. It was as if black pall had been cast far above us.

The air was absolutely freezing, which made warming our hands and feet by the fire most enjoyable. Swami Vidyananda, Swami Paramananda, Swati and I sat huddled around the fire, each of us wrapped in inners and woollens. Swami sat in a chair, clad in His usual cotton robe, indifferent to the cold.

Both Swamijis sang heart-warming bhajans in Kannada. While Swami Vidyananda's voice was filled with love and devotion for the Goddess, Swami Paramananda's voice had a distinctive quality that made one swoon with the Goddess's glory, and lose themselves in the Divine's lap. Soon Swami also joined in, and music like the murmuring river nearby began to flow ceaselessly. Suddenly Swami said to me, 'Why don't you ask Swati if she'd like some tea?'

I looked at Swami strangely, for none of the Swamis ever drank tea. Also, He knew well that I didn't take tea or coffee myself, and hated making it too. In fact, there's a little joke I tell very often that if only I had developed a taste for making tea, I would still be married. It was 9 p.m. We had already eaten our dinner. So it was with some consternation I replied to Swami, 'Tea at this time?'

'She's your guest, Dolly, ask her ...'

I looked from Him to my friend, thinking any second now Swati will say, 'No, thank you.' But just the opposite happened. Her face creased into a delightful smile and she said, 'I wouldn't mind some tea: the lemon-honey tea you make, Dolly.' I looked at Swami to find a smile playing upon His lips. And then it sank in that He had read Swati's mind; He saw her craving for a hot cup of tea in the cold weather as she sat around the blazing bonfire. With a sheepish grin, I rose to make tea.

Fifteen minutes later, I returned with a piping-hot cup of tea for Swati, some hot water for Swami to sip, and joined in the quiet celebration. 'I'm sorry, Dolly,' Swami said. 'I didn't mean to send you away just as everyone here is enjoying the bonfire. But your guest was longing for a cuppa.' I had been reflecting, while making the tea, on how Swami cared for the slightest comfort of those who came to see Him.

I had been friends with Swati since college, but it hadn't occurred to me to offer her something she really enjoyed. Swati's love for tea was well known to me. But Swami had read her heart's desire and in the proper tradition of looking after a guest, He had pointed out my folly in a gentle fashion.

About an hour into the delightful evening, a fat raindrop fell on my face. One look at the sky above, and we all knew that in a matter of minutes we would be drenched. Mighty winds began to blow, announcing the impending rainstorm. I was quick to squeal, 'It's going to rain, Swami. Please don't let it rain, we are having such a wonderful time!' Swami smiled at my childish request, but I persisted. Swati was amused at my insistence, and the Swamijis too, smiled. They had seen enough of my pleas and tantrums in the preceding few months. Nothing about me surprised them anymore.

As always, Swami didn't let me down. From the depths of His throat reverberated an ancient Vedic chant. It was both the roar of a lion and the sweetness of the nightingale singing on a full moon night. With every verse the tempo built up, and to everyone's surprise, the more intense it got, the quieter everything around us became.

The noisy crickets, the gushing river, our breaths, even the fire forgot to crackle in those moments; such was the power of Swami's chanting. We were all mesmerized. Facing Swami, I closed my eyes, for it was becoming impossible for me to keep them open. The moment I did so, a blankness like a dark moon arose between my brows, and merged into the tremendous golden light emanating from Swami. From the beginning of the Vedic chant, when the sky was as dark as night, to its merging with the golden halo of Swami – all transpired in perhaps less than seven minutes. I opened my eyes, and as always started rambling immediately. 'I felt this darkness ... It merged into you.'

In response, Swami tilted His face heavenward, and what we saw took our breath away. Millions of stars twinkled in the sky. The dark clouds seemed to have been swallowed by the bright twinkling stars. The sky was covered with countless stars, and not merely covered: it was as if the Milky Way had come down upon us. From where had they rushed at Swami's command to light up the night sky? Not a few stars, or a thousand but millions of them, as far as the eye could see, the sky was studded with stars sparkling, as if it were the Mother Divine's cloak itself, sequined so tightly that only a slight trace of black was visible beneath.

It was truly fantastical, unbelievable. It was magic. Even if we were to believe that the sky had cleared in a matter of minutes, would not the sky still be marked with the dark clouds drifting at a distance? But not a trace of the clouds existed in the open sky. It was as if the sky had flipped over.

I was reminded of the night of another bonfire a year earlier, when the raging fire had cowered in fear at Swami's command, and today water and ether had wagged their tails, bowed their heads. The beauty of that starlit sky was unparalleled. There was no denying the light amidst and the light above. In that holy quietude Swami said, 'Mother Nature is Mother Divine. You become one with either and the other is at once yours.'

Laughing with Swami

The most memorable moments with Swami were spent laughing, and in that laughter there was learning of a lifetime. The ashram was open to devotees for a week, and many came for Swami's darshan and discourses. The tiny discourse room was packed. After the usual evening discourse, it was time for a few bhajans.

On one such night, Swami Vidyananda very mindfully chose a bhajan that both Swami and he could sing together. They sang *janma-janma se main das tumharo*', a very beautiful bhajan whose title means, 'I've been your servant for many lives, O Lord'. In the third stanza there's a line: *Main guan hen, dosh paripoorna*', meaning 'I'm without any virtues, and full of flaws'. Swami Vidyananda would always point at me whenever he sang that line to tease me, like a brother would a sister. I once told Swami of this, and He joined Swami Vidyananda and we all laughed uproariously. 'Yes, Swamiji,' Swami jokingly said to Swami Vidyananda, 'this line is apt for Dolly.'

When Swami Vidyananda chose to sing this bhajan that night, I started smiling. As soon as they approached the line, the smile soon turned into silent laughter, with my biting on my lips to stop them from quivering with mirth. The harder I tried to suppress the laugh, the more a grin spread across my face. There were people all around listening with great devotion and rapt attention, as quietly shook with laughter. Swami saw my reaction to the line as He repeated it, and His lips curled into a smile. He looked away, looked back and I was still silently laughing. This time, His face broke into a wider smile. Swami Vidyananda noticed what was going on; He too lowered His face to hide his smile as he sang.

Now the three of us were locking down huge guffaws that were screaming to be let out; but with all the people around us immersed in Bhakti bhava (devotional sentiment), this wasn't an option. It was a priceless moment to see Swami trying to keep a straight face as He sang before an audience mesmerized by the soul-stirring bhajan. Somehow, we all got through the bhajan without breaking into peals of laughter.

After the discourse was over, the devotees stepped out to have their dinner, while Swami had His in the discourse room. Just as we did every day, Swami Vidyananda and I served Swami His dinner. The moment I put the tray down, He said, 'Why were you laughing, Dolly? Seeing you shaking like that with laughter, I couldn't help laughing myself. It's just as how one child in the classroom laughs, and no one knows why's he laughing, but seeing him laugh the other children start laughing too.'

He then looked at Swami Vidyananda and said, 'And you, Swamiji, are no better, you also started laughing. I didn't know where to look, I couldn't look at her, I couldn't look at you ...'

'I was only laughing because you were laughing, Swamiji,' Swami Vidyananda protested. Both of them turned to look at me -- the ball was back in my court.

'So, Dolly, will you tell us, why were you laughing?' Swami demanded.

'Swami, I thought that line, "*Main guna heen, dosh paripoorna*", both of you were singing for me -- especially when you repeated it.'

Swami replied, smiling, 'That's not true, Dolly, whatever gave you that idea.' Swami Vidyananda started laughing. His expression said it all: there couldn't have been a more fitting line to describe me.

'See, even Swami Vidyananda is laughing!' I exclaimed. Swami said with the utmost seriousness, 'No Dolly, we'd never do that, even if it were true.'

We all burst into laughter. Swami is the wittiest person I have ever met. He is as sharp as a razor's edge, never letting a single opportunity pass to make everyone laugh. It is His nature indeed to laugh and sing, living in the moment like a playful child. And since this night, every time they would sing this song, they would both sing the line '*Main guna heen, dosh paripoorna*' three times, with Swami avoiding looking at me lest I made Him laugh.

The truth is, since I had come to the ashram, there were enough moments when my anger and ego had got the better of me. Countless times I had hurt Swami with my careless words and callous indifference. Swami bore it all, without ever raising His voice or showing me the mirror. He would simply go quiet, become unwell, lose His appetite and the very next day forgive my trespasses as if nothing had happened. It was only in time that I understood He was truly equanimous. Whether you were a sceptic or an ardent devotee, He was the same. His conduct was never dependent on the behaviour of the person before Him.

He owed me nothing. In my remorseful moments I would ask Him, 'Why do you put up with my trespasses?'

His reply was always the same, 'Swami never abandons the one who seeks Him.'

He would then tell the story of the drowning scorpion which a saint tried to save three times, and each time the scorpion stung him. A passerby saw this and said to the saint that it was foolish to try to save the scorpion a fourth time, as it was only going to sting him to death. The saint replied, 'If a lowly creature like the scorpion, at the lowest rung of evolution cannot let go of his nature to sting, then how can I being a saint forsake my dharma (essential nature) to save a life?'

So while I was a bit of a menace, Swami and the Swamijis in the ashram had accepted me as I was. Swami Vidyananda even joked about how not two days passed and there I would be, sulking in some corner like someone had died. It was so liberating to be accepted for what and who I was. To be allowed to make mistakes; to be forgiven and loved with nothing expected in return but that I slowly learn to let go of my fears.

This is Swami's way.

He loves and laughs, and makes everyone and everything around Him beautiful. His grace is like a waterfall cascading to barren rock beneath, till it is soft and pliant as the muddy earth ready for new life.

His tinkling laughter, filled with kindness, melts many a hardened, blackened heart. I would say if innocence had a face it would be like Swami's, if gentleness had eyes they would be like Swami's, and if compassion were a person it would be Swami.

The Absolute Reality

In December 2013, we embarked on a multi-city book tour. After the memoir's launch in Delhi, we were headed to Chennai. The venue for the book signing was the Tattvaloka Centre, an impressive building in the heart of the city. It was ten minutes from our hotel, ITC Grand Chola. The first thing that hit us as we landed at the airport was the scorching heat and humidity. While the whole of north India was experiencing the chill of winter, people in Chennai were perspiring as if it were the middle of summer.

We were received at the airport by the sprightly eighty-one-year-old T.R. Ramachandran and the gracious Sarla Panchapekesan. They had been running Tattvaloka, a popular monthly spiritual magazine, for the last few decades. What was most commendable was that the magazine wasn't run with the intention of generating profits. On the contrary, the magazine's staff had devoted their entire lives for service to their guru -- the Shankaracharya of Sringeri. Tattvaloka is a magazine sponsored by the Sringeri Peetham.

Swami was here at their invitation for the book signing event, as well as to guide their thirty-six member staff -- comprising mostly retired people as editors, the design team and marketing team -- to spruce up the magazine in keeping with the times.

The day before the book signing event, Anju and I dropped Swami at the Tattvaloka Centre for a meeting with the staff. Anju, an ardent devotee with unparalleled devotion, was with us on the book tour. She had specially come from Canada to manage Swami's schedule for the book tour, leaving her two teenage daughters and a son in the care of her husband. Everyone who has read Swami's memoir is aware of how Arun, Anju's husband, and her family had welcomed a year-old Swami when he first landed in Australia in 1999.

Both Ramachandran Uncle and Sarla Aunty were present downstairs to receive Swami. Their eyes lit up as they saw an ochre-robed Swami stepping out of the car, His entire being brilliant like the vermillion tilak on His forehead. With His usual briskness and a swoosh of His robe, Swami walked into the lift with them, asking us to pick Him up at 2 p.m.

Anju and I had a little over two hours, and we were going to spend it shopping. We made our way to the nearest shopping arcade, equally excited at the prospect of browsing through the shops. It is any woman's delight, no matter where she is and what she's doing; say the word 'shopping' and you have her undivided attention. As we travelled up the escalator inside the arcade, the first store to my right was one selling stoles and scarves. They had a colourful display, but definitely nothing worth a second glance. Or so I thought.

I was never a 'scarf' person. The last one I distinctly remember buying was in the year 2005. The idea of anything around my neck -- be that an accessory, chain or scarf -- made me uncomfortable.

But that day, not only did I pause outside the store, I walked right in, making a beeline for a cotton stole in ivory decorated with tiny pink stars. I pulled it off the hanger, showed it to Anju and was happy to get an appreciative nod from her. I pulled out my wallet to pay. Just as the sales lady was bagging my new purchase I said to her, 'You know what, I'll just wear it.'

She was happy to hand it to me after removing the tag. I draped it around my neck. It looked very chic with the comfortable black singlet and jeans I was wearing. It looked as if it was meant to go with this attire all along; like the missing piece of a puzzle, it fitted right in. A couple of hours later, Anju and I walked out of there laden with shopping bags, poorer by a few thousand rupees. For some strange reason, despite the stifling humidity outside, I didn't feel the urge to pull the scarf from around my neck.

We rushed to be on time lest we kept Swami waiting. Luckily, the meeting had gone over time, and we were escorted upstairs and seated outside the big conference hall. Ten minutes later, we were invited in as Swami introduced us to the Tattvaloka staff: Anju, as His long-time devotee and an important member of the team that managed His travel schedule and video feeds in Canada, and I as His editor.

We must have been the youngest people in the room, for there was not a single person there under fifty years of age. Soon there was a group photo with the staff, with Swami standing majestically in the centre. With His hands locked just below His chest, His head tilted slightly to the right and His lips parted in a benign smile, Swami looked like little Krishna surrounded by His herd. Shortly afterward, we took our leave.

'I rarely buy scarves, it's not my thing,' I said at the dinner table. 'I don't know what got into me today.'

Swami let out a loud chuckle in amusement and said, 'When you dropped me at Tattvaloka, I figured, "Oh she'll walk into a roomful of traditional devotees, clad in that thin black singlet", and I thought to myself it'd be wonderful if there was a nice scarf to go with it.'

I nearly jumped out of my seat. 'You did it! Didn't you, Swami? You planted that thought in my head. I don't care for scarves, let alone look at them and buy them, and yet the first thing I do as I enter the shopping arcade is stop dead in my tracks right outside a store that sells stoles!'

Swami laughed and said, 'Well, the scarf served its purpose.'

It was most uncanny for me to retrace the processes of my mind – analysing every thought, every impulse – to understand where the thought of buying the scarf had originated. In my musing, I also recollected a few incidents where He had sent Swami Vidyananda on some errand, making it appear as if it was Swami Vidyananda's idea all along. I took the latest demonstration of His power in my stride. In addition to His reading my thoughts, I was coming to terms with His ability to plant them in my mind, too. Soon I was to be bowled over by another feat, another reality. Just as I had witnessed numerous instances of His omniscience it was time to bear witness to His omnipresence.

Our next stop was Bangalore. Apart from the book launch event, several interviews with journalists of leading dailies and magazines were packed within our tight schedule of three days.

Requests from many people began pouring in for a personal audience with Swami. Bangalore has a very strong devotee base, and it was next to impossible to accommodate hundreds of people in three days. At the very outset, Swami had made it clear that for this visit there would be no discourses or private audiences, as His schedule was packed from morning to night.

But there are always people whose need is greater than others. Some are going through a personal crisis that singles them out in Swami's eye, and so once again, despite our resolution to keep His schedule lean, there were quite a few extra meetings scheduled over the three days. To this day, I have been unable to comprehend how Swami gets so much done within the same number of hours as everyone else. No meetings were cancelled with the journalists, yet He was finding time to meet those who absolutely needed to see Him.

One amongst them was a devout Devi-worshipper, Naren Shivappa, who had been practising Sri Vidya and meditating on Mother Divine for quite some time. Naren had specially driven all the way to Chennai, and along with Ramachandran Uncle, had come to our hotel to invite Swami to visit his home in Bangalore. Seeing his love for Devi and his eagerness to know more about Sri Vidyasadhana, Swami had agreed to briefly visit Naren's home in Bangalore.

We were a small group of three or four people who were accompanying Swami on the book tour. On the appointed evening, on the second evening of our stay in Bangalore, all of us visited the devotee's house along with Swami. He welcomed Swami with great reverence, prostrating himself before Him and performing arti at the door. Once inside the house, he washed Swami's feet with water, applied sandalwood to them, offered flowers at His feet and eulogized Him. I noticed how Swami never gave anyone both His feet. He only gave his left.

Naren showed us his altar, with its meticulously laid out yantra and resplendent Kali holding a goad in one hand and a head dripping blood in another. That the man was a Devi worshipper was evident from the vibrations emanating from his altar. His wife bustled about the kitchen fetching prasadam and other delicacies for Swami. He partook of very little -- no more than a couple of bites -- as is His habit, and asked them to simply drop everything and sit with Him.

There is nothing in this world that touches Swami more than a pure, pious heart. It is the love of a bhakta (devotee) alone that pulls the glorious and mighty side of our Swami out of hiding. That evening, Swami's divinity was evident in all its glory as He basked in the devotional sentiment of His bhakta, emitting a radiance, an energy that filled us with awe and wonder. Swami called upon the Mother Divine, sang a few bhajans, and I suddenly found myself overcome with great emotion and reverence.

I gathered a few rose petals in my palms, and offered them at His padukas, while He continued to speak. In the face of His divinity, my whole existence just crumbled. Though I was utterly convinced of the magnitude of the cause I had committed myself to, there were times when I would challenge Swami openly. But in that moment, I felt like nothing more than a pebble by His feet, and happily so.

With that glorious, heady feeling, we said goodbye to the family. Prasad Parasuraman, another dear and ardent devotee, was driving us back to the hotel. There was a divine quietude in the car, because everyone was still basking in the extraordinary radiance Swami was exuding.

Suddenly, Swami started singing a eulogy to Lord Narasimha. An astonished Prasad turned his head to look at Swami. He would recount later that just a few seconds earlier he had thought of requesting Swami or His Holiness, as he usually addresses Swami, to sing the Narasimha Stuti. Swami simply smiled at his apparent bafflement and delight and continued to enthral us with Narasimha Bhagwan's glories.

And so our merry caravan reached our hotel, JW Marriott. The small group did their pranams in the hotel lobby and the cars departed for the night. There were only four of us left: Swami, Anju, and the competent Narendra Anand, the devotee who had ensured at every step that our stay was a most comfortable and pleasant one in Bangalore. Like a sweet child he lingered at the door of Swami's suite. Anju and I were right behind him.

He asked in a low voice, 'Swamiji, please come home for dinner tomorrow night after the book signing event. And then of course there's breakfast at my place before you fly out to Mumbai the day after.'

Without thinking I blurted out, 'Dinner would not be possible, there's simply no time. Swami will be very tired. Tomorrow, the whole day He has meetings with journalists and devotees. And then there's the event itself.'

Narendra went quiet. Despite being well built and robust, his face fell, and he looked like a child whose favourite toy had been taken away. He had bought a new house and had been waiting for Swami to grace it first before he would move in.

Quickly casting a glance my way, Swami spoke up, 'Don't worry, Narendra, for you Swami will take out time.'

Swami chided me good-naturedly, 'Children shouldn't interrupt when the elders are talking.'

Needless to say, Narendra was thrilled. I had made a mistake by speaking out of turn, but it was quickly rectified, and with a minimum of fuss. An elated Narendra walked out the door. Swami beckoned Anju and me to sit. We had barely settled on the floor when He said to me in a kindly tone, 'One can never be too careful with others' sentiments, Dolly. A single misplaced word is enough to hurt them.'

He was about to continue, but I requested Him in my mind to say no more. My eyes had suddenly welled with tears, and I knew that with another word from Him I could not hold them back. My ego was as strong as ever, and I didn't want to make more of a fool of myself than I already had. As if reading my mind, He smiled most gently and pacified me, saying, 'It's not your fault. Breathe.'

I struggled to contain my tears and parked myself by the corner of the long couch Swami was seated on. There were some important things that Anju needed to discuss with Him regarding the next day's schedule. I sat quietly in the corner, on the floor, looking out of the huge glass window that offered a view of the forested park facing the Marriott. The view was magnificent from Swami's suite.

Anju and Swami were deep in discussion. It had been a very hectic and tiring day for Swami. He lay on the couch in the famous Vishnu pose, with one hand propped under His head and the other resting lightly to the side. His divine feet, formed as if carved by a master sculptor of classical times, were about two feet away from where I rested my head on the edge of the couch.

Lost in thought, I stared at the tufted green canopy the tall trees formed, and the luminescent glow the street lights beneath emitted from the vast line of trees. Dejected, I wondered how I had managed to ruin a perfectly delightful evening. I felt terribly alone, just like the trees outside; but even they had each other.

Suddenly, I felt as if someone was very gently stroking my head. I quickly looked to see who or what it was. Anju was seated closer to where Swami's head was and Swami's feet were resting in just the same place where I had seen them last. Thinking it to be my overactive imagination, I rested my head back on the couch. And there it was again: an unmistakeable sensation of my hair being stroked most lovingly. My hand quickly went up to my head. No, I wasn't imagining it -- it was as real as touching my own head with my hands.

Once again I lifted my head and glanced in Swami's direction questioningly. While He seemed engrossed in what Anju was saying, a playful smile lurked on the corners of His lips. This time, I dismissed the idea of speaking my mind. What could I possibly ask Him? I had made enough of a fool of myself for one day. I kept my peace, put my head back and waited for them to finish. And there it was again: the calming touch, a mother's gentle pat -- draining away my sadness, taking away the emptiness -- filling me with love. And this time, I realized it was Swami's foot that was tenderly stroking my head.

I could feel the big toe sliding down my hair, and yet between His feet and my head there was a clear distance of at least half a metre. I stayed put, unable to get over this amazing occurrence. How was it even possible to touch someone when you are not within physical reach? His foot continued to stroke my head most lovingly.

Ten minutes later, we did our pranams and left Swami to rest for the night. The next day, still perplexed by the unusual phenomenon of the last evening, I said to him, 'Swami, may I ask you a question, please?'

He looked at me penetratingly and smiled. For a moment I felt intimidated, because it was just not possible to hide anything from Him. It was impossible to veil my feelings with carefully chosen words; He would just look straight past them to the truth. Expecting Him to nod so I could continue, I was still forming the question in my head when He said, 'Don't wonder about how I stroked your head from a distance of two feet.'

I stood there, gaping.

'Experiences lose much of their divinity when we try to explain them, Dolly.'

I wanted to bow down at His feet to offer my pranams when He said almost immediately, 'I've accepted your devotion.'

I felt I had stepped into a world where the lines between the existing reality and that which I thought of as unreal and impossible had blurred. How could anyone reach out to another human being – let alone give them warmth and affection – without actually having touched them? Yes, it was possible – through words, a gesture, memories or a display of affection – to stir or trigger these emotions; but that is not what had happened.

Swami had manifested His touch without having touched my head in my physical reality. It was unbelievable. It was miraculous. It defied everything I knew and held to be true. I knew of a few devotees who claimed that Swami manifested in their dreams to warn them of impending danger or to guide them through a crisis situation, and He had been doing it for years now.

But what I had witnessed wasn't a dream, or a vision in a dream. It happened with my eyes wide open. It had happened in my physical, waking reality. Once again, this was merely dipping my toe in the cool waters. Soon, I would completely fall under.

The Silent Face

In His soon-to-be-published book on Kundalini, the origin of Kundalini, its practices, practitioners and the stories that have been told vibrate with an energy that is compelling. From Daksha's *yagya* to Ma Parvati turning to ashes, and Prashar Rishi's imparting the knowledge of Kundalini to Ved Vyasa, to the young yogi disappearing in the mountain with the King's horse: these are powerful stories. They are vivid beyond a storybook description. What would normally appear fantastical strikes you as the absolute truth. As I edited the book, reading and rereading it, I realized these didn't seem like stories merely from ancient scriptures; they were more like a first-hand account of events.

Swami's reluctance to share the source of His knowledge or answer any questions pertaining to the scriptures that document these details, has only reinforced my faith that He was indeed a witness to these events, and sees them as clearly as if He had seen them yesterday. It is this mighty consciousness that inhabits Swami's slender form. A consciousness so ancient and divine that it makes one believe that there is a God up there, and He exists just like you and me.

And yet, God needs looking after too. Those of us who are constantly around and in touch with Swami are protective of Him. The one who keeps us all safe, needs to be protected too, for He doesn't know how to protect Himself. He is often coerced into giving His time: meeting scores of people in a day, speaking for six–seven hours at a stretch, continuing to write and taking care of administrative matters. All this, and the constant asthma attacks brought on by fatigue, put a strain on His health. We find Him almost immediately on His feet after a severe asthma attack, though, giving a discourse, ever smiling, and listening to people's problems all over again.

One may well assume that such a powerful saint could fix His own health. I posed this to Swami once, and in response He cited the example of Ramakrishna Paramahamsa, who developed throat cancer and died a year later. 'Should I bother Mother Divine for such a petty thing, when this body is nothing more than a paper doll with a hole in the throat?' was Ramakrishna's response to his disciples when they urged him to ask Ma to cure his cancer.

Swami will move heaven and earth to help His devotees, but barely lift a finger to ensure His own well-being. It is this selflessness that makes us want to shield and protect Him. He is pure and guileless, offering His lunch box to anyone who asks for it. On numerous occasions, I have marvelled at His artless nature. I've been intrigued by his simplicity, the kind that usually only a child can feel and display. It seems as if after His darshan of the Divine, Swami is born anew, and feels quite vulnerable. In the last two years, I have seen Swami adapt to the ways of this world and insulate Himself. Just as a newborn learns to live in this world, He grapples with the pettiness, anger and hatred around Him.

Without a doubt, Swami's delicately tuned sensitivity is as much a cause for discomfort as it is inspiration. One time during the summer months, Swami was inspecting the area around the ashram to see the possible sites for construction of a gaushala (cowshed). The heat was scorching, as if the sun was merrily firing away at us in the open valley. As always, Swami was holding a black umbrella. In the early days, I found it a bit odd to see Swami carrying the umbrella about. No matter how mild or gentle the sun, Swami never left His cottage without His black umbrella. Some days, if the umbrella was left behind, He'd simply cover Himself with His robe. It had seemed to me back then that He was being too overprotective of His skin.

That morning after we finished His rounds of the ashram, He went and sat down in the discourse room. In the cool discourse room, Swami immediately turned on the wall and a table fan directing its cool breeze at us. It was a welcome change from the unbearable heat outside. As always, He took off the black slip-on shoes He wore and slipped His feet into wooden padukas. As He came and sat down, He started massaging His feet. It was then that both Swami Vidyananda and I noticed Swami's feet had turned a bright red. The skin seemed burnt and about to blister around the soles.

'Swami, did you hurt yourself?' I asked, looking at His discomfort.

Before He could respond, Swami Vidyananda said, 'Ayyo, Swamiji, your feet are burnt.'

I immediately responded, 'How did that happen?'

'Gurudev went out in the sun. It's so strong today. He went out without wearing socks.' Swami Vidyananda took some moisturizer from a bottle that was lying nearby and began massaging it gently onto Swami's feet.

'But Swami was wearing shoes,' I said. I looked from one foot to the other. How could His feet be sunburnt when He had shoes on? It seemed a little strange. 'Our Swamijis' skin is like a little baby's. Mahapurushas are tender like a lotus and hard like the Himalayas,' said Swami Vidyananda while massaging Swami's feet.

A soft smile full of love for His disciple spread across Swami's face. He tried to stop Swami Vidyananda from applying the cream, but to no avail.

Later, I had the opportunity to see pictures of the cave where Swami had His vision of Mother Divine. A couple of devotees had trekked all the way up there to pay their obeisance, and the photographs they brought back shocked me. It was no more than a cowshed; moreover, a cowshed in the most pitiful condition. My heart cried at the sight of those pictures. To visualize Swami living in this hovel for more than a year was quite a mental stretch, for it was simply not fit for habitation. Indeed, it struck me more as a place where desperate hikers would huddle to wait out a blizzard, than a place where a person would choose to stay. I can scarcely contemplate one surviving the harsh winter there -- especially one clad in the simple cotton robe that Swami wears.

There was no doubt in my mind that the soft and affectionate Swami was at once resilient and tenacious, with an iron will that even the gods couldn't shake. And yet, upon meeting Him, one would only experience His remarkable gentleness, His manifestly tender nature. As months passed, I found out just how tender He could be. Once, I was hurrying toward the discourse room carrying a warm drink for Swami when I stubbed my toe at the threshold. My big toe throbbed a little, but I ignored it. It wasn't painful enough to warrant much attention.

'That must have hurt,' Swami said, slightly rising from His asana.

'No, it didn't, Swami. I'm fine.'

'It's hurting, isn't it? Tell me the truth.'

Again I said it wasn't hurting at all, which was a partial truth.

'I know it's hurting, Dolly, because I can feel it in my foot.'

I stood speechless for a few moments. I had witnessed numerous such events in Swami's presence; but His capacity to experience others' pain -- either of the mental, emotional or physical kind -- profoundly, as if it were His own, was still baffling beyond words.

I have seen Swami radiate love and warmth, and dazzle with great humour and wit. He can reduce grown-ups to little children hankering for His one glance. The master coddles them all. A first-timer or a long-time devotee, it matters not, for He knows their innermost thoughts. The troubled soul finds peace in His presence and the anxious, questioning mind knows bliss. Just as one needs to stand in the rain to know how it feels to be soaked to the skin, the coolness -- the luxurious serenity of being in Swami's presence -- can only be understood by experiencing it.

It is the way His face breaks into a smile: a knowing smile; a kind and loving smile; a smile that disarms you. It makes you believe in the goodness of all things. It makes you smile in return; for those precious moments, your heart runs clear as water from a mountain spring. Who you are, what you've done, or what it is that plagues your spirit -- it is all forgotten, as He laughs and smiles at you. You laugh with Him, you smile with Him. You silently thank Him from the depth of your heart for having graced your life.

If I have witnessed Swami's playfulness and penchant for humour, I have also witnessed His silence – moments in which He is utterly quiet. As He withdraws from the world, a strange quietude surrounds Him. The energy around Him changes too, and you feel it strongly, as if you're walking in shallow waters and suddenly feel the riverbed's rapid falling away to its depth. His is the same divine form; but it now strikes a slight fear in your heart. The gaze that was so loving and soft becomes as piercing as the point of a needle. The chemistry of all things changes, and you start to experience the futility of your desires – their smallness contrasts with the gigantic proportions they have assumed in your life.

In silence, though, Swami exudes a rare tranquillity. His withdrawal from the demands and sorrows – the maddening, exacting pace of the world – is usually followed by a period of great contemplation. This may last anywhere between a few days and a few weeks. In His selfless life, there is not the slightest place for pettiness, distrust or manipulation of any kind. He gives without wanting anything in return. 'It's my dharma to give,' He would say, as if it were one of the countless mantras He chants.

It is a great burden for those around Him – and I call it a burden advisedly – to keep their hearts and minds pure of ego, selfishness and lies; for He is sensitive to the slightest change in human emotion. He knows even before you and I utter a word the intention with which it is said. It saddens Him if in our small, constricted hearts we cannot find kindness or compassion to share with those around us, equally desirous of Swami's time and attention.

These periods of silence are often triggered by small acts of selfishness, envy or deceit by the people around Him, which strike a blow to Swami's tender heart, making Him question whether His teachings are really changing lives. In these quiet stretches, He often ponders the reason He chose to come back from the Himalayas. He could have easily given up His body after the vision of Mother Divine, attained samadhi (union with the Divine) and be gone.

It certainly seems it was destined so in the distinct creases of His palm. Etched deeply in His fair, pink palm, the lifeline just stops midway, denoting an abrupt end to His life at the age of thirty-two -- His very age at the time of His vision. Swami's delicate hands, with long and slender fingers, are like the hands of Devi raised in blessing. The nine weapons of the Devi mark His palms -- scissors, goad, conch, trident, bow and arrow, lotus, discus, thunderbolt and mace.

They started to appear one by one as He carried on with His sadhana, undeterred by the freezing cold and frightening hailstorms. Devi doesn't merely speak through Him: She is Him. His Devi swaroop (divine self and form) is most distinct after a kirtan, where in His devotional sentiment, He is one with Her as He sings Her glories.

Swami has, in the past, stopped His heartbeat in a matter of seconds in the presence of a hall full of devotees. He has demonstrated this amazing capability to surgeons and doctors on numerous occasions. This is not merely a display of His psychic or spiritual prowess; it is proof of the power which runs through Him. Time that's a ticking clock for everyone is but a slave that stands with it's hands folded by Swami's bed side. This is not a clever expression on my part but a reality that's far beyond your and my understanding.

Swami is here by His own will.

He admitted as much publicly, for the very first time, at the book launch of His memoir *If Truth Be Told: A Monk's Memoir* in

Delhi. The auditorium was packed with booklovers, devotees and the HarperCollins team, including their CEO at the time, Mr P.M. Sukumar. Mr Sukumar posed a question regarding Swami's accurate prediction of His maternal uncle's time of death, prior to Swami's renunciation. Mr Sukumar wished to know if it were truly possible to predict the time of someone's death. In response to his question, Swami revealed this:

'I'm here at my own will. I can give up this body anytime.'

There are stillborn babies who have come to breathe upon calls for His intercession, and there are those who have been lingering on deathbeds for months, only to be delivered by His presence. These incidents are but bookmarks in the beautiful and mystical journey of Swami's life, a life that is truly devoted to serving mankind. It is His only purpose for being in this body. Swami's return from the Himalayas was motivated by two selfless reasons, as the world will witness.

He wanted to guide all those who were longing to seek God, as He had once sought God Himself. His extensive knowledge, of meditation, chakras, Kundalini awakening, the sonic science of mantras, ancient scriptures -- and many forgotten vidyas that have been reduced to myth and lore -- would have all died, disappeared with Him. And so He chose to return, to disseminate a plethora of knowledge that would help people lead better, happier, richer and more spiritual lives.

The second important reason He returned was for the only woman He has ever loved like the Mother Divine Herself: His birth mother, or Mata Rani, as He fondly addresses her. A queen no less in her own right, only a woman of her spiritual stature could have borne a son like Swami. She barely slept a wink for five months, praying day and night for His safety, remembering Him in every moment. Her son had set out to achieve the unachievable — to seek God, not merely in thought or theory, but to manifest the divine energy. How many have actually seen the face of God, let alone talked to God or manifested God at their will? This was Mata Rani's son's goal. It was virtually unimaginable to the human mind; and the only thing that she had ever seen Him desperate for.

She always knew that her son was highly clairvoyant. He could sense many happenings beyond ordinary awareness, and He often predicted events before they occurred, even as a child. As a young man in His twenties, He had created enough wealth to lead a lifetime of luxury; yet it wasn't enough to keep Him in this world. What do you do with a son like that? You set Him free. You let Him go where His quest takes Him. This is precisely what Mata Rani did; and she humbly bore the pain of separation and uncertainty that this entailed. For eighteen months, she didn't know of Swami's whereabouts. The countless nights she lay awake, worrying, wondering, praying for His safety; Swami experienced it all as He sat still in His sadhana, day after day. He felt her tears, her cries, her pain and her fears.

He came back for the mother who loves Him like no other. He had to come back for her.

The Divine Mother

I first met Mata Rani at Swami's birthday celebration in the ashram in 2013. She seemed a kind and thoughtful woman: she spoke to everyone and took pains to ensure they were comfortable. There's a striking resemblance between mother and son. At that point in time, though, I only knew this resemblance to be physical and in their shared gentle nature. Her face glowed just like her son's; she possessed the same gentle manner, and was soft spoken to a fault. It was hardly a surprise that the tree that bore the fruit was as sweet as the fruit itself.

Over a period of time, my interaction with her increased. She would often come to the ashram to hear Swami's discourses, waiting her turn like everyone else, and would be content with the ten minutes that Swami spared for her. Sometimes when I would demand – and demand not too politely – that Swami give me more time because I was an ashram resident, He would say in a quiet tone, 'Dolly, even my own family barely gets a few minutes with me. They are just happy to see me. How do I bypass the queue of devotees outside to see you? Can you come up and say in front of everyone that you are more important than the others, and hence should get more time with Swami?'

I couldn't answer Him. I knew I was wrong, but at that time I didn't have the courage to admit it. Instead, I remained tightly coiled, like a wire about to snap. He steadily and patiently broke my ego slowly and steadily until a time came when I was at peace, and I knew without a doubt that Swami could do no wrong. That was the beginning of the most wondrous phase of my life. Mystical experiences of all kinds began to manifest before me.

Mata Rani is an important figure in Swami's life. He would often tell of how she put a roof over her maid's head and helped her buy a piece of land and build a proper house; all on her meagre government salary. This is the same maid whose son's leprosy Swami had cured with a consecrated rudraksha, when He was barely eight years old Himself.

Mata Rani is the epitome of unconditional love. She once made a jar of panjiri for a pregnant woman, a labourer she had spotted in her neighbourhood. She just walked up to her and handed it to her with her best wishes. She has donated to just causes most generously, from her limited means, throughout her life. Anna-dana, gau-dana, swarna-dana, bhoomi-dana, vastra-dana, kanya-dana, vidya-dana; she has done them all. Her life is filled with instances of goodness and kindness.

So often, she would remind me of Swami – the same gentleness, care and generosity. She appeared to be just as patient with me as Swami, too. Anyone who had occasion to spend more than a day with me would learn of my foibles. I would be laughing and enjoying myself one minute and the very next I would withdraw into a dark, sullen silence, sadder than anyone I knew. She seemed to view this with equanimity and accepted me as I was, much as her son did. But although I knew her to be a kind and affectionate woman, and felt a certain affinity for her, we did not yet share a close relationship.

As I spent time in Swami's grace, my episodes of moodiness became less frequent, and the darker side of my nature began to wither. Like a pale new leaf, I now shook with laughter in the breeze of His love. Six months later, I moved to the city. The months I had spent in the ashram were transformative. It was the most blessed period of my life, for it prepared me for all the wonderful things to come, and the role I would play in these. I moved out to the city in March 2015.

It was during the time of the second retreat in Rishikesh in July that I had my next major spiritual experience. I couldn't go for the retreat, as there was plenty of editing work that I needed to finish. While I was busy working, my heart was there, at the retreat. I envied all those lucky people who were getting to see Him everyday, hear His voice and bask in His presence. 'Please sometimes visit me too, Swami,' I prayed to His picture. And then on the fourth day, Swami visited me.

I woke up in the wee hours of the morning, laughing and smiling, unable to believe what I had just experienced. I was barely older than a baby of six months, held high in the air by a pair of strong arms. Like a mother lies down and lifts her child high above her, shaking the little one as it gurgles and laughs, Swami was holding me up in the air. He was clad in white.

I was wearing a pale green crochet dress, like the woollen ones our mothers dressed us in when we were babies. There was a black thread tied around one of my tiny wrists, and a bangle with little silver bells on the other.

He was laughing too, but in that laughter there was the warmth of the sun, as if He had poured the love of all the earth into my being. I felt a mother's love as I had never experienced before, and like a bolt of lightning it ran through my tiny body. I gurgled some more, my tiny body shaking with mirth, as He brought me down in one swift movement and lifted me high. He did it many times, till our laughter synchronized, becoming one.

Who hasn't seen a child's delight at being swung high in the air -- her innocent laughter, her ear-splitting squeals? I was that baby. And not just that -- I was the silent witness seeing it all. The eyes of my soul could clearly see Swami holding the baby that was me! When Swami had previously manifested in my slumber, I had experienced a similar phenomenon: I was watching myself both sitting and lying at the same time.

But the vision didn't end here. His love was the light that came from Him. I was bathed in that light. Just as the tremors of an earthquake travel for miles and miles, His light travelled back with me into my wakeful state. It was now in my physical reality, and it consumed me, elated me as I laughed and smiled, unable to believe that I was a baby in His arms. I experienced such love, in every fibre of my being, that I couldn't sit still.

One of the first things I did upon waking was email Swami. Nothing could negate the excitement and bliss I felt in my every bone and sinew. A couple of hours passed, yet the euphoria didn't leave me; it was as if I had been infused with love. It burnt; it glowed inside me. A constant feeling of joy overpowered me. I could no longer contain this bliss. I felt I would explode if I didn't tell someone.

But who could I tell? No one would understand the feverish elation that ran through my veins. I was melting from the inside. This is what Mira, Kabir, Surdas and Rahim must all have experienced as they sang the glories of the Lord. The sheer bliss they experienced in His refuge made them unfit for any worldly pursuit. This was my state. It occurred to me then that with God's grace, the devotee experiences such profound bliss that everything in this world turns to dust.

Morning became noon, and yet the desire to proclaim my experience hadn't subsided. I wanted to run out on the road and tell people, strangers, that I had just experienced love in its purest form. I now understood why Krishna -- the child, the lover, the warrior, the protector -- were all the same. Love was in its entirety the face of God.

A faint thought had been waiting to be heard since morning, and each time it rose to my attention, I would dismiss it as sheer foolishness. There was only one person in this entire world who would understand that Swami was the Divine Mother indeed. I wanted to pick up the telephone, but I was reluctant to place that call, hoping the euphoric state would eventually wear off. But it refused to go away, so I finally called Mata Rani.

Her lyrical voice crackled with affection as she recognized mine over the telephone. In between laughing and talking, I managed to tell her the morning's episode. What happened next was equally amazing. Her voice, brimming with love and happiness, floated over the phone, her honeyed tones like soothing music in my ears. She was so ecstatic; I couldn't believe that someone could be so happy for another. My happiness was important to her. I had not felt more important and loved than I did just then.

She said something very beautiful: 'This world is false, every relation is false. The one true relationship is with God. It's the only one that matters.'

I felt stupid for not having called her all those months. I felt proud, too, for listening to my instincts and calling her now, sharing with her the love Swami had showered upon me. He had lifted me, not just figuratively but within another dimension, to a place where love was not an emotion or a need but a soft, mellow light that our souls emanate. I calmed down a little after speaking to her, and slowly my mind returned to its normal state.

I thought about Mata Rani and how graceful she looked when she sometimes sang a bhajan on my request. Her voice is a natural lullaby, immediately putting the listener at ease. It's from her that Swami has inherited His deep love for devotional music. He would often say that while growing up He only ever heard Mata Rani sing bhajans; no other song ever played upon her lips. There's a loveliness about her that comes from loving God. She has passed it down to all her children in equal measure. Swami's elder sister, whom He lovingly addresses as Didi, is an ethereal being. She radiates goodness like a light bulb emits light. She has a natural ability, like her brother, to make light of a situation, laugh and smile and yet appear quiet and reserved. Of all the wonderful people I've met in the ashram, Didi by far is the dearest to me and not on account of being Swami's sister, but the sheer love and consideration she has always shown me. I would be huddled in a corner of the temple trying to catch a glimpse of Swami as He gave a discourse. The temple would be packed with devotees with little space to even place a foot and out of nowhere Didi would call me to where she sat in the front row. It was as if she knew how important it was for me to be near Sri Hari, near Swami. It's a freedom like no other to be loved and accepted by Didi and Mata Rani. Their hearts are made of gold. It's the kind of gold that I've yearned for all my life. I light up in their presence, just as I light up in Swami's.

Then there's Rajan whose love and yearning for Swami, his younger sibling, is remarkable. Many days would go by without hearing a word from Swami. Being far away in Canada with his lovely wife, Pooja and two adorable kids, Rajan was the furthest from Swami. Between discourses, private audiences, ashram administration work, travel, answering hundreds of emails everyday, writing and editing, Swami would be so tired by the end of the day that He seldom had the energy to speak or even write back home.

He would often say, 'Like a brother, Rajan has always stood by. He had sold his only car when my business was down once to lend me money.'

A quietude would descend on Swami's face, as He would recount, 'Rajan never let me pay rent or anything else for the home when we lived together first in Sydney and then in Canada. Pooja and Rajan followed me wherever my business took me. She once told me that I was Rajan's whole world.'

But Swami's life was now devoted to the world, everyone was His family. And yet, with those whom He had grown up missed Him more than ever. Their affection for Him was unlike the love of His new family, it was a love without any demands. They were just happy to stand aside and love Him from afar.

I had a long way to go before I could be as selfless as them. Though these new experiences had begun to instil humility in me.

The logical, questioning human mind would simply dismiss my experience as a dream. But it was not merely a dream. There are three dream states in which Swami is known to appear. One is where He consciously visits those who have been calling out to Him for guidance or simply to quench a devotee's thirst for a vision of Him. The love and reverence of such devotees makes Swami appear to them. What makes these dreams distinct is that the devotee remembers each and every detail, as clearly as if it had happened in a wakeful state. It takes them a while to slip back into the reality of their lives. Swami's presence lingers like a favourite fragrance from the past.

With the second state, devotees may have been constantly contemplating Swami. As their devotion grows, their own thoughts at times manifest in the form of Swami in their dreams. These dreams may contain other people and images, and He may appear in the background. These dreams are vague, abstract, and may or may not make sense to the devotee upon waking up.

Then there is the third dream state, which is brought about by the devotee's ardent desire to have a darshan of the master. In this case, the devotee may have never set eyes on Swami in person, but hearing His glories or having read about Him has developed a strong reverence for Him. As his desire to seek Swami becomes most compelling, one of Swami's companion energies may appear in his dream, bearing Swami's grace and showering blessings upon him.

One of the characteristics of such dreams is the extraordinary surge of devotion for the master that ensues. I have experienced the first dream state numerous times, but I was still startled by the experience of someone who had never met Swami in her life.

His Grace

I had moved into my new apartment in March 2015. At the far end of the corridor lived a family of five: husband and wife and their three beautiful children. The middle child, Ashu, a twelve-year-old girl, would just drop in from time to time to play with Benoo (my adorable black Labrador). Most people — not just children, but adults too — are afraid of Benoo. Her sheer size and weight scares them off. Ashu was not the least bit intimidated by Benoo, and Benoo seemed thrilled to have a new playmate.

Eventually, both Benoo and I started looking forward to Ashu's visits. It was during her summer holidays that we would write essays or read a good story or a poem from her course books. I really wanted to inculcate the habit of reading in her; and what better book to begin with than Swami's memoir? I asked her to read a couple of pages every day. It so happened that her father picked up the book.

He would come home from work as late as ten, or sometimes even eleven at night. After finishing his dinner, he would settle down with the book and read it, late into the night. The next morning, he would gather all the children around and tell them the story of Swami's youth, His struggle in Australia and His longing to see God. The children would listen in rapt attention, and so would their mother. Until that time, I had no clue that theirs was a deeply religious family. They visited the temple each morning, read Ramcharitmanas and kept regular fasts – especially the Thursday vrata of Lord Narayana.

Both husband and wife were great devotees of Lord Vishnu. The wife would make prasada every Tuesday and Saturday morning and distribute it at the Sanatana Dharam temple.

On hearing Swami's tales, Ashu would come to me, excitedly telling me of how inspired her mother and father were with Swamiji. I had a hearty laugh when she came home from school and said, 'Today I remembered Swamiji before my exam, and it really went very well.' Or when she accidentally broke her father's brand new phone and prayed to Swamiji fervently to fix it. And He did, according to Ashu. It started working in a matter of moments after her prayer. A couple of days later, I bumped into Deepa, Ashu's mother. I had spoken with her briefly on a couple of occasions, but I didn't really know her very well. That day, she approached me.

'Swamiji's book is so wonderful! I can't read English, but my husband tells me the story. He's sometimes up till 2 a.m. reading the book. We are all so inspired by Swamiji. He's God Himself.' Her eyes welled up with tears. She tried to stifle her emotions, but the tears just ran down her cheeks. Ashu stood close by. Seeing her mother in tears, her small face became even smaller. Deepa dabbed her eyes, while I stood there not knowing what to say.

I was stunned. Here was a woman who had never heard of Him until a few days earlier. She couldn't even read the book, and yet here she was, so completely overwhelmed. What a clear-hearted person she must be, I thought. It had taken me more than a year to actually see beyond Swami's persona, and this woman had recognized His divinity instantly.

Over the next few weeks, my neighbours opened their heart to Swami. Whenever Deepa would see me, she would say in a voice filled with longing, 'I hope we can also have Swamiji's darshan someday. My husband doesn't get much leave from work. He has five mouths to feed.'

Ashu had told me many times, in her quiet and determined way, that she really wanted to grow up quickly so she could ease her father's financial burden. He worked very hard, and she was so proud of Him. I didn't know this kind of people existed, especially in these times. Yes, when I was young, our family was not too different from Ashu's; maybe that is why I felt an affinity towards them.

In a short while, their reverence for Swami grew astonishingly. In fact, from the day he had started reading Swami's memoir, Ashu's father would place the book in their home's temple. Soon, they began to pray to Swami. Ashu would ramble on about how her parents longed for Swamiji's darshan. She would then also give me a list of things she would like Swamiji to materialize for her on her birthday. My heart would warm just listening to her innocent chatter.

And then the unimaginable happened; or should I say, the inevitable. Swami visited Deepa in a dream. In her dream in the early hours of the morning Deepa, her husband and Ashu were seated in the living room, when there was a knock at the door. Deepa asked, 'Who is it?' It was Ashu who responded, 'Mummy, it's Swamiji!' On hearing His name, Deepa quickly stood up in attention. She felt goose bumps up her arms. Before she could reach the door, she recalls, Swamiji breezed in like a gust of wind. A radiant white light, bright and blissful, followed Him as He swiftly went by. She saw no limbs but an energy, His energy moving through the house to the kitchen, where He placed a white sack right next to the gas cylinder. She ran after Him, wanting to prostrate herself before Him. A feeling of disbelief and great joy flooded her being.

She knew without a modicum of doubt that it was indeed Swamiji. There was only one thought that dominated her mind – and that was to touch His divine feet. She stood right behind Him, hoping to offer her pranams. But the bright light disappeared as quickly as it had appeared. She woke up remembering the minutest details of the Swami in her dream. She even went to the kitchen, looking for the white sack He had placed there. She told her husband and children excitedly that Swamiji had visited.

The same evening she shared her dream with me, she asked in a troubled voice, 'Why did Swamiji not let me prostrate myself before Him? I can never forget that dream – every detail is etched on my mind. My only grievance is that He did not accept my pranams.' She crinkled her pert nose; a deep frown marred her attractive round face.

It bothered her that He had left before she could offer her pranams. It somehow detracted from the bliss she had experienced at Swami's darshan. I remembered my own first vision of Swami where I, a city girl, who barely even touched His feet in person, had an overwhelming urge in my dream to touch Swami's feet.

I was surprised beyond words that my neighbour, who had never laid eyes on Swami, experienced the same feeling of wanting to offer her obeisance at His feet in her dream state. It is as if the soul recognizes the divinity of the manifestation and loses its own existence. The only burning desire is to lay oneself at the master's holy feet; a complete surrendering of the ego, as the atman (soul) recognizes the Paramatman (supreme soul).

Understanding a little of Swami's ways, I knew that He never went anywhere empty handed. The sack He had placed in Deepa's house could only mean prosperity -- affluence and abundance. For Swami grants His devotees that which they need most, and Ashu's family now had it all; even if they didn't know it yet. And I wasn't too far off the mark. A couple of months passed when Deepa confided in me that not too long before Swamiji appeared in her dream there was not a grain of wheat or rice in her kitchen. Her husband had been out of work for seven months and they were in dire straits. Things had only started to improve recently. Sobbing softly she recalled how for days altogether she would make the children porridge for lunch and dinner. The more she cried the more she thanked Swami for protecting her family. I stood marvelling at the simplicity of this pious woman. At the time I could not have known that soon Deepa would become my closest friend, her family would become my family and my dog would become her dog. Much later I had this realization that often miracles manifest in the form of people, to transform you and your life.

Ashu was now remembering Swami, day and night, praying to His picture in their temple; summoning Him for all the little worries she had. The answer to all her difficulties at school was Swamiji. According to Ashu, every time she prayed, He answered.

Look at the innocence of a child, I thought. She believes He is the reason her class teacher didn't change her seat, or that she was included last minute in a dance programme for which she had been overlooked. The conviction with which she would say, 'Today Swamiji heard my prayer again,' was both endearing and amusing. Ashu came to me a few weeks before her birthday. She said, 'I've one wish on my birthday that I want Swamiji to fulfil. That'll be my birthday gift from Him.'

'Tell me, what would you like Him to give you, Ashu?' I indulged her.

'Can you please ask Him to come in my dream on the night of my birthday? It's the one thing I want the most for my thirteenth birthday.'

'Well, I can't ask Him that, it's your birthday, you invite Him.'

It was decided that Ashu should write a letter to Swami. I promised to email the letter to Him. In her elegant, cursive handwriting, this sincere child wrote a two-page letter that began with 'Dear and Respected Swamiji'. She had very thoughtfully slipped the letter in an envelope and lined it with a shiny green wrapping paper. I took a picture of the letter and emailed it to Swami. I was as excited and anxious as she was that her letter reach Swamiji.

Just as Ashu was leaving after we had sent the letter, she said that I could read it too. When I read the letter, I was once again amazed at the purity and innocence of the little girl, for much of the letter was about me: how we met, what we did together. It was only toward the end that she had asked Swami to come in her dreams and that her family wanted His darshan. I gently chided Ashu for not writing more about herself and instead filling the pages talking about me.

She waited the whole day for Him to respond. Swami wrote back a most touching email to Ashu, wishing her happy birthday in advance. He wrote how proud He was of her, and asked her to give the utmost respect to her parents. Toward the end of the email was a line that read, 'One day I will give your family my full darshan. Please tell your mother that I will always protect her family.' Need I mention the response of Ashu and her parents — they were moved beyond words by the simplicity of this saint whom they had never met. Their joy knew no bounds as they offered their prayers to Swami.

Over the next two weeks, Ashu continually asked me — pestered me, actually — 'Will Swamiji still come in my dream?' 'He has a lot of important work to do, and He did reply to you, what more can I ask for?' I replied. She was undeterred, though. A day before her birthday, as she was unwrapping her gifts in my living room, she said, 'Today's a very special night, because Swamiji will come in my dream.'

'Sure, you pray to Him before you go to sleep.'

'Yes, that's why I'm going to sleep early tonight.'

While I had said what she needed to hear, I didn't really believe that He was going to come. Several times before going to bed, I thought of dropping Swami an email. It would mean so much to the child. I also remembered how Lord Shiva had appeared in His dream when He was a child Himself. That one dream had changed the course of His life, and in some corner of my heart, I felt that maybe Ashu's belief in God would be reinforced forever if Swami did come to her in her dream.

But I didn't write those things to Him. It seemed silly to ask Swami, the saint, the divine being to indulge a child's wish. Even grown-ups — people of power and importance — didn't have that privilege; and here, a mere child wanted Swami's darshan in her dreams — what's more, she wanted His darshan tonight.

The next morning, Ashu came over before going to school. She had brought her little cousin. With Benoo jumping all over them, I somehow managed to wish and hug her. I scanned her face to see if she had something to tell me, but she was busy playing with Benoo. I mentally braced myself, thinking that soon she would be asking me, 'Why didn't Swamiji come in my dream?'

But she didn't bring it up for a good five minutes. 'So, were you able to sleep all right?' I asked.

'Oh yes, Swamiji came in my dream,' she replied with the carefree air of a child as she busily played with Benoo.

'He did? Ashu, tell me everything!' I commanded her.

'He gave me a gift, a white gift-wrapped box. I took it from Him and bowed.' She enacted the whole thing, accepting the gift and then bowing in front of Him, as a child would walk up to the school podium and accept a prize. 'Everything around us was white. He was in His orange robe, with a red tilak and another one, pale yellow, high up on His forehead. He looked all round and cute just like in His picture. Oh, and He was wearing these wooden slippers ...'

'You mean, padukas?' I was very excited by then. Even though Ashu had glanced at a couple of Swami's pictures in my house, she had absolutely no clue that He wore padukas whenever He visited someone's home in real life. She had not seen a full-length picture of Swami.

All the devotees who have had the honour of hosting Him know that Swami never enters anyone's house without His padukas. Ashu carried on with her description of the padukas. 'They looked like they were made of wood, or painted like that, and there was a knob-like thing in the front, in which Swamiji had slipped His toes.'

This was incredible: she had described Swami's padukas most accurately. In the ashram, while cleaning the pravachan room before the discourses, I had cleaned the padukas countless times. 'What about you, Ashu, did you see yourself?'

'I did see myself, but I really didn't have a body. Swamiji was right there, smiling at me. I remember the dream as clearly as seeing it with my eyes open.'

I was astounded. A child had called upon Him with all her faith and might, and the loving Swami had come running. It was so easy to win His heart, to lure Him into our lives with love and devotion. I felt so humbled in that moment; if somewhere He had heard Ashu's plea, He had also heard mine. It meant the world to me that this child was granted her wish. Sitting in my home, I marvelled at how life was so filled with delights; that such secrets were hidden in each unfolding moment.

The gods we had placed in our temples, believing them to be an idol or a picture in a frame, actually walked among us. It was our lack of conviction in calling them that kept us separated from them. Ashu had called, and Swami had come; this was the truth, a simple truth that most lacked the faith to comprehend. A child's purity and innocence is needed to behold the Divine.

A Glimpse of the Divine

The next opportunity to be in Swami's presence came in the last week of May 2015. The first youth retreat was being held in Rishikesh. Swami Vidyananda, Swami Paramananda, Mani, a most devout and steadfast devotee and I were travelling with Swami from the ashram to Rishikesh by road. It was a six-hour-long, wondrous journey through undulating terrain. On the way, Swami sang many devotional songs of Mother Divine and regaled us with the story of Lord Narasimha.

He described all the tiniest details of the Lord's form, from His sharp talons to His piercing eyes. This avatar of the Lord was taller than the tallest trees found in the deepest mountain valleys. And with His long hair flying in rage, His was a form so vengeful and immense that it struck fear in our hearts. Swami's voice and presence seemed to extend far beyond the confines of the Innova in which we were travelling. It was as if Swami was seeing ahead, far ahead, reaching into the recesses of His mind as He narrated how Lord Narasimha had torn Hiranyakashyap apart with His bare hands, only to become more wrathful than before.

I had read many storybooks in my childhood of this ancient battle between good and evil, but none could match the vividness, the clarity of Swami's monologue. It was as if He was narrating from His own memories.

'Bolo Narasimha Bhagwan ki Jai,' said Swami, in a voice that commanded us to repeat these words with fervour. A sudden hush fell in the car after the jaikara (ovation). None of us dared ask any questions -- for once, even I had none. The energy in the car, palpable and elevated, was such that each of us sat quietly, thinking about the story. All this while, Swami continued to stare straight ahead, unblinking. It felt like a ball of fire, a body of energy was seated ahead. I felt its heat; we all did. Some twenty minutes later Swami spoke, and immediately the tension was diffused. He smiled and spoke of innocuous things, like checking Google maps to see if we were on the right route.

The teenagers' retreat was a four-day affair. They liked the carefully put together handouts, which listed the core virtues that would enable them to study better and make more informed choices. They asked Swami all sorts of questions, ranging from what kind of car He owned to whether He had girlfriends in His youth. Swami had them in fits of laughter from the outset. Nothing was off-limits in His sessions; no question was too silly or unimportant for Him.

There were kids from various walks of life, and between them, they shared the gamut of teenage woes. Some came from homes where their parents fought constantly; others just felt lost or unable to handle peer pressure. There were those bogged down by relationship issues and child abuse, and a few had taken to substance abuse to numb their pain. Swami met them all one by one, healing some, inspiring some, motivating them to spend their youth studying and working hard so that they could have a better future.

Sitting in the audience as a volunteer, all I could think of was: I wish I had this guidance when I was a teenager. Someone to tell me to read better books, to work hard, to have a passion and a hobby to pull me through tough times. Someone encouraging me to work hard in school and college so I could enjoy an easier and more rewarding adult life. All of us -- adults and teenagers alike -- were deeply moved by Swami's inspirational talks during the four days.

On the fourth day, it was time for us to return. Swami was headed to Uttarakhand, where He would retire for a period of solitude, in which He would finish some of His writings and take a break to recuperate. Exhaustion had crept up on Him over the preceding eight months, mostly from meeting devotees and tending to their needs without respite.

Since only a handful of volunteers remained, Swami decided to join us all for lunch in the hotel's riverside restaurant. As soon as He walked in, some eight or ten of us rushed to claim the chair closest to Him. Someone kindly nudged me to get inside as we had joined two tables together, and to my delight I ended up sitting in the chair opposite Swami. Everyone knows Swami's fondness for cottage cheese, and an entree of it was ordered.

The waiter placed two sizzling-hot plates in front of us. Swami offered, as usual, the first morsel to Mother Divine. He very gently put a grilled juicy cube of cottage cheese on His plate, offered it to the Divine and asked everyone to help themselves. He picked up the fork again to slice the cube, when a thought crossed my mind.

A small bowl of fresh chutney was sitting right in front of us, and I thought that if Swami had the cheese with the dip it would taste so much better.

'Please have the chutney, Swami,' I said in my head. 'It'll taste much nicer.'

Between that thought forming in my mind and Swami acting on it, there was a lapse of barely a few seconds. Without looking up at me, He pulled the chutney bowl closer and put a spoonful on His plate! A faint smile played upon His lips. I could neither control my disbelief nor my laughter as it rang through the dining hall. My companions looked at me strangely, but they were used to my bursting into laugher in Swami's presence for no apparent reason every now and then. Perhaps some even considered me frivolous, but they all set about enjoying the meal nonetheless. If only they knew these recurrent bouts of laughter -- these sudden bursts of energy -- were because Swami would so often read my mind when I would least expect it.

A word would flash in my mind during a discourse. I would think that Swami could have used this word in His talk instead of the word He had just uttered, and the very next second Swami's powerful mind would pick that word itself and weave it into His discourse. It was as if His mind was everywhere. I have often felt that the energy field around Him is so vast that all our individual energies present are then connected to Him. I have seen so many miracles of His profound connection to those seeking His comfort that I have lost track of them.

It was around 4 p.m. when we finished lunch, and it was time to do our pranams and take Swami's leave. The very thought of undertaking a six-hour-long journey back home without Him filled my heart with dread. I said to Him, 'Oh, we are all going to miss you. The journey won't be the same without you.'

He was fatigued from the routine of the last few days, but still, His smile was as delightful as the late afternoon sun. He raised His palm in the air in blessing and said, 'Go, I'll be with you. You won't miss me even one bit.'

Still unconvinced I said, 'Who'll tell us stories now?'

He laughed, and pointing to Swami Vidyananda, He said, 'Swamiji will tell you stories on the way, Dolly.' I mentally rolled my eyes. Swamiji is a very learned monk: His knowledge of the puranas and legends is no less than anyone's, but his story-telling skills are somewhat hampered by his broad Kannada accent.

Swamiji's idiosyncratic pronunciation would sometimes delight us, and occasionally give rise to confusion. When Swami was away in solitude during my early days at the ashram, Swami Vidyananda took me under his wing, and imparted to me as much of his vast spiritual knowledge as time permitted. Swamiji became my spiritual brother and guide, and we would spend many mornings talking after he had finished teaching me bhajans and Vishnu Sahasranama (song of praise of the God's thousand names). Mostly, we would talk about Swami, life at the ashram, spiritual books and literature. Swamiji had read some of the finest Telugu writers, and his knowledge of classical music and ragas was impressive. On one such morning Swami Vidyananda asked me, 'Why don't you start writing again? Gurudev says you are a published author and a good writer.'

'I don't feel like writing fiction now, Swamiji, and I'm too immature to take up writing spiritual stuff.'

'What kind of stories did you write?' He asked.

'Mostly dark stuff -- murder, love, revenge and deceit were the themes of my previous three novels. It was all fast paced and edgy. My books would entertain readers, but they wouldn't make a real, lasting difference to their lives.'

He leaned forward in his chair, trying to get a better grasp of what I was sharing, 'Omelette, like omelette,' He said.

'Swamiji?' I thought I had misheard him. Again, he said, 'Omelette, you write stories like omelette.' He couldn't be talking about omelette in the middle of a conversation about books; and all the more so with his being a staunch vegetarian, I thought. Once more he repeated the word with the same confidence. And then I understood. '*Hamlet*, Swamiji, you mean *Hamlet*, Shakespeare's play *Hamlet*?' He nodded and said, 'Yeah, yeah, that's what I said!'

Lord, how I cracked up that day. It took me quite some time just to find my voice. There were many such fun moments with Swami Vidyananda, so while I knew that we would have a wonderful road trip, I also knew it was not his storytelling skills that would keep me enthralled.

After a wistful goodbye, Swami Vidyananda, Mani and I got into the car and departed. Soon, all of us started talking. Swamiji then began telling us the story of Markandya Rishi, who was sentenced to death by the King, after a thief had laid a part of his loot at the noble saint's feet while he was in dhyana (deep meditative state). Swamiji's erudite mind had no shortage of such tales, and they kept his tiny audience in rapt attention. Just as Swami had predicted, I was so engrossed in Swamiji's telling of stories from the puranas that I didn't think of Swami even once.

Around 8 p.m. we made a pit stop. There were still a couple of hours more of travel ahead before we would reach home. Exhaustion hung heavy on us all. For the preceding few days, we had been waking up at 5 a.m. daily, attending talks throughout the day and sleeping late. This day had been long and hectic too, and we were fatigued beyond our wills to stay awake. My eyelids began to droop, and I readied myself to nap. Though it was the peak of summer in May, due to exhaustion, hunger and travel sickness, I felt cold. The air-conditioning in the car was adjusted, but I still felt cold. I pulled a scarf out of my bag, the same one Swami had subtly urged me to buy in Chennai, and wrapped it around my head.

The next two hours passed in keeping my head from hitting the window as I drifted in and out of sleep. Bone weary, I just wanted to get home, to sleep in my own bed. We reached Chandigarh at around 10 p.m. I had a quick meal and dropped Swami a brief note thanking Him for a wonderful journey and how I had the most amazing time listening to Swami Vidyananda's stories.

'There was not even one uninteresting moment in the journey, Swami, just as you had promised. Thank you for travelling with us today.' I teased Him in my email.

Swami's short reply just a few minutes later took the wind out of my sails. 'Really, then who was sleeping like a baby with a scarf wrapped around her head, bumping into the window now and then?'

A shiver passed through my body, and coursed through my heart with disbelief. His piercing gaze had seen through the curtain of time and distance to check where we were, if we were travelling safely. He had been looking out for us all along. How do I even begin to explain the magnitude of His powers or His compassion? It was then I realized that I may have been parroting that Swami sees and knows all but today was unlike any other day, His reach was beyond the scope of my rational thinking mind.

The Wish-Fulfilling Lord

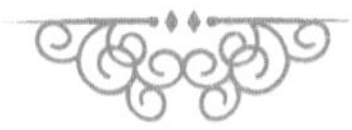

I no longer lived in the ashram. But its pull was such that every couple of months I found myself crossing the river and walking the familiar, uneven path to its sanctuary.

In October 2015, I was assigned the task of looking after the book counter. The meditation camps in Hindi and English were scheduled back-to-back. It was the first time that such an event was being organized in the ashram. I reached there a few days early, as did the other volunteers.

The volunteers laboured under the guidance of Swami's dear disciple, Ma Shamta, a gentle but resilient soul who had endured much in life with the grace and poise of a saint. They worked hard to organize bedding, allocate accommodation, draw lists, and clean rooms, bathrooms and the outdoors. The temple hall, lined with bright red cushions facing Sri Hari, was converted into a mediation hall.

Once the camps started, the days flew by. Swami would take us all on a joyride, full of mirth and laughter. There were many first-timers who had signed up for the camp after reading Swami's memoir and didn't know what to expect.

Within the first couple of days, their avalanches of questions and doubts swiftly melted away under the warmth of Swami's presence – not to mention his infectious humour and no-nonsense approach. It was heart-warming to see the temple hall reverberating with laughter.

After the morning discourse while Swami gave private audiences to people, a small crowd would gather around my tiny book counter. Many were keen on knowing more about Swami. The regular question that everybody asked each other was, 'Since when have you known Swamiji?' In every corner of the ashram people were only talking about Swami.

It was also the first time we had set up the book counter. I remember Swami Vidyananda's excitement as he arranged and rearranged the books on the table. For eight years, he had looked after the book counter at the Bangalore ashram. He had quite a few tips to impart to a newbie like me. As always in these light-hearted moments, I felt really grateful to Swami for bringing me into His fold, amongst people whose hearts were pure and truly childlike. Even as the books sold like hotcakes, I marvelled at how Swami, the author, had produced four books in less than a year.

The memoir was released in December 2014 and a mere eleven months later, we had four titles on display:

If Truth Be Told
The Wellness Sense
A Fistful of Love
Satya Kahoon To (the memoir's Hindi translation)

Only He could have pulled off a feat like this. Swami's simplest thoughts invariably manifest. So when Swami decided that writing would become one of the vehicles to foster change, how could Nature be a silent spectator?

One of the things that I enjoyed most at the ashram was dressing in traditional clothes. Most evenings when I attended Sri Hari's arti, I would wear a simple bindi and colour my lips red or pink. I relished wearing vibrant colours. It was sheer bliss to look beautiful for my Lord both in flesh and stone. To me, it was no less a divine act than singing the glories of the Lord. If for others closing their eyes in prayer was worship, then for me, staring at the vigraha (idol) lovingly, daringly, asking the Lord to look at me and smile at me was worship.

I would stand near the chrome railing that separates the garbhagriha from the rest of the temple, gazing at the idol of Sri Hari as Swami would raise the conch and blow it three times. Like golden wheat swaying in the breeze, His lithe body moved with the divine eulogy. He would lean forward on His toes and raise His hands high as if welcoming the ever-smiling stone idol into our hearts.

After the arti when Swami would settle down on His asana and face the crowd, I would be sitting right in front of Him. While the purity of my sentiment was clear to the Divine, it did not seem to be so for everyone. Sometimes I caught stray glances from other devotees which would betray their wondering, their silently questioning of my zeal for dressing up for the occasion. It was an ashram after all -- a place where one forswore all pretence and quietly remembered the Lord. Many came dressed in white, in pastels -- in sober clothes -- covered from head to toe. And here I was, flashing like a neon sign on a highway at night. Perhaps it was hardly surprising that they saw me as ostentatious.

The night before Diwali, Swami joined us for dinner in the dining hall, as He would do sometimes when there were only a handful of devotees present. After we finished our meal and Swami left, the remaining devotees got up from the floor and carried their plates, glasses and spoons to wash them outside. Shakti, a volunteer from Chennai, had stayed back for Diwali. He had been working tirelessly during the ten-day-long camps. For our limited interactions, I had found him to be amicable; a decent chap. He had a frank, genial face, and behind his heavy spectacles were smiling eyes. His English was coloured with an accent not too different from Swami Vidyananda's.

Shakti and I were sitting side by side. I had finished eating but he had just begun, as he had been serving all of us. I decided to sit with him till he finished his meal. We got talking, and soon the most common question – one that I had been asked at least a hundred times – was again asked of me.

'How did you meet Swamiji?' Shakti asked.

I smiled at the question. I told him to wait till my book on Swami comes out and he can read all about it there. He persisted, asking that I share something of my experience with him.

'Swami appears to you in the sentiment in which you revere Him. If He's merely a guru to you, then He'll play out the role most beautifully, but if He's your God, only then and then alone will you experience His mystical and divine side. He's all pervading.'

I must have spoken non-stop for twenty minutes as I recounted vignettes from my time at the ashram. All the while Shakti sat, his mouth agape.

'Swamiji reads our minds?' He uttered in disbelief.

'He does, Shakti.'

'Oh that's why ...' He said, 'Yesterday, while we were having dinner, you were laughing loudly for no apparent reason. I thought to myself, why is she laughing like this in Swamiji's presence when everyone else is sitting quietly? It's disrespectful. The second I had this thought Swamiji said to me, "Shakti, she's like a child."'

And suddenly it all became clear to me. On the previous evening, they were serving two different kinds of sweet, and I had only been served one. I was hoping someone would give me the other sweet, when Swami called out to the person serving us, 'Please give the coconut barfi to Dolly.' I had started laughing, thinking how even my greed wasn't hidden from Him. Swami had smiled and then suddenly He had looked up in the other direction, where Shakti and a few others were sitting, and said, 'Shakti, she's like a child.'

He had read Shakti's judgemental thoughts as clearly as He had read my rapacious ones.

Suddenly Shakti became serious. 'I have a confession to make. Please don't take it to heart ...'

In his delightful, broad accent, he continued. 'Swamiji had come to Chennai for the memoir's book launch in December 2014. The event was organized in the Tattvaloka auditorium. It was you who introduced Swamiji before the event, right?'

'Yes, it was.' I was most curious to know where he was going with this.

'I asked Ashish, an IITian, another young devotee of Swamiji, if he knew who this girl was. Swamiji was so simply dressed. "Who was this girl all dressed up in a bright dress and pink lipstick?" I asked Ashish.'

It struck me then that people notice everything, especially things that don't fit with their mental framework or conform to their notion of right or wrong. Perhaps we are all prone to being judgemental, in one way or another.

Shakti hastened to apologize. 'I'm sorry. I didn't mean to think badly of you. But in the south, girls don't normally dress up like that.' I smiled inside because all he had seen me wearing since the Chennai book launch was traditional Indian garb, in which I had been covered from neck to toe. Having spent time with Shakti for the few days prior to this, though, I knew he had a faithful heart, full of love and reverence for his Swami.

'There's no need to apologize, Shakti, I understand your thinking. But even in the olden days when families went to the temple to offer worship or celebrate festivities, they donned their finest clothes and ornaments. Like every other offering made to the Gods, one made an offering of himself or herself.

'During Lord Krishna's time, Radha Rani and the Gopis spent hours adorning themselves with exotic flowers and ornaments, making themselves attractive for the Lord. It's the same sentiment with which I line my eyes with kohl, or place a bindi on my forehead. Do you think it's wrong to do so?' I smiled and he smiled back.

In a gentle voice he said, 'I now feel bad for thinking such things ...'

'It's all right, Shakti, no harm done. Anyway, tomorrow is Diwali and I'm going to wear a sari!'

'Oh, so you'll walk into the temple like an angel tomorrow,' he said, shaking his head in a teasing manner. Soon we bade each other goodnight.

The next morning, I woke to a glorious sunny day. I felt the festivity in the air. In the afternoon after serving Swami's lunch, I headed to the temple, where I found Ma Shamta decorating the garbhagriha and Swami's asana. She was kneeling on the ground as she arranged each flower, opening its petals before placing it most lovingly near Swami's paduka.

In Swami, she had found the son she had lost a decade earlier. She saw little Lord Rama in her guru and worshipped and cared for Him just as a mother would busy herself caring for her little one. Her favourite line every time I exclaimed that Swami seemed exhausted was, 'Chote se to hai mere Swami, my Swami is so tender. At such a young age He looks after all of us.' Ma's affection and devotion to Swami is the stuff of legend.

Seeing her working with such care, I offered to help with the flower decoration. Ma teased me for always being absent when some work was waiting. We shared a warm relationship: she loved and accepted me with all my flaws, and I could not help but love and admire this dedicated, sensitive lady.

I carried a basket of rose petals to the main temple door, and scattered them on each side. All the while, the Lord's beautiful idol kept smiling at me. I finished and walked over to the corner where the sound system was kept, and placed the remaining rose petals near the windowsill. Swami Raghavananda was in the garbhagriha, holding two angavastrams in vibrant mustard and red silk in his hands as Mani stood near the railing. They were both eagerly discussing which colour should grace Sri Hari on this auspicious day.

'Will a red angavastram be too bright for the Lord?' Swami Raghavananda asked Mani, lifting the red one higher.

'Not at all, Swamiji, it's Diwali, a bright colour will look quite nice. Let's drape a few angavastrams on Bhagwan's shoulders and see which one looks best.'

I didn't hear Swamiji's response, as my mind was occupied with questions of my own. Gazing at the life-size idol of Sri Hari I said to Him, 'O Lord, I'll be dressed in hot pink in the evening.

Give me company, please be dressed in pink. I don't want to be the odd one out.'

As this monologue played in my mind, I walked out of the temple. I could hear Swami Raghavananda and Mani settling on the red silk. But so strong was my anxiety to not be judged and looked down upon that I dared the Lord, 'If you really listen to all the things I say to you, if you are indeed alive and present, O Lord, then surely you can do this much for me: Please dress in pink.' Even while I was pleading, I realized how childish my plea was. Besides, it seemed like they had already decided to go with red silk.

A couple of hours later, I made my way to the temple's main door. Touching my forehead to the dust, I looked up at the idol of the Lord. Lo and behold, Sri Hari too was draped in pink! As alluring as ever, He stood resplendent in a pink angavastram of the finest silk, and a garland of white and violet flowers hung around His neck. The most loving and mischievous smile played on His sculpted lips.

I could only stare at Him. Goosebumps crept up my arms as I realized that the words so casually formed in my head, the divine Lord had honoured. How I had teased and questioned His presence, and He who needs no proof had manifested my wish. Tears washed over my eyes as I remembered how Swami always said that both Lord Narayana and the Adya Shakti resided in the idol. I rushed into the temple and bowed my head at the Lord's feet.

The villagers were already there and some of the volunteers, too. I found it difficult to control my emotions, the sudden surge of love that coursed through my veins. I quietly got up, and went behind the garbhagriha to thank Sri Hari. Pressing my face to the wall behind the garbhagriha I cried softly, thanking Him with all my heart for listening to me. I had always prayed with the belief that whatever I said to the idol in the temple somehow reached Swami. And today Sri Hari had indeed come alive for me.

I composed myself and went back to take my seat on the floor. I sat there, humbly basking in His love and grace, happier than I had ever been. Swami came in a few minutes later, dressed in His black robe, looking all-powerful and breathtakingly elegant. He blew the conch three times, and the evening arti began. He gave a short discourse, did kirtan and distributed gifts to the village children, cracking jokes and thanking and honouring everyone who had been of any service to the ashram -- no matter how minute or momentous.

The whole evening passed in a blur of happiness as I gazed adoringly at Sri Hari's compassionate form in flesh and in stone.

The celebration came to an end two hours later. Swami Vidyananda followed Swami into the discourse room, while Ma Shamta gave the finishing touches to the simple but delicious dinner of freshly made saag, cabbage and dal. I took the prasadam and rushed to the discourse room to tell Swami the evening's incident.

To my astonishment, as soon as I knocked and entered, the first thing Swami said to me was, 'Dolly, see how Bhagwan heard you and wore pink as well?'

'You heard me, didn't you? You heard my prayer in the afternoon.'

Swami started laughing. Swami Vidyananda looked from one to another. He had no clue what we were talking about. I then narrated to him how I had asked the Lord to dress in the same colour as I. Swami Vidyananda was most pleased to hear about Bhagwan's leela (play). I hadn't seen Swami since lunchtime, yet He was privy to my every wish.

The Truth

My work as Swami's editor conferred upon me a certain privilege. It allowed me ample opportunity to experience both His divine and human aspects as I worked with Him on the book. Swami is a great tantric, a brilliant meditator, a being with an uncanny and most powerful mind capable of complex software coding to manifesting a wish, a desire in a heartbeat. I would now see glimpses of His worldly talents. He could have chosen to be anything: the finest musician, artist, scientist, politician or businessman -- or all of these combined -- but He chose to renounce material pursuits and become a monk, donning the robe which is testimony to the path He placed above all.

Swami, the author, is a perfectionist, a prolific writer, and most thorough and intuitive. His deep understanding of a gamut of human emotions and the mysteries of the universe are reflected in His writing. Inspiration leaps at you from His words, holding your mind and heart captive, and the simple truths of life sink into your consciousness like a pebble cast into a still pond.

One thing that is especially remarkable about Swami's writing is His ability to view and review feedback. He is a writer who is utterly unafraid of criticism, and He accepts it with the same equanimity as if one were heaping praise on Him. He would write and rewrite -- and rewrite some more, ten times if need be -- till He was convinced that He had composed His very best work. His view is very simple, just as He told me once: 'Readers invest not only money but also their precious time in reading my books. It must be worth it for them.'

The discipline with which Swami sets out to finish a book in a matter of weeks -- often no more than three -- is admirable, if not astonishing. His frequent disappearances in solitude allow Him to write night and day, accomplishing that which would engage lesser minds for months. Swami often says, 'Writing is a matter of discipline.' And I haven't seen anyone undertake writing with anywhere near His diligence. It may only be His commitment to the welfare of our race that drives Him to work day and night in such a manner. I truly believe that in times to come, His works will be considered some of the finest and most relevant literature of our times. It shall be His legacy, and will inspire people long after He is gone.

I no longer see Swami as a person. I see Him as a movement, a phenomenon. On average, Swami works eighteen to twenty hours a day, with little regard for His health. A grave dearth of rest and His unusual sleeping pattern, influenced by a near constant state of samadhi, doesn't allow for His complete recuperation. His health suffers. Many mornings in the ashram, we would find Him unwell and listless, which was sometimes a prelude to an asthma attack. He would dismiss His condition as a seasonal allergy, lack of sleep or simply fatigue. The truth is that all the ailments -- the physical and mental suffering He elevated from others -- would, in some form, find their way back to Him.

I asked Him once if it were true that He took people's pain and suffering upon Himself. His reply was simple and unassuming, yet no less cryptic: 'What is a mountain for an ant is but a tiny mound for an elephant.'

While I am away from the ashram, I cherish my memories of the soulful evenings spent singing the Lord's many names in Swami's presence. These weren't merely feel-good evenings where everyone sang and danced as Swami's delicate fingers played the cymbals -- these were moments filled with inexplicable joy. There was always the glorious, inscrutable presence of a divine being in our midst. From pubs and clubs to watching Swami sway to the kirtan, chanting the holy Hare-Krishna Maha Mantra, I had come a long way.

Bhava Samadhi is as natural to Swami as a bee seeking nectar from a flower. So often, He would slip into a deep devotional sentiment while singing an eulogy of Mother Divine and Lord Narayna. He would slip into it as quietly as the burnished sun disappears behind the mountain peaks. Where moments ago the discourse room was filled with merry laughter and devotional singing, a sudden quietude would prevail. It would emanate from Swami's face, particularly His forehead where the samadhi sensation is concentrated. A divine red hue would spread across His face as He would struggle to keep His eyes open. Sometimes a tear would roll down.

The stillness in the air would begin to flow directly from His body, affecting those sitting in front of Him. It would feel as if someone suddenly got up and changed the thermostat of the room. The intense feeling of change in mood, sentiment and energy is unmistakable.

A few minutes would pass in which Swami would sometimes pick the digital clock nearby, look at the time, glance around to see, by seeing I mean through His mind's eye, if everyone was satisfied with today's session. The devotees came from far to see their Swami. When the samadhi would become unbearable He'd simply apologize humbly saying, 'My samadhi is very deep today. I'll see you all tomorrow. Please have your dinner and rest.'

Swami would then breeze out of the room in the dark of the night singing a devotional song in praise of the Adya Shakti, 'Ambe hare, jagdambe hare, jai jai jagjanni, ambe hare.' Swami Vidyananda would run after Him to ensure that Swami reached His hut safely. Because in that bhava, Swami does not stop to even wear His shoes. A few times I feared He might just run straight into a wall. Once I even thought that He might just go into a wall and not come out.

We swayed toward Him as He swayed toward the idol of Sri Hari behind Him. The idol and the master appeared to be one. And the whole congregation in the temple would somehow be transformed into fragrant flowers that sought to rain themselves on their master. As Swami raised His hands heavenward, His dark-lashed eyes would briefly shut us all out, His lithe form immersing itself in the enchantment the Lord's name had ignited.

In the depths of winter, He would start to sweat even as all of us shivered in the cold, layered in warm, woollen clothes; He wore a thin black linen robe or an even thinner ochre robe. His body would soon begin to tremble as the Divine energy passed through Him. In one such moment, an image of Chaitanya Mahaprabhu lost in ecstasy flooded my mind. Swami Vidyananda stood closest to Swami, lest His trembling cause

Him to fall off His asana. Although it seemed He could topple at any moment, Swami continued to stand, chanting the Lord's name. My heart skipped a beat, and I took a step forward as His body shuddered visibly with the force of the divine energy inside Him. He carried on singing and dancing, oblivious to our world.

This divine energy would not remain confined within Him. His palms, like chalices brimming with God's love and grace would soon turn upon us, pouring out their boons and blessings. At first, I was taken aback as my eyes welled up with tears at this sight. Conscious of what others might make of the softness of my countenance, I would hastily wipe away my tears, only to find every person in the room looking at Him with as much love and adoration. In God's home there was nothing to hide. What had once seemed surreal, I now recognized as the only reality.

It was a realization that I had ached for. In my old life, when I had cried my eyes out alone, the cold floor my body pressed against would feel like a door nailed shut, barring my entry into another world. I would ask God every single day of my sorry existence to call me to Him. Sometimes I pleaded and prayed: at times in anger, in absolute helplessness, I would beg Him to take me. In its own time, something strangely beautiful started to happen. I began calling out to God with love. My heart, dry as a desert creek, would at times flood with a torrent of bliss, a calm surge of love. I came to know that Swami was the water my parched being had sought; He was the very rain that nourished barren earth, sating my thirst for meaning, bringing me back to life.

At first, I confess, Swami fascinated me. He fascinates everyone who lays eyes on Him. This is a fascination that deepens till one's very soul is engulfed, immersed in and experience of His love. A new remembrance is thus born, as powerful and compelling as the tenderness within a child held in a Mother's arms, and this remains. You are drawn to His presence with this remembrance.

And just as water flows in a perennial river, Swami's love flows endlessly for anyone who seeks Him.

His Protection

Over the last four years I've taken countless troubles to Him, my own and others with the belief that Swami will fix them. I'm sharing a notable few.

There was a dear friend who had been accused of shoplifting. The laws of that country were very strict, the police had seized her passport, and though out on bail, the case would go on trial soon enough.

Frantic with worry she confided in me how a small misunderstanding with the sales staff of a famous makeup brand had led to a situation that could have easily been avoided. Through no fault of hers she was now doing the rounds of the police station in a foreign land. Her fate hung in balance and she could go to jail. It was a very lonely and harrowing phase where she even contemplated ending her life.

Moved by her plight, I appealed to Swami. I had been spending hours speaking to her, consoling her as best as I could. Her situation weighed on me heavily. Sometimes all that worrying caused me severe headaches. It had only been a few months since my mother had passed away and small things rattled me. Any situation that made me feel helpless would put a strain on my nerves.

In response to my urgent plea, Swami sent a short reply.

'No harm will befall your friend. Her case will be dismissed without any demerit on her person. She'll stay in that country.' There followed a period of great anxiety and uncertainty for my friend, but I reassured her that Swami would make it go away. After a couple of weeks of intense sessions with the officer in charge, he dismissed her case. She never even had to face a judge. Her passport was returned to her and she could safely travel back home.

After I had moved to the ashram, a wonderful family I was close to inspired by Swami's memoir asked me to seek blessings for their daughter, who was preparing for the Civil Services exam.

I asked Swami if I may ask Him a question.

In response He took the name of the girl.

I was stumped. I had never before mentioned the girl to Him. And then even before I could pose the question about her predicament, He uttered a single word, 'No.'

'But I haven't even asked you the question yet, Swami.'

He replied quietly, 'She won't clear the Civil Services exam. I don't see it happening.'

I felt just like a deflated balloon. Shock and disbelief coursed through my veins at the same time. Shock because He just took the name and stated the exact question I was planning to ask Him out of the blue. Disbelief because I had been so hopeful that surely there would be some wonderful news to give to the kind and gentle elderly couple. Seeing my anxious face, a tiny smile surfaced on Swami's lips.

'I'll consecrate a Rudraksha for her. It's just for their well-being. Rudrakshas don't write on the answer sheets. The candidate has to do that.' Keeping out the part about Swami's prediction I gave them the Rudraksha and asked them to leave everything to the Goddess. When the result came out a couple of months later, sure enough she hadn't cleared the exam. But their faith in Swami only increased.

Once I sought Swami's blessings for a young man who had a head-on collision with a truck. Before I could fully explain the extent of the situation, Swami very gently conveyed to me that it was just a matter of time before he passed away. It was the same with an elderly person who had been recently diagnosed with throat cancer. Though, it was at the early stages, soon complications arose making the illness difficult to treat.

Over and over again I noticed that Swami truly has no agenda of His own. When listening to the problem or concern of a devotee He only states the truth as He sees it. I could never see even a hint of desire in His eyes, words or gestures. No matter how personal a question may be, you ask Him and He gives you the truth. Every word that falls from His mouth is nothing but the truth. Three pieces of unstitched robe, vermillion and sandalwood mark on His forehead are His only covering.

It isn't devotion that has led me to this conclusion. It's His response to every situation, with every person, young or old, rich or poor, weak or strong, ordinary or capable, ugly or beautiful that has forced open my eyes. One thing I can tell you from my own experience is that only when you experience a meltdown, a complete annihilation of your ego, identity and desires that you really get a glimpse of a different side of Him, a side He keeps mostly covered. The fearlessness I experienced from being under Swami's shade was completely unimaginable to me before I knew Him.

The First Disciple

Whether it be writing, giving discourses, attending endless meetings and listening to people's pains and troubles -- or any of His other myriad activities -- Swami is relentlessly moving like the wheel of time, striving to make this world a better place. For those already in His sanctuary and those who will surely seek Him out in time, He is set upon leaving behind a legacy of truth and saintliness.

Swami's playfield is through the eyes of His foremost disciple, Swami Vidyananda, or Swamiji, as I call him. Swami Vidyananda is a saint in his own right, and is devoted to Swami like no other. The grand purpose of Swamiji's life to be sure, is service. He has been in Swami's personal service since He came back from the Himalayas, constantly ensuring that Swami eats well, gets enough rest and remains in good health. He has no other desire but to care for Swami's well-being. And this perhaps is what makes him unique.

Swami Vidyananda can be seen everywhere in the ashram, scurrying on cracked heels in his open-toed sandals to complete daily chores and accomplish all manner of other tasks. Be it washing and drying Swami's robe in the sun or fetching vegetables from the kitchen, cooking Swami's meal, cleaning His cottage, singing the arti, doing abhishekam (puja) to Sri Hari on ekadashi (the eleventh day of each fortnight in the lunar month) and amavasya (new moon), or enthralling Bhagwan and the devotees with his melodious bhajans – Swamiji never seems to pause much for rest.

Like the thick layer of cream that forms over a glass of warm milk, Swami Vidyananda's devotion to Swami is pure and untainted. He doesn't put a morsel in his mouth till Swami has eaten. In my time at the ashram, it has happened on several occasions that Swami, despite being unwell, worked ceaselessly the whole day, and finally when His body couldn't take it anymore, He collapsed into a deep sleep. In those critical times, be it in the scorching heat of the day or the dark of the night, Swami Vidyananda would wait outside Swami's cottage well past midnight, patiently sitting like a child waiting for his mother to wake up.

The master-disciple relationship is a unique one. Swami Vidyananda is Swami's heart. They are inseparable. Swami loves to feed Swami Vidyananda in the best of places, especially when they are travelling together, for Swami Vidyananda's penchant for good food is well known. Swami often says, 'Swami Vidyananda has the heart of a child, and that's why Mother Divine's grace has fallen upon him.'

When the master and disciple sing together, they only have eyes for each other. The synergy of their voices – of their hearts – is visible like moisture on a glass, and the hall packed with devotees is mesmerized. What Hanuman is to Lord Rama, Swami Vidyananda is to Swami: always willing and eager in His service.

One day at the ashram, I saw Swami Vidyananda marching towards me in his usual brisk manner. He was clutching something in his hand. It was a pair of bundled up black socks. He thrust them right under my nose and said, 'I just found these. They have been missing for six months. There's a little fungus and dampness; but see, fragrant as ever!'

By that time, I had got over my initial reaction of what-does-he-think-he's-doing, and figured out that these were Swami's socks. Swami Vidyananda was absolutely right: the socks had the same divine fragrance that comes from Swami. 'Only clothing of a Mahapurusha, a divine being, can smell like this despite the fungus and the dampness they have been rotting in for the past six months,' Swami Vidyananda declared proudly. I could only smile at his loving observation. That is how sweet he is.

But it wasn't merely an observation; I had experienced this phenomenon, too. Since Swami Vidyananda did most of the cooking, washing and cleaning for Swami, I offered to iron Swami's robe. Swami Vidyananda would soak the robes in a mild detergent for twenty minutes. Swami's robes were always clean. I never saw a dirty mark or food stain on a single robe. After Swamiji's hand-washing the robes and letting them dry in the sun, they would come to me. What was most surprising was that despite the washing, the robes still had the same distinct fragrance that I had so often inhaled in Swami's presence.

It was amazing how it lingered. I remember picking up the robe and smelling it a few times to check if I wasn't just imagining the scent. I would spread the three pieces of unstitched ochre cloth, iron away the creases and fold them neatly. Every alternate day there was a robe to iron, and each time I would smell it to check for that fragrance.

A couple of weeks had passed when Swami said to me out of the blue, 'Swami Vidyananda tells me that you've been ironing my robes. Thank you, Dolly, this is the first time I'm wearing ironed robes in the ashram. Swamiji has so much work as it is, I don't like to saddle him with more.'

'I haven't really ironed clothes before. It's pure cotton and hence a little tricky to iron out the creases. I know it's not exactly rocket science; still, forgive me if they don't come out right,' I replied.

Swami started to laugh, and with a little to and fro movement of His body He said, 'No, you are doing an excellent job. I feel the love with which you're ironing them, and also how lovingly you smell them before you iron them.'

If I could, I would have died of shame. 'How do you even know that, Swami? You are not supposed to know that!'

Swami didn't answer, and just smiled. It was one of those moments when I just wanted to disappear. In His teasing mood, Swami could be relentless.

He was like that with both of us – teasing us, sometimes even goading us to defy Him. Like a true disciple, Swami Vidyananda would always agree with what Swami would say. With construction and other work going on at the ashram, sometimes Swami would remark about a certain person. If He liked somebody and would say, 'Such-and-such person is an honest worker,' Swami Vidyananda would instantly add, 'Yes, Swamiji, I've also noticed how he helps out with the ashram chores as well. A very fine man, indeed, what great devotional sentiment he has for you.'

A couple of days later, Swami would express His annoyance with the very same person, 'He still hasn't given the report regarding the development plans we drew last week. Why don't people keep their word?' Swami Vidyananda would be quick to agree, 'Yes Swamiji, you are right, that person has no sense of time or responsibility. He has no regard for the words of a saint.'

Swami would look at Swami Vidyananda with feigned concern, trying hard to suppress the smile lurking at the corners of His mouth. 'Why, Swamiji, only days earlier you were saying this person's devotional sentiment toward me is remarkable.'

Many times Swami would carry on with this charade of expressing His displeasure with someone, only to have Swami Vidyananda display an equally displeased reaction. Swami would quickly change His stance and immediately start praising the same person. And no prizes for guessing: Swami Vidyananda too would have an immediate change of heart. It was not just hilarious, but extremely endearing to see how quickly Swami Vidyananda would change his stance to match Swami's. Swami would then tease His disciple by calling him Akbar ka baingan, or Akbar's brinjal, and tell us this Akbar–Birbal anecdote.

Once Birbal was dining with the Emperor Akbar. The royal chef had made a delightful vegetable dish of stuffed brinjal. Akbar told Birbal what a delicious and nutritious vegetable it was and how delectable it tasted. Birbal thoroughly agreed with the emperor, going so far as to call the humble brinjal the king of all vegetables, pointing to the little green crown on its head.

After a couple of days, the royal chef cooked mashed brinjal for lunch. Birbal was also eating at the palace that day. When the pulpy dish was served to Akbar, he refused it, saying that it was a tasteless vegetable, full of seeds; it lacked proper nutrition and was unfit to be served to a king. He then asked that it be served to Birbal, who loved brinjals.

But Birbal, too, refused it saying, 'I've no taste for such a fat, unpalatable and ugly-looking vegetable. Take it away.'

Annoyed by Birbal's response, Akbar said to him, 'Not two days ago you sang praises of this vegetable, sitting right here at this table. You even compared it to a king. And now you can't even stand to look at it! You are deceitful, Birbal.'

Birbal replied most humbly, 'I'm his majesty's obedient and loyal servant, and not the brinjal's. When you praised it, I praised it – when you criticized it, I felt no love for it either.'

Swami tenderly reminds Swami Vidyananda of this particular story from time to time. It very beautifully sums up the love, loyalty and devotion that Swami Vidyananda carries in his heart for his master.

The love and devotion in Swamiji's heart carries into his music. After the evening arti when Swami Vidyananda would sing eulogies to Mother Divine, involuntary rivulets of tears would run down my cheeks. The poignancy, the longing for Jaganmata (Mother Divine) in Swamiji's voice would immediately open the floodgates of my emotions. During my first months at the ashram, I cried almost daily. It hadn't been that long since my mother had passed away. Sometimes, the crying overcame me, and I avoided going to the temple during arti time. Instead, I would go and sit by the river. Only after I had gathered enough strength to bear another emotional outpouring would I venture back to hear Swamiji sing.

I loved Swamiji's voice; but even more, I loved his love for Swami, the sheer yearning with which he called out to Him – especially when Swami would be away in solitude. We both missed Him intensely and sought Him in our prayers. It is our love for Swami that made us bond.

Swami was in Canada when I moved to the ashram. He had been travelling extensively in the US and Canada for discourses at devotees' requests. It was Swami Vidyananda who welcomed me, and he mentored and cared for me at the ashram. He would cook delicious meals for me day after day and take care of me. If I returned from my run after dark, he would scold me, too. I had much to learn, especially in the ways of being in the presence of saints. Swamiji became my guru, teaching me bhajans and Vishnu Sahasranama in the temple. He also related the most wonderful accounts of Swami's miraculous powers. In no time at all, we became a team.

On Swami's return, He joked in His customary manner, 'People serve the saints so that they can earn some good karma, and here Swamiji has been serving you all this while, Dolly.' I chuckled. This was so true. Sitting two continents away, Swami had been keeping His vigil, and He knew exactly what we were up to in the ashram.

My first weeks in the ashram had shown me that despite his formidable knowledge of scripture and robust frame, Swami Vidyananda is a truly childlike monk. His love for Swami is unmatchable, and it is this quality above all that is most endearing. He is the only person with a blanket permit to see Swami at any time of the day or night. He is also the only one who has had the privilege of hearing from Swami's mouth the past life connection he shares with his master. Because Swamiji's devotion to His master is extraordinary, his experiences too, are extraordinary.

Swami needs Swamiji's tender and protective care. Those familiar with Swami's powers sometimes make the mistake of assuming that He can be approached to fulfil their petty desires. This may involve a search for a lost piece of jewellery or a misplaced document, or even the desire to shirk labour and effort, yet attain success in the material world. While such matters are child's play to Swami, some people have the audacity to casually ask of Him the likes of these trivial and meaningless favours. They make demands as if it were their right to dip their hands in the grace that flows from Him; as if His powers exist simply to serve them.

It is true that Swami merely has to direct His consciousness toward a wish, and the wish is granted. It comes to fruition, just as a seed buried deep in the ground sprouts in seemingly barren land with the correct tending. I have seen this happen more times than I can possibly enumerate. But without the right devotion for the Divine in your heart, it is not possible to receive Swami's grace. Your readiness allows Him to make your dreams come true. Standing at God's door, you can only kneel and pray, surrendering to Him. Beyond that is His will.

It never ceases to amaze me how countless contemporary spiritual books, even biographies of great masters, proudly adorn the shelves of bookstores, and yet for all the talk about Him, not one can claim to have seen the face of God, let alone speak to Him. And here I am, in the presence of this divine being in a human body, who carries both the Divine Mother and Lord Narayana in His being.

Swami's remarkable power doesn't merely rest with His spiritual prowess, which allows Him to know people's past, present and future, grant years of life to ailing devotees, cure deadly diseases, grant material wealth, heal sadness and work miracles. It is as much in the humility, gentleness and love woven into His every gesture and every glance. His word melts you or breaks you, more often than not into a crying mess of devotion or peals of laughter. Swami is venerated by His devotees for the sheer bliss and joy that flows from His very being. His goodness calls out to you. You experience in His presence the calming energy you perhaps sometimes sense in the deity in your altar, or the ancient temple (mandir) you have visited since childhood.

It is Swami Vidyananda's earnest wish – as much as it is mine – that the world know the truth behind the young saint who likes to call himself, 'a simple sadhu in a complex world,' for there is a truth behind the simplicity that is beyond our expectation, and is yet to be revealed to the world.

This book is an amalgamation of events and incidents that have transformed lives. More than this, it is a book of faith. I hope the glimpses it renders of Swami's love, goodness and power – real power that heals, mends, revives and brings the ever-elusive God out of hiding – will ignite His grace within you.

My only qualification for writing and compiling this book is Swami's acceptance of my tainted love and reverence. In my heart, despite my failings, I find Him seated day and night. His grace has simplified my life; and it all began with my writing. When I wrote poetry just for God, I did it for the sheer bliss His remembrance evoked. Whenever I was alone with my thoughts or as I sat in meditation, bliss rose from the deepest part of me such that the love for God would spill itself into verses. I hadn't the slightest inkling that my verses would reach Him, that the One for whom I wrote had read every line. And I couldn't have known that Nature was preparing me for this day, when I would be in Swami's service, singing and writing of His glory.

Words, at any rate, cannot do justice to Swami, for He speaks the language of the heart. But words are the language the world understands, for now, even at the cost of sanity and reasoning: Holy is the ground on which Swami walks. His power is limitless and not of this world.

I've come to realize that not only does He read my thoughts like scribbles on a child's slate, He weighs each one to see if it's what I truly wish for. If the fulfilment of a wish makes me happy, His response will always be in agreement. It's the sole reason why devotees experience such bliss in Swami's presence; He speaks the language of the heart. He peeps inside you and gives you what you want.

Omniscience is no longer a word, but an occurrence that I revel in. You will surely now understand that Swami is, for me, no longer a cool monk or a sharp guy whose vast intellectual reserves amaze me at every moment. He is the one I pray to.

Make no mistakes, our thoughts, intentions and desires are like water in a glass tumbler, apparent, evident to Swami. At least, that has been my unfailing experience.

With great gratitude and reverence, I bow my head at His beautiful and divine feet. He listens, He grants.

The temple at night

Another view of the temple

Swamiji's old cottage

The view from Swamiji's ashram

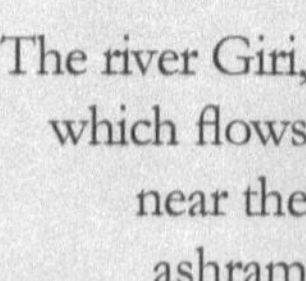

The river Giri, which flows near the ashram

Left: Bhagwan's murti in the temple
Below: Swamiji performing arti

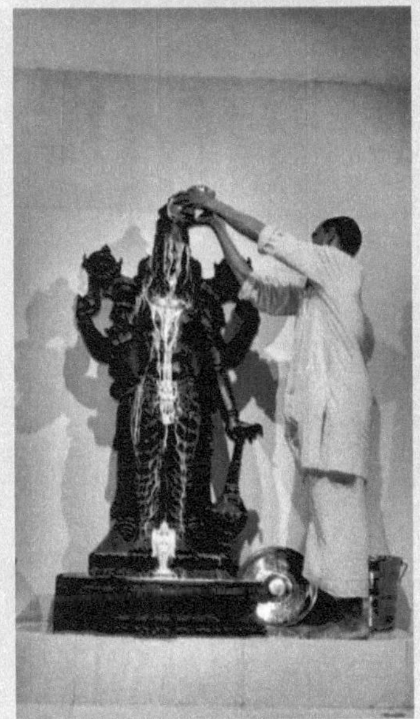

Above: Swamiji deeply immersed in singing for his god

Left: The performance of Bhagwan's abhishek

Right: Swamiji performing kirtan

Bottom: Swamiji at his ashram

Swamiji on a walk near his ashram

Swamiji on
the banks of
the river Giri

The simple discourse room where Swamiji
meets his devotees

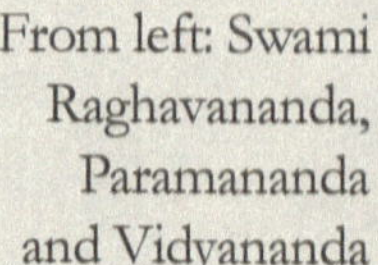

From left: Swami Raghavananda, Paramananda and Vidyananda

Swamiji meeting devotees under the shade of a tree

Devotees as audience when Swamiji performs kirtan

Ismita and Swami Vidyananda

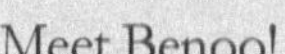

Meet Benoo!

The pink sari episode
on Deepawali

A bonfire at the ashram: This was the very first
time that Swamiji read Ismita's mind

Book Two

MY MASTER, MY LIFE

Swami Vidyananda Om

Let me tell you at the outset, before I begin narrating my experiences with Swamiji, or Gurudev as I sometimes call Him, that my world begins and ends with Swamiji. You may or may not believe the experiences I share herein, but if you are fortunate enough to be around Him, you will know that anything is possible in His presence.

I have not shared my experiences for the sceptics or those who have no affinity towords my Gurudev. I have written of my experiences because so many times devotees have asked me about my time with Gurudev. I have written this work primarily for the devotees who worship the very ground Swamiji walks on, or for those whose curiosity about Swamiji brings them to these pages. If you harbour doubts about the existence of the Divine and its power to transform one's very existence, then this may not be a book for your reading. In any event, I don't feel that I am capable of doing justice to the writings about Gurudev. He is Tathagat, the one who has gone beyond. Whatever good there is in this book is only by His grace.

I hope you rejoice in reading about the virtues of my spiritual father, my Gurudev, my world.

All glories to my Gurudev.
Swami Vidyananda

The First Meeting

Haridwar is a holy place in the foothills of the Himalayas. It is one of the seven holiest places (Sapta Puri) for Hindus, and with good reason. Its name literally means 'gateway to Lord Vishnu' in Sanskrit. Originating from the lotus feet of Lord Vishnu -- after Bhagirathi's great penance and by the grace of Lord Shiva -- the holy Devaganga flows from Gangotri, and it is at Haridwar where it enters the plains, purifying the land and giving it life.

Every twelve years, innumerable pilgrims flock to Haridwar to immerse themselves in Devaganga's blessings, and the town of a few lakhs plays host, for a few brief days, to the greatest peaceful gatherings in history. Haridwar is the dwelling place of countless great sages of yore, and devotees and monks throng here throughout the year. It is also the famed city where the Brahmajnani sage Shuka preached Srimad Bhagavata Purana to the dying King Parikshit.

Sadhana Sadan is a very famous ashram in Haridwar's Kankhal area. It is nestled there in a delightful locale which is mostly dedicated to worship. There, spacious buildings on both sides of the road serve the faithful, and wide bathing terraces on the river bank, popularly known as ghats, are flanked by temples. The beauty of the Devaganga flowing below can make a believer out of even the most affirmed atheist. For three years, I offered prayers and performed arti at the ashram temple, after which I would chant the Durga Saptashati (story of the Goddess Durga's victory over the demon Mahishasura) and Lalitha Sahasranama (song of praise of the Goddess's thousand names).

The ashram temple has idols of the five-faced Shiva, Radha-Krishna and Ram-Sita Bhagwan. Every day upon completion of my Durga Saptashati chanting, I would pray for a guru who would be the guiding force for my sadhana; a guru who was a Shakti Upasak (Goddess Worshipper). I read Durga Saptashati thrice a day during Vasanta Navaratri and Sharat Navaratri (nine holy nights of spring and autumn). In the auspicious nine days of these festivals, I consumed only fruit and milk or just water, and I prayed ardently to the Goddess Mother.

My dedication to the Goddess Mother was a closely guarded secret, though. I wore a tripundra, three horizontal lines of vibhuti (sacred ash) on my forehead, indicating that I worshipped Shiva; ostensibly, I was dedicated solely to Him. I thought if I met a true guru, he would know just what I really wanted – he would instantly recognize my hidden yearning for the Divine Mother.

Three years passed offering prayers to the Divine Mother, asking for Her grace in the form of a guru. My desire to find a guru became my reason to pray. On 9 November 2010, the Goddess Mother heard my prayers and graced my life with Gurudev.

In my more pensive moments since, I have often pondered: Had I been guided by the Divine Mother to this sacred town, and were my devotions of the intervening years preparation for my meeting Him? Or was Gurudev, in His kindness, there to find me so I may be guided to the Divine Mother?

There is, in any event, no dearth of sanyasis and sadhus in Haridwar. Since it is on the way to Chota Char Dham -- the pilgrimage route of Yamunotri, Gangotri, Kedarnath and Badrinath -- Haridwar is always bustling with holy men and women from all over the country. Sadhana Sadan ashram provides facilities for the passing sadhus to stay at the Sadhana Kutir. These cottages on the outskirts of Haridwar offer solace to wandering monks. Sadhana Kutir is divided into four cottages arranged in a row. The third of these has a beautiful Shiva temple in its environs.

On the morning of 9 November, a sadhu from Kerala invited me to join him in visiting another Keralite sadhu, who was staying in one of the cottages. I finished my daily routine of puja and chanting and closed the temple doors. The temple remained closed from 12 noon to 3.30 p.m. The cottage is about four kilometres from the ashram. At first, we felt that we might not be able to return in time for me to open the temple gate, and we decided to go there the following day.

The Goddess Mother seemed to have different plans for me. I felt a strange and powerful urge to meet this sadhu, and by 12.20p.m., we had resolved to go that very day anyway. As if some divine force had taken hold of me, I felt impelled toward Sadhana Kutir, and we briskly walked the four-kilometre distance there, as if it was no effort at all. We passed the Shiva temple in the third kutir just as its doors were being closed, and we bowed to the Lord from afar and entered the second cottage. There was a small room near the entrance gate and a Bengali sadhu was staying there. We spent some time talking with him and another sadhu.

Soon it was time to head back, and there was no sign of the Keralite sadhu my companion had sought. The Bengali sadhu mentioned that there was another sadhu from Tamil Nadu staying in the next cottage. He suggested that we meet him. I was reluctant to linger, for additional to my duty of opening the temple gate, I had to pluck flowers for the evening puja. The sadhu insisted though, saying that it wouldn't take more than a couple of minutes.

We entered the kutir and saw two sadhus, one sitting on a cot and the other sitting opposite him in a chair. The sadhu from Tamil Nadu, who was sitting on the cot, told us to wash our feet before entering, which we did. My companion greeted the other sadhu warmly, since he knew him, and they began to converse in a friendly manner.

All this time, I was preoccupied, as I would so often be; lost in musing about my lack of spiritual fulfilment. When would I find my guru? It had been eight years since I had left home to walk the path of sadhana. I had followed the spiritual calling assiduously, and had no complaints for renouncing material pursuits. But apart from prayers and chanting I knew little, as did everyone I knew. Among them, there were old sadhus, experienced sadhus and senior sadhus, with their grey hair and wrinkled skin. Years spent in the Himalayas may have enriched and elevated them spiritually, but beyond that, they had little to show for their endeavours. I wished for more than spiritual elevation: I wished for a miracle, for Her darshan.

Immersed in these thoughts, I stared at the floor. Suddenly, I felt someone's attention upon me. I looked up and got my first glimpse of Swamiji's eyes, shining bright with tejas. I just stared at Him, spellbound by His direct and piercing gaze, His divine radiance. He was regarding me deeply and quizzically, as if He were reading me like a book.

Swamiji then uttered a single sentence to the sadhu next to him: 'We spoke about Sri Vidya yesterday'. He then fell silent. He was no longer looking at me. He knew, however, that He had ignited a fire in my heart with those few words. They were the crux of all that I had desired.

Sri Vidya, the discipline of Devi worship, was the sum total of all I wanted to learn. It was my heart's longing. Gone was the lethargy that hung on my mind and body upon hearing these two sweet words. I could barely wait to speak to Him. But how would I approach Him? As if on cue, the other two sadhus stepped outside, and Gurudev signalled me to come closer. I hastened to sit near Him.

'You wear a tripundra to mask your sadhana,' He said, with a gentle finality in his voice. 'You are a Devi worshipper.'

I was stunned. He knew my secret; the deepest wish that I had never uttered. Even in the preceding three years at Sadhana Sadan, nobody -- not even the spiritual head there -- had seen my burning desire. I clasped His feet immediately.

'You pray to Durga,' He said, 'when what you really want to do is learn Sri Vidya.'

I was overawed because He had, in those few moments, gently unpeeled the facade, the pretence that I had been living. I knew in that very moment that I had found my Gurudev, but I wasn't sure if He would accept me.

He smiled and said a few words about Sri Vidya. My time had run out -- it was past 3 o'clock, and I had to be back at the temple. I invited Gurudev to come to Sadhana Sadan, but He declined.

'I'm staying at Sri Vidya Mandir for only two days,' He said. 'Come and see me there tomorrow at 10 a.m.'

Waves of happiness rose and fell in my heart. I had been dreaming of this moment for so long. How did He know that it was the one thing that I had wanted most in this world? Would He take me into His fold? With His shining eyes and quiet manner, I felt confident that He could teach me real sadhana. I silently thanked the Goddess Mother and took His leave.

As I walked back to the ashram, my mind was blank with the enormity of our meeting. Just like a tired, disheartened explorer stumbling into a lost city in the jungle, I was at once thrilled and overwhelmed by my discovery. Only a few days earlier, I had prayed fervently to the Goddess Mother during Sharat Navaratri for a guru. My prayers had finally been answered. I slept fitfully that night; I anxiously awaited daybreak so I could leap out of bed.

As was my routine, I woke up at the Brahma muhurtha (the auspicious period beginning at one hour and thirty-six minutes before sunrise), finished the morning arti, recited shlokas, and offered naivedhya (food for blessing) and special prayers at the temple. Despite my haste with my morning duties, I was running late. By the time I had finished, it was around 10.30 in the morning. I borrowed a cycle from one of the students and, peddling feverishly, reached Sri Vidya Mandir in a matter of minutes. Gurudev was sitting outside on the temple platform speaking to another sadhu. As soon as He saw me, He said, 'You've come. Good.' He had waited for me.

We went to His room where he was staying. Gurudev told me in brief about His stay in Varanasi at Naga Baba's place and His sadhana in a cave near Badrinath Dham. As we spoke, another sadhu came to Gurudev's room and called Him for lunch.

Gurudev asked if I had eaten anything since morning. I shook my head. In my rush to meet Him, I had left without bothering to eat. 'Then let us have prasadam together,' He said.

After lunch, Swamiji told me that before Sri Vidya sadhana, certain preparations had to be completed: chanting holy mantras; knowing the hidden secrets of the mantras, the special aspects that take place in the puja, their essence, and how Jaganmata (Divine Mother) had given all the aspects and powers to achieve the Sri Vidya sadhana. Gurudev explained everything elaborately.

His gentle and loving manner was encouraging. I couldn't help but ask Him, 'Will I get the opportunity to see Jaganmata?'

'If you believe Jaganmata to be real, speak to her, pray to her with all your heart -- then, and only then, is it possible to see her.' He replied.

'Swamiji, please accept me as your disciple,' I urged Him.

'It is not possible at the moment, but I'll help you achieve what you need to for you to get there. This is my solemn promise to you.'

Swamiji then said to me, 'I will chant the holy Lalita Sahasranama, and you just listen to it.' He sat on the bed in a siddhasana posture (sitting upright with legs crossed in on themselves and hands in the appropriate mudra), while I sat on the floor listening to the mantra in Swamiji's deep and powerful voice. I had never heard anyone chant the Goddesses' names with such love and conviction before. It was hypnotic.

Somewhere in the middle of the Lalita Sahasranama, I was certain I could see the outlines of the Goddess Kali around Him. I quickly rubbed my eyes. It was broad daylight, yet the vision persisted. I immediately bowed my head and maintained this posture of reverence for a few minutes.

He continued chanting. He didn't read from any book. He just chanted everything from memory, as if all was within Him and was merely pouring out of Him with the Goddess Mother's grace. After Lalita Sahasranama, Swamiji was already in His deep bhava (state of being). He went on to sing glories of Devi in her various forms. I was spellbound.

I had lost all sense of time. Swamiji enthralled me with one beautiful chant after another. When it was finally time to leave, I asked Him, 'When will I see you again, Swamiji?'

'I'm going to the Himalayas to complete one of my sadhanas,' He said. 'I'll see you when I'm done.'

I went quiet. How was I to know how long it might be before he would be done?

'At the most two years,' He said, as if reading my mind. 'Most probably, a few months.'

I offered Gurudev some fruits which I was carrying with me, but He gently said, 'Sorry, I do not accept any material offerings.'

I was surprised to hear this. I remembered the famous lines from Chandogya Upanishad, *tyagenaike amrit-tattva-manashu*, meaning, 'It is only through sacrifice that we can attain immortality.' Gurudev placed a hundred rupees in my book. I tried to refuse His gift, but He would not have any of it. He told me to accept it as a blessing. I was deeply touched by His gesture. Gurudev then did namaskara, pressing His palms together, and tears spontaneously rolled down my cheeks. I had never seen a guru do namaskara.

I asked Him, I implored Him, not to leave me. I didn't know how long it might be before I would see Him again. I felt utterly dejected. I left with a heavy heart, slowly peddling the bicycle back to the temple, as I had left my heart and mind with Gurudev. On the one hand, I was happy that I had been given the chance to meet Him, and on the other, I was completely overcome with sadness upon leaving Him.

As the days passed, my yearning for Gurudev was almost beyond bearing. My eyes would frequently mist over, just at my thinking of Him. Sometimes my pillow would be soaked with my tears. Now that I had found my guru, two years away from His presence seemed interminable. I even contemplated assigning my puja work to someone else and heading to the Himalayas, closer to Gurudev, and staying there till His return. But I didn't want to do anything against His instruction.

Many months passed, and it was Sri Shankaracharya Jayant in May 2011. This is an important celebration at Sadhana Sadan, and it is accompanied with anna prasadam (the partaking of blessed food) and dakshina (donations) for a thousand sadhus. In the main auditorium, there was a special programme from 9.30 in the morning to noon.

After the puja celebration concluded, the sadhu from Tamil Nadu whom I had first met with Gurudev approached me to say that Gurudev would be arriving on the 9 June. He elaborated that another Swami who had been serving Gurudev had asked him to convey this news to me. That was in a telephone call in December 2010. The matter, he said apologetically, had completely slipped his mind until he saw me at the puja. The news thus reached me five months late; but I was no less overjoyed for this. Indeed, I was ecstatic. I felt like dancing with joy. In less than a month I would see Swamiji again!

On 9 June, I had finished puja and gone to the banks of the holy Ganga to collect flowers, when the driver from the ashram came rushing to me and said, 'A sadhu from Sadhana Kutir wants to meet you.' I immediately borrowed a bicycle and hastened to Sadhana Kutir, but Gurudev had gone to Rishikesh, which is approximately twenty kilometres from Haridwar. After thirty eager minutes of my waiting, Gurudev returned. I ran to Him, and prostrated myself before Him.

'It's so good to see you, Swamiji,' He said to me in His sweet voice. From Gurudev's holy lips, I heard how on 13 February, He had received Jaganmata's complete vision.

Nistula nilachikura nirapaya niratyaya (nistula: she is peerless; nilachikura: whose locks of hair are shining black; nirapaya: she is imperishable; niratyaya: who is indestructible).

This is how one verse in the Lalita Sahasranama describes the form of Jaganmata. Just as waves bring the sea's bounty to the shore, it was my punya (merit) that I was listening to the description of Mother Goddess. Swamiji told me she was brighter than a thousand suns. I was the fortunate one to whom Gurudev was first telling of His realization and vision of the Mother Goddess.

Later, Gurudev chanted the Mahishasura Mardini Stotram (the hymn recounting Durga's slaying the demon Mahishasura) and I first enjoyed the darshana of Jaganmata in Gurudev's divine voice. The vision of this epic battle stayed with me throughout the day, long after I had left Swamiji's serene presence.

I returned the following day. The sadhu from Tamil Nadu and Gurudev were in the same kutir. I wasn't sure if he would cook for Gurudev, so I had prepared some chapattis for us. When the Tamil sadhu came to know that I had brought food for Gurudev, he became angry. He started shouting, 'Who will eat the food that I've already prepared here? Why didn't you tell me that you were bringing food?' I was crestfallen. My kind and merciful Gurudev took my part, though, in the most subtle and gentle manner. He told the sadhu that He would eat the leftover food for dinner. The humble way in which He defused the situation showed me His sensitivity and magnanimity, which

I would become accustomed to over time, and which would endear Him to all those whose lives he touched.

After our lunch -- which proceeded happily for all, as Swamiji's diplomacy had immediately mollified the sadhu -- we stepped outside the cottage and spoke about Gurudev's experience of the Divine Mother. The mere remembrance of those conversations always fills my heart with bliss. Swamiji then told me that He had to go to Kamakhya Kshetra for two months for a special sadhana and would be back on 9 August.

On Swamiji's return from Kamakhya, He shared the details of many tantric aspects of Sri Vidya. My reverence for Gurudev grew a thousand fold because I could now see beyond any doubt that He was not just a talker -- He was a doer, a practitioner.

After Kamakhya, He must go to the eastern Himalayas for a month, He told me, to do another sadhana. He was here only for a day. He had come here specially to see me, He said, and was now going to Rudranath to meditate once again -- at an altitude of 14,000 feet. I was amazed that He could survive in such a cold place.

My wonderment at his sadhanas in the mountains never ceases. All He ever had was one small bag with two sets of robes in it. He was always clad in His thin ochre robe, in terrains and at altitudes where others would invariably be swathed in woolly clothing. He seemed quite unfussed by the sheer physical hardship these sadhanas entailed, leave alone the remarkable feat of simply staying alive under such inhospitable conditions. I struggled to comprehend why He would subject Himself to all this.

But then again, I never claimed to understand Gurudev. How far can you ever see, standing at the water's edge, looking out across the ocean?

The Ashram

On 24 September, Gurudev descended from the Himalayas and met me in Haridwar a day later. 'I will meet you in the ashram on 11 October,' Gurudev said to me, just before departing for Rishikesh to conclude another short sadhana. I spent the next fifteen days in rapture, my heart filled with pure joy. I knew that it was just a matter of days before I was to embark on my path to the Divine Mother.

I would travel with Swami Raghavananda (known as Brahmachari Pradeep before initiation) to the ashram in Himachal. It was Swami Raghavananda who had looked after Swamiji during His intense sadhana in the Himalayan woods. During those six months, he cooked, cleaned and carried heavy pails of water for Swamiji, as Swamiji sat in intense dhyana. Swami Raghavananda's dedication to his master was next to none. He is the very embodiment of the word devotee.

As the bus lumbered from Haridwar to Solan, expectation filled my heart and charged my imaginings. I was leaving the blessed plains of the Ganga and moving to more elevated surrounds, far into the holy mountains above. There, I would finally dedicate myself to knowing the Divine Mother. The spiritual quest which had long eluded me was now imminent with Gurudev's grace, and I couldn't help but envisage my life at the ashram as I travelled. I warmed at the thought of serving Gurudev, doing sadhana, learning shlokas and hearing His inspirational words.

On 11 October, Swami Raghavananda and I woke up at Brahma muhurtha and left for Gurudev's ashram. Located on the scenic banks of the river Giri in the lap of the Himalayas, the very countryside is imbued with the presence of God. As we hiked through the rugged wilderness into the valley, I felt one with it. All the elements seemed in harmony: the earth in its sculpted forms rose above the waters it fed, and fresh wafts of new growth that Mother Nature Herself seemed to tend to evoke with the promise of growth of my own. And though we must walk the Giri's bracing waters, we were headed towards the holy fire at the ashram, our prayers rising like smoke to the firmament.

As it happened, we weren't alone as we crossed the powerful river's gently flowing currents. A bhajan mandali had also arrived from Varanasi. We all reached the ashram in under an hour. And at the ashram, we were anything but alone. My eyes scanned the crowd for Swamiji in a gathering of more than a hundred people, as my heart ached in my disappointment. I didn't know that there was going to be a crowd. In my ignorance, I had assumed that Swami Raghavananda and I would be living in the ashram in Gurudev's service and doing sadhana like the sadhus of olden times. That is why I had left my home eight years earlier: to have a darshan of the Jaganmata, and in meeting Swamiji, my hope had been reinvigorated.

And yet, the scene here was no different from the bustling ashrams I had moved in and out of over the years, each one seeming no closer to my dream. My hope pined within me in these moments, and my heart cried silently for here, it seemed, I would be just another monk in a line of hundreds of devotees who had thronged to be by Swamiji's side.

My eyes sought the divine presence that had called me here amongst the bustling, joyous throng of devotees; but He was nowhere to be seen. I stood quietly waiting for my turn, trying not to think what the future held for me. And then just as suddenly, Gurudev was at my side, uttering words that brought forth both tears and a smile.

'Swamiji, Jaganmata will give you darshan here. This is the place.' He said in a firm voice, His eyes looking deep into mine. What else does a sanyasi need to hear? I quickly offered my pranams at His holy feet and rose, feeling humbled by His consideration. Soon Gurumata, Swamiji's mother, walked over to where we stood. She had the same kind, satvic face as Gurudev -- with bright eyes filled with love and merriment -- replete with the same divinity as Swamiji's. Only an enlightened mother could give birth to a great saint like Swamiji, I thought. I offered my pranams to her, and fell quiet. Even though she spoke most kindly, I felt shy. I had this habit of clamming up when meeting people for the first time.

Soon, a small and learned brigade of pundits began chanting Vedic mantras. The puja started with mantraghosha (recitation of mantras). Swami Raghavananda and I performed the dhwaja pratishthapana (hoist the temple flag), as we recited the Hanuman chalisa (a devotional hymn). The flag, with its compelling burnt-orange field surrounding an embroidered gold sudarshan chakra (discus) emblem, now heralded the divinity here, its proud colours of renunciation and glory holding sway along this stretch of the Giri. The bhajan mandali from Varanasi began singing the most soulful songs of the Lord's glory. In Swamiji's divine presence, the land beneath our feet vibrated with peace and bhakti (devotion).

At 3.00 p.m. the programme finally concluded. I brought lunch for Gurudev's naivedhya and offered it to Him. I sat near to Him, my palms pressed together in my lap.

'Swamiji, you too have lunch. It is already very late. It looks like you haven't had anything since morning.' He was right: I hadn't eaten anything for all those hours, but out of shyness I denied it. At that time, while He had clearly perceived my hidden dedication to Divine Mother, I had no clue that for Gurudev all my thoughts and desires were as apparent as to one looking through a window to my soul.

His voice, filled with tenderness, brought my gaze to His face. He said, 'Please come, let us have lunch together.' The devotees sitting nearby seemed surprised -- almost as much as I was -- at the gentleness in Swamiji's voice.

After lunch, I said to Swamiji a little hesitantly, 'Swamiji, I have to do my daily recital of shlokas ...'

'Please do,' He replied. He was sitting on a cot outside having a satsang with the devotees. I finished taking my bath and reciting shlokas at around 6.45 p.m. and rejoined the group to hear Swamiji's pravachana (discourse).

The dinner was ready to be served at 9.30 p.m. There was puri, lentils and a vegetable dish. In the afternoon, Gurumata had asked me to organize the preparation of two or three chapattis for Swamiji's dinner. I was in a new place and I did not know whom to ask, and eventually, it slipped my mind that I must convey the message. I could thus only give puris to Swamiji, and they were thick and unpalatable and all but dripping with oil. I watched, bemused, as Swamiji struggled to eat. He ate only one puri -- and that too, I suspect, so as not to hurt my feelings. He left the rest of the food. It had been a long day for Him, and there were signs of fatigue on His face; but I didn't see the loving, considerate smile waver even once.

It was the night of Sharad Purnima (the autumn harvest festival on the full moon). The bhajan mandali were in fine form. All the devotees huddled around Swamiji, enraptured with the heart-stirring bhajans of Lord Krishna's birth, life and battle. Despite the divine surroundings and music, my mind and heart were far away. Although the ashram's locale was doubtless picturesque and Swamiji exceedingly gracious, I felt that I was somehow out of place. And my letting Swamiji go hungry by not properly arranging His meal niggled at me. He had welcomed me most warmly and brought me close to Him, and I hadn't even managed to get Him two chapattis to sustain Him after such a gruelling day.

I went to bed absorbed in these thoughts, unable to still the churning emotions inside me, fear and disappointment their bitter fuel. I was mortified at seeing so many people around Gurudev. I had envisioned a quiet new ashram life with just Swamiji and me; but here, no less than one hundred people were in attendance -- and they all sought His attention, His darshan. What I didn't know was that they would return to their city lives in just two days.

In the Ramakrishna ashram in Bangalore, where I served for many years, I was in the habit of reading a great many religious and spiritual texts in Kannada. I had read how the Himalayas were a densely forested range covered for much of the year in snow; how for countless miles its lofty peaks, snow-capped and reaching into the sky, gave way to one another, nurturing in their cool valleys a few hermitages by the banks of the Ganga or deep in the woods.

As I read these descriptions, I had imagined being in this holy, majestic land a couple of years later, well on my way to becoming a big rishi or tapas (sage). But when I arrived in Haridwar, all I saw were people and buildings. It was not too different from Bangalore, only the streets were filthier. I was heartbroken for some time, until fate brought me to a lonely kutir on the banks of the Ganga, where I spent the next three years looking after the temple in Sadhana Sadan. I was happy in my quiet life.

Meeting Swamiji had awakened again my idealized dream of a hermitage in the realm of the Gods, and just as I had nurtured an idyllic vision of Haridwar, I had imagined Swamiji's ashram to be secluded and tranquil. As I lay in my bed that evening, I sadly reflected on my dashed hopes. It was Haridwar all over again. The ashram was all but overrun with devotees, and Swamiji seemed so far from my reach. In my ignorance, the dam of tears I had held at bay since I arrived broke. Soon, I was sobbing like a child, and I struggled to dampen the sound with my blankets.

In the midst of my grief, I felt a loving touch on my head. I looked up in surprise to see Swamiji's countenance above me. He was sitting near me, stroking my head. There was such compassion and understanding in His eyes, as if He knew what went on in my small and impure heart. For He had always known, from the first moment He met me.

The next morning after we awoke, Swami Raghavananda and I readied ourselves for the homa (ritual of offerings in a sacred fire). This was to be a momentous day for the ashram. As I sat close to Swami Raghavananda near the fire, we made arghya (offerings) to the fire god, Agni Deva, as Gurudev continued to chant mantras in His deep voice. With His heavenly baritone so close to me, my heart melted, and my eyes blurred with tears. I kept thanking the Jaganmata for this wonderful opportunity to be in Swamiji's service.

With resounding cheers from the assembled devotees, the ashram was named 'Sri Badrika Ashram' in these auspicious moments. Sri stands for Jaganmata, Badrika means Lord Narayana. Both were present amongst us, in the form of my Gurudev.

The Foremost Yogi

Winter soon brought its chill and beauty to the land, and I was happily settling into my new life at the ashram. Despite the unpromising first meal I had provided Him, my work included preparing Gurudev's food. In one sense, at least, this was no great undertaking. With the diet of a mere child, Gurudev eats with the grace of an Emperor. The soft and round chapattis the size of a child's palm are enough to fulfil Swamiji's hunger. His frugal diet is a habit from His sadhana time, where He took only one meal a day, and sometimes not even that. As much as anything, this was due to the remoteness of the place of His sadhana, and a serious lack of provisions. For days on end, He would meditate twenty-two hours daily, sustained only by snow.

In His memoir *If Truth Be Told,* there is some mention of the hardships that Gurudev experienced in the harsh Himalayan weather at an altitude of 14,000 feet. These privations, however, pale to insignificance beside the tolerance and discipline I have seen Gurudev exercise. Enduring cold, hunger and heat -- deprived of even the most basic comforts of a proper roof, a bed and a washroom in the ashram — Gurudev lived happily, gratefully immersed in the Divine Mother.

While preparing His meals, I would pray to the Goddess to purify me so that the meal would be befitting of Gurudev and Her, for He offered everything to the Supreme Goddess before He partook of it. Not a drop of water ever touches His lips before it has been offered to the Divine. Anxiety tugged at my heart as I cooked, reminding me to keep my thoughts pure and focused on Swamiji's prasadam (food). Moreover, I could not taste it to ensure that it was satisfactory, because He would not accept food that had been consumed by another before Him. If the offering was impure in any way, He would politely refuse it and forgo His meal.

One time, two devotees, young men, came to the ashram with a small bag of apples. They insisted that Gurudev take at least one of the apples.

Gurudev took out one apple from the bag, whispered a mantra on it, but just as He was about to bite into it, He put it back in the bag.

'I'm sorry,' He said. 'I can't eat this because fruits have been taken from this bag and eaten already, before I could offer the first one to Mother Divine.'

The two men hung their heads in shame. 'We are very sorry, Swamiji,' they said. 'We were hungry on the way so just before crossing the river, we had an apple each.'

Gurudev laughed heartily and said that was good — only He could no longer eat from that bag.

Another time, a woman had made sweetmeats for Gurudev and brought them carefully parcelled to the ashram with her husband and young son. Once again, they insisted that He partake from her offering.

'Has it been tasted at all?' Gurudev asked as soon as He lifted a laddoo.

'Not at all, Swamiji,' they said. 'We knew that you would not accept it otherwise.'

Gurudev smiled and murmured a mantra. But before eating it, He put the laddoo down and said, 'I'm sorry, but it's not fit for offering.'

'We swear, Guruji,' the wife and husband said in unison. 'It has not been tasted.'

'You are not lying, but you don't know,' Gurudev said.

He looked at the child sitting next to them and called him closer. He stroked his head.

The child said, 'Sorry, mummy. I had one laddoo when you left them to cool down and stepped out of the kitchen. I couldn't resist it.'

The woman rose to scold him, and the child cowered in fear. Just then Gurudev drew the child closer to Him.

'Don't!' He stopped the mother. 'He ate means Mother Divine ate.'

Gurudev lifted the box of laddoos and gave one to the child and ate one himself.

The family left, but Gurudev's face had become sombre.

'From now on,' he said, 'I'll offer my food differently to Mother Divine so that no one ever gets scolded or has to worry about offering any food to me. It wouldn't matter then whether it has been tasted or not.'

Still, if for some reason the food I prepared was unsatisfactory or impure, He would simply push the meal away, thank me lovingly, and eat nothing till it was time for the next meal. This was crushing for me. The thought that my Gurudev would go hungry if I was remiss in my duty – even in the most subtle of ways, some not of my knowing – weighed heavily on me. It was not as if He needed to skip meals, as many of us do, either. His lean form carried the minimum of reserve.

I had cooked many a meal at ashrams before – cooked for hundreds of disciples, devotees at a time. But here, preparing one small, rudimentary meal for Gurudev had butterflies fluttering wildly in my stomach. Even after four years, I still experience this same sensation, though less obtrusively, as I enter the kitchen to prepare Swamiji's meal.

One afternoon in that winter of 2011, I moved about the small mud cottage as usual, preparing a simple lunch of chapatti and lentils for Gurudev. As I went about kneading the dough, I could hear the famous *'Niranjani narayani'* by Pandit Jasraj playing in Swamiji's room. It was the perfect soundtrack for my work. As I rolled the small chapatthis, I was almost carried away by the sounds of the glorious bhajan. When the chapatthis were cooked and the lentil dish was steaming, I went to Swamiji's room to inform Him that lunch was ready.

The door was ajar, and as I was about to step inside, my gaze fell upon the image in the glass window opposite to where Gurudev sat. I was startled to see the reflection of a yogi, a saint who appeared to have been deep in samadhi for thousands of years and would now manifest before me. To say I was startled would be an understatement. I stood frozen in the doorway for some time, the reality of the reflection in the glass dawning slowly. The image was as real as my own in the mirror. It wasn't the reflection of Gurudev as I knew Him, but a glimpse from another time, ancient and mystical. He was a yogi of yore: deeply immersed in meditation, and completely oblivious to his surroundings. The ambience in the small room felt thick and powerful, like a cooling flow of the river, and I was immersed in peace.

In essence, the reflection I beheld in the window and Swami were the same; but the reflection was the secret behind the human form -- the divine truth beneath the layer of flesh and bones, blood and marrow. My feet felt heavy as I stepped back so as not to disturb Swamiji's samadhi. I have seen many facets of Gurudev since that winter, but the image of the yogi is still fresh in my mind.

The days in the ashram were filled with quietude. The pace of the world outside had no meaning here as Swamiji spent His days in writing and deep contemplation. Many evenings after dinner, Gurudev and I would walk together under the awning of the stars. How could creation be silent in the presence of a holy one? Night after night, the whole sky would put on a show, as if ablaze with a million fireflies. He would point out the many constellations, and my whole existence would drown in His deep, sonorous voice. His presence filled me with supreme joy. Living far into the wilderness, without even the means to so much as produce a bag of wheat or rice, I was happy to be by Gurudev's side, serving Him.

The living conditions were far from ideal, though. The ashram had only one modest mud cottage, which comprised a small lobby that served as our kitchen, two tiny rooms and a basic washroom. Gurudev stayed in one of the rooms and I in the other, while Swami Raghavananda slept in the lobby. For the first fifteen to twenty days, we cooked food outside with firewood, as we did not have a stove. During winter months, sometimes only semi-frozen water would flow from the water pipe. In spite of these shortcomings in our amenities and the resulting hardship, Gurudev would always praise our service.

He was most hospitable and accommodating with visitors, too, despite there barely being room for just the three of us. When devotees stayed overnight, they would sleep on the floor in Swamiji's room, while He slept on a rickety cot. There was insufficient space in that small room to move about freely, and yet Swamiji didn't mind the intrusion as, he said, people had travelled from far to see Him.

When devotees were staying, He would wake up as usual between 4 a.m. and 5 a.m., and then quietly step over their slumbering forms in the dark and head outside. There, He would take a bath in the freezing cold in icy water, simply because the washroom was next to His room, and bathing there might disturb the sleeping devotees. He would then come into my room (which was no more than six feet by six feet) to change His robe. At such times I was deeply moved, even saddened by the lack of basic comforts we had for my Gurudev. He wasn't just another monk who had renounced a mediocre life to walk the path of spirituality. He had renounced enormous wealth, a multi-million dollar business and a life of success and luxury that most people can only dream about. And here He was, living happily in the most pitiful conditions.

Perhaps this had much to do with the Divine Mother manifesting for Gurudev. He needed nothing; He was truly desireless, a living idol of love. All that I had read and knew about God -- the truthfulness and righteous conduct of Lord Rama, the playfulness and merriment of Krishna -- seemed to shine forth from my Gurudev. His mysterious forms didn't reveal themselves at once; it was a sweet, baffling and startling journey as I experienced His grace along the way.

There were enough indications from our first meeting, however, that I was serving a great saint indeed. There were numerous instances where He would accurately read my mind, foresee unexpected events and visitors and predict the problems and questions with which people would approach Him. It was an intriguing period of my life. I had stumbled upon gold only to realize its glory wasn't the sparkling of a shiny metal, but the effulgence of the sun.

One evening, as we strolled after our meal, savouring the lights of the universe that seemed to unfurl nightly above the ashram, I could not help but reflect on my good fortune, my idyllic existence. I wanted to bask in these moments; I wanted this time to last forever, just Him and me living peacefully in our hermitage. Here, as I learnt many vidyas and sadhanas from Him, I was following the spiritual path that I had longed for, and in His company, nothing was left wanting. Gurudev was quick to read my mind.

'These are golden moments: this time, the quiet, peaceful ashram life will not come back, Swamiji. Enjoy these moments to the fullest,' He said. The magnanimity of my Guru is such that He always addressed me as Swamiji. At that time, I couldn't grasp the significance of what He had just said. Much that Swamiji speaks of has a meaning deeper than one can fathom, or simply seems enigmatic or even unimaginable at the time. His words are as the clouds building before rain -- they are material portent, a promise of what will transpire. As I was new to His ways, I simply pressed my hands together in gratitude, and left it at that.

Certainly, Swamiji already had many devotees. Some devotees He had known from His purvashram (prior to renunciation) days. A large circle of people had believed in His divinity, even in the days when Swamiji wore fitted suits and travelled the world doing business. His taking to the ochre robe only reinforced their faith in Him, and they still sought His blessings. But while the village folk from the district surrounding the ashram had heard that some babaji had come to live in their midst, they didn't really disturb us. A few of them crossed paths with us from time to time, and our relationships with them were genial. But for the most part, we saw no one for days. All that was about to change as Swamiji had rightly predicted; and change in such a drastic manner that I would never again experience the luxury of having Him all to myself.

Not even two weeks had passed since I had come to permanently live in the ashram; but it felt as if I had spent a lifetime in Swamiji's presence. It was the usual morning routine. I was inside the cottage, attending to my kitchen duties, and after enjoying a light breakfast of upma, Swamiji was sitting outside, writing an article for His blog. The Internet connectivity was very poor in these parts. The simple task of uploading an image or an article that would normally take less than a minute elsewhere, would routinely take anywhere between ten to thirty minutes. Gurudev would patiently sit through it all, for He knew how eagerly devotees waited to hear from Him.

I was busy clearing the kitchen when a piercing female voice rang out across the mountains above the ashram, breaking our tranquillity. 'Please help, help me please, somebody ...' There was great desperation and urgency in the voice. The words were punctuated by wailing which continued, growing louder by the second.

Swamiji rose to His feet and I quickly emerged from the cottage. Together we tried to see where the voice was coming from. We peered into the hills, but there was nobody in sight. Swami Raghavananda ran up the nearest hillock to find out more. He returned after a couple of minutes.

'Swamiji,' he said breathing heavily, 'There's a house above here, and a woman and her daughter stay there. This morning when they went to get hay for their cow, a whole swarm of poisonous wasps bit them all over. They are swollen and blue. The child is in excruciating pain and the lady doesn't know what to do. They are crying for help.'

Swamiji closed his eyes momentarily and then looked faraway, as if surveying distance beyond our realm. 'Let's go and see what can be done.'

We all walked up a tortuous, slippery path to the house. It was a run-down hut, little more than a shed. Indeed, I wasn't sure, at first, if it was cattle or people who inhabited it. As soon as we neared the hut, we saw a woman lying on the ground outside, moaning softly. Her face had turned a livid purple from the insect bites; her forehead, hands and feet were horribly swollen, and one eye had completely shut because of the swelling. It was a terrible sight. There was no doubt in my mind that the insects' poison was indeed deadly, and it was spreading rapidly throughout her body. She obviously needed urgent medical attention. Swamiji quickly went to the child, a girl of about nine or ten, who lay semi-conscious nearby. Her symptoms were much the same as her mother's, only worse.

An old lady, with gnarled hands and feet, limped out of the hut and begged us to save the lives of her daughter-in-law and granddaughter. As Swamiji knelt by the child's side, the old lady fell at His feet and pleaded with Him.

'Please save my child, Swamiji. She'll die like this. Please help her, do something.' She started crying loudly. 'These are poisonous insects. We lost a dog only a few days ago with just one bite.'

The old lady howled in fear and grief. Her husband, who had by now heard his wife's cries came running too, leaving his goats behind.

'My daughter-in-law will die, Swamiji,' the old lady cried. 'Please save her.'

We carried the little girl into the hut. The child turned to Swamiji and her tiny hands reached out for Swamiji's divine hands. She seemed to be hanging by a thread, and yet the innocence of children is such that they accept and embrace the goodness that life brings them.

Reflecting on this moment, I am reminded of the puranic story where the child Markandeya clings to the Shivalinga when Yama, the god of death, comes to take him. Death seemed to be lurking nearby that morning, and the young girl was clinging to Swamiji lest she be taken. I wasn't sure what we could do. There was no road to the ashram; the nearest hospital was at least an hour away, and one had to travel on foot for the first thirty minutes. I didn't think the child would last that long. The lady's condition was grave indeed, but the child's was positively dire.

The two women fervently implored Swamiji to save the child. The mother's condition too was deteriorating; but her love for the child seemed foremost in her mind. Swami Raghavananda and I stood behind Swamiji, awaiting His instructions. It occurred to me that we had little option but to summon medical aid. It seemed, though, that the child might be beyond helping. She appeared to be slipping away, the bluish purple of her small, swollen face covering a deathly pallor. I felt it was just a matter of time now. Little did I know that Gurudev's mercy and power knew no bounds; anyone who sought His sharan (refuge) would not be turned away.

Gurudev was suddenly very quiet. His countenance had changed; the ever-laughing eyes closed in dhyana and his curved lips quivered as He softly chanted a mantra. I had never heard the mantra, let alone have any clue what it meant. Every sound in the little hut stilled as the gentle vibration of His voice resonated against the four walls. The effect on the mother and child was immediate and palpable. Their agitation and pain seemed to flow out of them like water into a drain, and they began to look more aware of their surroundings. It was amazing how the mantra carried with it a strange healing power that almost instantaneously granted relief to the patients.

I had never seen anything like this in my life as a renunciant. I knew many stories of sadhus healing the ailing with the power of tapas (intense meditation), but to have witnessed this first-hand was unnerving, to say the least. For Swamiji hadn't merely healed the child: He had snatched her from the very jaws of death.

'Nothing will happen to your child. Both of you will be fine, this is Swami's word.' He spoke in quiet tones to the women huddled on the floor, looking up at Him with reverence and awe. Every word that fell from His mouth felt like a blessing, driving out the gloom and illness that lurked in the damp and dark corners of the little hut. Once again, I could only marvel at Gurudev.

He then instructed Swami Raghavananda to call a devotee, a doctor to find out how to drain the poison from the body. The doctor advised a drink of tulsi and honey. The old woman had tulsi but no honey. I quickly ran back down the path to the ashram kitchen to fetch some honey.

By the time I came back – and I was gone no more than a few minutes – that horrible purple hue on their faces had mostly cleared, and the swelling had started to subside. I couldn't believe what had happened here. Still, Swamiji asked us to prepare the mixture. He patiently waited as we made the concoction, and He administered it to the child Himself.

Satisfied, Swamiji turned to the mother and gently told her, 'Your child is out of danger now. When she's a little better take her to the nearby hospital.' As Swamiji rose to leave, the women once again fell at His feet in gratitude, thanking Him, crying tears of relief and joy.

Needless to say, news of Swamiji's miraculous healing of the woman and the girl spread in the local and neighbouring villages more rapidly than a summer bushfire. By evening, everyone had heard of how Swamiji had saved the life of a lady and a child with His mantra. From that day onwards, people started flocking to the ashram for Swamiji's darshan and His blessings. They came with sick children in their arms, an ailing parent or an infertile wife in tow. From wealth and prosperity issues to extreme medical conditions; from mental and physical ailments and addictions to being childless, they came seeking Swamiji's divine blessings.

This event marked the beginning of a continual, steady flow of devotees. For word of Swamiji's ability to give relief to all manner of life's woes spread almost as swiftly across the land and to other continents as it had through the surrounding countryside. The ashram would never be the quiet, tranquil place where I had Swami to myself – and it was all for the better. I had my cherished memories of my time alone with Him. The ashram gates were thrown open to anyone who came seeking His grace. Swamiji had predicted as much, for He had returned after His vision of the Supreme Goddess only to help mankind. This was His only mission.

Vision of the Mother

Just a couple of days after the incident of the wasp stings, Gurudev asked me what chanting I did for three hours every morning. 'I recite Sri Durga Saptashati,' I replied.

'How long have you been doing this?'

'About three-and-a-half years,' I said.

'So that means, you have recited it more than a thousand times ...'

I bowed humbly. 'Yes, Swamiji.'

'You don't need to do it from tomorrow. If you wish to do it I have no objections. But I will tell you a sadhana now. It'll take twenty minutes and you can do it at the same time in the morning instead of your routine recital. You can start from tomorrow. Results will come through within one month.'

He then gave me the details. This was the sadhana I had been awaiting from Him – and He gave it, too, on one of the most auspicious nights of the year. In Haridwar, a senior Swamiji had once told me that three days of the year – Akshaya trithya, Vijayadashami and the night of Deepawali – are very auspicious for giving diksha (initiation in to a spiritual practise) or to begin any sadhana. It was the night of Deepawali and by the grace of the Goddess, I was fortunate to receive the sadhana from Gurudev.

This was Jaganmata's greatest boon for me. Just a few hours earlier, Swamiji had been worshipping the Goddess with Sri Sukta (a devotional hymn to the Goddess Lakshmi). Now I, mere humble devotee that I was, had received sadhana from Him. I was numb with joy, and didn't know what to do or say. I held my hands together and sat down quietly by His side.

Seeing my quietness, Gurudev said affectionately, 'Look Swamiji, till now you were worried about finding a guru and you did sadhana, japa (chanting of mantras) in the way you thought was correct. But from now on, I am with you. I am with you till the day you have the darshan of the Jaganmata herself.'

I was overwhelmed with Gurudev's sincere promise to lead me to the Goddess, for in today's world, there is perhaps no one else who can give such an assurance. Adi Shankaracharya said in his epic poem *Vivekachudamani* it is rare to find three things, other than the grace of God: human birth, longing for liberation and the protection and care of a perfect sage.

After my fruitless years of searching, I was indeed fortunate to have found all three. My life was complete, and I eternally offered my sashtanga namaskarams (prostrate devotions) at the feet of Gurudev for this.

On 5 November 2011, like any other day, I woke up at Brahma muhurtha and did my morning sadhana that Gurudev had given me two weeks earlier. The day passed as usual. Gurudev had promised me that I would have darshan of Mother Divine.

At around 8.30 in the evening while we were having milk, Swamiji was snuggled in His quilt when He received an email. Having read the email His demeanour changed, and He fell silent. He wanted to write back to the devotee, but the Internet was playing up. We had a very poor signal in the ashram. It was a constant struggle just to remain connected.

Gurudev asked me to put His chair outside.

'Swamiji, it's very cold outside ...'

Without looking up from the screen, He replied, 'This devotee is in trouble. I must reach out to him. He's waiting to hear from me.'

I put the chair outside with a heavy heart. It was extremely cold; the winter in the ashram can be harsh and unforgiving. Swamiji tried numerous times to get a signal but to no avail. This was, in fact, a most common occurrence for Him. Uploading an image or an article for His weekly blog post would sometimes take three or four hours. On some good days, it would happen quickly and He would be done uploading within an hour. He would keep changing the position of His laptop, tilt it high, and sometimes even walk a considerable distance where He could get a faint signal and complete His work.

On one such occasion, I asked Him 'What's the need to inconvenience yourself? What is so important that it demands your attention right away?' Partly closing the screen of the laptop in front of Him, He replied, 'There are people who wait for my weekly post as if their life depends on it. Many troubled devotees check their emails constantly to see if their Swami has replied. How can I let them down, Swamiji?' He then promptly reopened the laptop screen and turned His attention to finishing His work.

Throughout these tiresome, prolonged hunts for a signal bar on His laptop, He never displayed any kind of impatience or annoyance. He endured this with just the same aplomb that He evinced in dealing with the bitter cold of winter, the searing heat of summer and the ascetic living conditions at the ashram. Even in those cumbersome hours He seemed at peace. Nothing seemed to ruffle Him.

On this particular evening, it was difficult to get even that one vital signal bar. Gurudev was only wearing His thin cotton robe in the biting cold. He stood up, sat down, changed position, restarted the device, tried walking around with the laptop in His hand, but nothing seemed to work. Three hours had passed, and He still wouldn't give up. The cold appeared to seep through my woollen socks all the way to my bones. How he must have felt, clad only in His cotton robe, I could only guess.

A layer of mist had settled in the valley around the ashram like a white, ethereal river. Even the chirping of the crickets seemed to have frozen in their throats. Swamiji had been asking me to go inside for a while now, but I didn't want to leave Him. Finally He ordered me to go inside and sleep and said that He would follow as soon as this work was done.

I couldn't disobey Him, so I went inside, but I didn't go to sleep. How could I sleep when my Gurudev was outside in the cold? It was as if my body was here in my room, but both my heart and my mind were outside there, with Him as He walked in the darkness, searching for some response from the device He held. I stayed awake to switch on the light when He finally came inside. Sitting in my dark room, I quietly waited for Him. The clock showed 12.30 a.m. when Swamiji came inside.

He realized that I was sitting in the dark, waiting for him, and He walked into my room. I hurriedly stood up and gave Him a seat. I was at a loss as to what I should offer Gurudev. This was the first time He had stepped inside my room at night. He cast a loving eye about its tiny space.

'It's very late. Why didn't you go to sleep?' He asked me gently. I kept quiet. He picked up a framed photograph of Sri Ramakrishna Paramahamsa from the small temple I kept that also held a picture of Devi.

He stared unblinking at Sri Ramakrishna's photograph for some time. A few minutes passed, but He still kept looking at the saint's image. Soon tears started flowing from His eyes; not just a tear or two, but veritable streams wetting His cheeks. It felt like the two great avatars were deep in silent, profound conversation. Try as I might, I couldn't look away from Gurudev's face. I stood transfixed by the love that emanated from Him for the great Bengali saint. Some fifteen minutes later, Gurudev quietly put the photograph down and without uttering a word, went to His room.

I switched off the bare bulb above me. My mind flowed as silently as a river pouring into the divine ocean, for I knew had witnessed something extraordinary. I just didn't know what. I woke up at Brahma muhurtha, had my bath, and sat down for my sadhana. As I said my prayer and chanted a mantra just as I did on any other day, a small girl appeared next to my room's temple.

I was agog. My eyes just stared at her exquisite, tiny form. She was lovely like a doll, a little princess doll. Around three feet tall, she was clad in a rich green top, with a crimson dress flowing from her waist to her ankles. Exquisite gold earrings hung from her ears, and tiny bangles and anklets tinkled on her hands and feet as she moved. I was too astonished to make any sense of what I was seeing. Each unfolding moment was beyond my understanding; I kept still and watched, entranced. She came toward me and sat to my left and her fair, tiny arms slipped around my neck.

While her form was truly minute, she held me with unearthly power. Lovingly, she whispered a divyamantra, a divine chant in my ear. She walked to my right side from behind and sat down once again. This time, she placed both her palms on my head. The divine girl-child then blessed me, and vanished.

My mind and body were numb with rapture. Devi had appeared! I somehow managed, in my ecstatic state, to finish my remaining sadhana and prepare breakfast for Swamiji. Carrying the breakfast, I rushed to His room, and hastily sat down to do my pranams. But I could not contain the bliss that was bubbling inside me.

'Swamiji, today during my sadhana ...' I couldn't complete the sentence, for I was too overcome with emotion. My throat felt choked and my eyes misted with tears of elation.

'Yes, Mother Divine came in bala swaroopa (child form),' He said in a matter-of-fact tone. 'She has given you the permission, Swamiji. I'll give you the next step now.'

Still, I regained my voice, and the words tumbled out of my mouth as I recounted to Him my experience. I wanted Him to know everything all at once.

Like a mother looking at her child adoringly, Gurudev replied, 'She is satisfied with the Sri Durga Saptashati chanting that you've been doing for the past three-and-a-half years. You have now reaped the fruit of your earlier sadhana.'

He sounded so happy and pleased with me that I thanked Mother Divine again for her blessings. He then went on to explain the significance of the mantra and the Devi appearing in her child form. I listened in rapt attention. How Gurudev had turned my life around! Thousands of monks visited holy places, served in temples and ashrams, praying to the Divine with fervour day and night — and yet even in their twilight years, they had never received a vision of the Goddess. Here, barely a month in Gurudev's service -- and in a matter of days after Gurudev made changes to my sadhana -- I had been granted this heavenly boon.

Later in my room, I thanked my divine master again and again with all my heart, recalling with awe every detail of the previous evening when Swamiji had come to my room. He hasn't again, either, and it has been nearly four years since this episode. I couldn't help but wonder at the connection between the silent conversation that took place between Gurudev and Sri Ramakrishna Paramahamsa's picture, and the Divine Mother's visitation.

The divine girl-child had appeared only by the grace of Gurudev. His love for me had summoned the Divine to my door. Otherwise, who was I but another renunciant among the countless who called out to her? This thought filled me with even greater peace, for I realized the Divine Mother hadn't left at all -- she was present at all times in my master.

Living with the Master

Gurudev never let anyone do any seva beyond a few minutes. Even now, He does not accept anything for His personal needs from any devotee. He doesn't seem to need much for His personal needs, in any case. Through His own limited means, He built a hut, no more than eight feet by eight feet, with only a seven-foot-high ceiling. A bare tin roof and the mud walls keep out the elements. He wanted to do another sadhana lasting eight months. So in January 2012, He shifted into His new hut and began another intense sadhana that would end in August 2012.

In the gruelling heat of May 2012, He sat in meditation for the whole day in this small hut. Far from protecting Him from the sweltering conditions outside, its tin roof acted more like a hotplate, and the scorching summer sun would heat up the room to a fearsome degree. We didn't have proper electricity in the ashram. You couldn't even have tube lights. Only CFL bulbs would work. Fans would not work from 6 p.m. to 9 p.m. because of low voltage; but even this electricity would fail us, sometimes for five or six hours in a day -- and sometimes it would be gone for days. But Gurudev didn't complain once as He sat immersed in sadhana.

The tantric practise was so intense that Swamiji's whole body seemed to burn up. I could see that He was especially suffering the effects of this intense burning sensation in His feet, so one midsummer evening, I asked Him if I may massage them. He was working on His blog, but He allowed me to massage His feet and legs with oil as He continued typing. Barely had five minutes passed when Swamiji said to me, 'Your hands must be tired. I am not used to this seva. Please, stop.'

'No, Swamiji, I'm not tired at all. It's my good fortune to touch your feet. Please let me continue for a little while more.'

He shook His head, saying He felt shy and uncomfortable taking such service from me. It was a rare opportunity for me to massage His feet, though. I had no wish to let them go. In spite of having thousands of gods and goddesses in attendance, the Lord's feet are massaged only by Jaganmata Lakshmi. Likewise, thousands of devotees are scattered across the world, but it was I who was here performing this service. I had no intention of relinquishing this moment. I held onto His feet with the doggedness of a child clutching a favourite toy.

Needless to say, I continued to massage His feet and legs for some time. Gurudev's feet are pink and as clean as a little baby's feet. If I massaged them for a few minutes, they would turn red like lotus petals. I never let an opportunity to massage His feet pass, for they were my eternal abode. But one thing never changed: His reluctance to let me massage them for more than ten minutes. It is just not in Gurudev's nature to let anyone do any seva for more than a few minutes. One can see the burden on His face as He cajoles me to let go of His feet. It is difficult for Swami to order me to stop, for

He is well aware of the joy I derive from doing His charan-seva (feet massage).

Gurudev's company was, at any rate, pleasure in itself. In the early days at the ashram, Gurudev and I would often take a morning walk along the lively, noisy river Giri. A cool breeze from the valley would caress my skin, and I was at peace. In those silent mornings, each moment spent with Gurudev was precious. He was always smiling, sometimes talking about his writing – and often teasing me playfully, for my Hindi was terrible. Some days, Gurudev would say that Jaganmata herself accompanied us. I would be delighted to hear it, and even look across my shoulder to see if I could spot her. Swamiji would smile.

Once we were walking together, I accidentally stepped on a small anthill, scattering its tiny inhabitants and squashing them beneath my feet. Gurudev was quick to observe my error: 'Oh Swamiji, what did you do! These small insects build their home on the ground. Please look where you are stepping. Many minute living organisms move about on the ground. We should try to never cause them any harm or pain.' He surveyed the mess I had made on the ground with a pained expression on His face.

He seemed quite disheartened. The atmosphere changed, and a sort of gloom descended on my mind. I asked for His forgiveness. He reassured me, but I knew I had made a mistake. I then recalled how Gurudev always walked very carefully; He always looked down so as not to step on any small creature. The true paragon of virtue that He is – a guru of deeds as much as words – He never tells others to do that which He doesn't do Himself.

If there was much learning in Swamiji's example and serious tutelage, there was much laughter and playfulness, too. I first experienced His mischievous sense of humour little more than a fortnight after I arrived at the ashram. He was sitting outside writing His blog as I was sitting inside, quietly absorbed in my evening prayers, when a couple of village folk approached Him. Not knowing that they were addressing the Swamiji Himself, they asked if they could meet with Babaji.

'Is Babaji there, can we see Him now?' they asked hopefully.

Although they hadn't met Him, there had been incessant talk in the village about the Babaji who had cured a little girl and a lady with His mantras in a matter of minutes, and they had been moved by what they had heard and had come to the ashram to seek His help. Seeing His youthful appearance and unassuming demeanour, it didn't occur to them that He was the one whose audience they sought. Gurudev asked them to wait a while, and that Swamiji would soon be there. He carried on with His writing. When I emerged from the cottage after my prayers some ten minutes later, Swamiji stretched His arm in my direction and said, 'Here comes Swamiji.'

Immediately the men stood and rushed towards me, flinging themselves at my feet. Before I could open my mouth they began addressing me as Babaji, telling me their troubles and firing questions at me. I was completely nonplussed. Why were they asking me questions? I looked from them to Him, not knowing what to do. I looked again, and this time recognized the mischievous glint in Gurudev's eyes. I figured out what had transpired. I quickly told them that I was merely the disciple, and the guru was sitting right there in front of them. It took the men a moment to register that the young and slender Swamiji sitting in the chair was the real Swamiji. They looked in puzzlement at my burly frame and bemused expression, and then like lost sheep running home to their master, they went to Swamiji.

I stood nearby, pondering the strange experience of these men offering their pranams to me first in my Gurudev's presence. After they left, Swamiji noticed my reflections and let out a chuckle. I too joined in. He said to me, 'The look on your face was priceless when they started asking you questions.' I humbly pressed my palms together at His leela and vowed to be more alert to Gurudev's pranks in the future.

One day after breakfast, Gurudev asked me to assist Him. 'There is a small task that I need you to do, Swamiji. I have to record my discourse. Devotees have been asking for it. I'll teach you to operate this camera. Just follow the simple instructions and we'll be fine.' I nodded eagerly. There could scarce be better use for this technology, I thought, than for it to help others to get to know Swamiji. We went around the ashram premises looking for a suitable place for the recording. We finally decided on a spot: a huge rock from where the river could be seen flowing below, surrounded by tall hills on all sides. It seemed like the perfect place.

I fixed the stand, adjusted the focus so that Swamiji was in the centre of the frame and pressed the record button. This first session lasted twenty-two minutes. It was the most wonderfully inspirational twenty-two minutes, as I absorbed every word that Gurudev uttered. In that scenic setting, filled with Gurudev's divine voice and insight, I felt my life's mission was complete. It would be the beginning of a great many discourses to come.

Soon, we began to record Hindi discourses in the morning and English discourses in the evenings. After every recording, Swamiji would look at the footage and make camera or sound adjustments if necessary. His eye for detail and pursuit of perfection in everything He undertook was commendable. In the months that followed, we recorded discourses on Tapas, Purity, Where are you going, What you want, Bhaja Govindam Series, Karma and many more topics.

During this time, there were three dogs in the ashram that followed Swamiji everywhere. They would come running, wagging their tails the moment they spotted Him. He was very fond of them. Not once did they disturb the recording by barking or fighting amongst themselves. They were happy to sit quietly near Swamiji. In their frail bodies and loving manner, Swamiji would see Lord Narayana.

Their names were Shangri, Binny and Kaalu. Swamiji insisted on making extra chapattis so we could feed them. Some evenings, He would feed them tenderly with His own hands and even give a chapatti from His own plate.

In some of the old videos, the dogs can be seen moving about as Swamiji is giving His discourse. Sometimes He would remove His shoe and fondly pat one of the dogs with his feet. Immediately, the other two would come near Him, as if demanding similar treatment. It was a delight to watch them seek Gurudev's attention and bask in it when it was granted. He would then keep His feet on all three of them, and they would just fall at His feet in complete surrender. These animals were fortunate indeed.

Anyone who was drawn into Swamiji's presence, for whatever reason, was fortunate. Once, an aged shepherd had fallen unconscious near the ashram in the scorching heat of the day. Swami Raghavananda was returning from the river after his bath when he stumbled upon the shepherd's stricken form on the ground. He rushed back to tell Swamiji, who was busy with His writing. He was always working, either writing His blog or recording the discourses. As soon as Swamiji heard the news, He immediately put aside His laptop and headed toward the spot where the old man was lying.

He knelt on the ground beside the old man, without caring for the mud and dirt beneath that now soiled His robe. He checked the shepherd's pulse. It was beating slowly. He touched the unconscious man's forehead delicately and whispered a soft mantra, reviving him. Having seen Him do all kinds of things, I wasn't surprised anymore. Gurudev asked me to fetch drinking water from His room. In the meantime, He had made the old man sit in the shade.

I handed the water bottle to Swamiji. He held the water to the man's parched lips. The shepherd seemed too frail to drink the water by himself, so Swamiji continued to gently pour from the bottle for him. He then opened His umbrella for the elderly man, asking him to rest till he got his strength back. Swamiji knelt on the ground in that heat for nearly an hour before the old man's son came to take him home.

After having spent time in the cave in Rudranath, not seeing the sun for months altogether, Gurudev's body burns up instantly if He steps out in the sun without an umbrella. Any part of His body on which the sun's rays fall develops a blister. His body is a storehouse of energy, always emanating heat, and to sit there in the scorching sun holding up His umbrella for the old man was heart-warming beyond words.

Gurudev could easily have chosen to go inside after His initial ministrations. Swami Raghavananda or I could have watched the old man. But Swamiji stayed by his side till he was delivered to the care of his son. In His eyes, everyone is deserving of His attention and love. This is the sign of the last stage of samadhi — to see the Lord in every living being around you. Only great souls and stithaprajna (one with Godly wisdom) can live a life of such purity and austerity.

Only a stithaprajna could abide the demands that were now placed on Swamiji's time and energy, too. People were coming everyday to seek Swamiji's blessing. The continuous flow of visitors disturbed Swamiji's routine. We fixed times on Tuesdays and Saturdays for people to come and see Gurudev between eleven and noon. Sometimes, there would be so many visitors that it would extend till 1 p.m. Swamiji would talk to every one of the visitors and answer their questions most simply and patiently.

Some of the common queries were about a cow not giving enough milk, the desire to have a child, children failing in exams, bad dreams, fighting couples, no peace of mind, pain in some part of the body, etcetera -- people's common, everyday concerns. Some of the questions and problems were bordering on inane, but Gurudev would never turn anyone away. He would answer with the utmost sincerity, never ridiculing anyone's troubles as small, insignificant or irrelevant. These were simple village folk with simple problems and He was here to serve, He would say.

After a while, Swamiji began conducting English classes for village children every Sunday morning, from eleven till noon. At first, only about twenty students attended the English classes. But as the days passed, word began to spread of the simplicity and humour with which He was teaching the children, and soon the room was packed such that several students were sitting outside in the hall.

Though the class started at eleven o'clock, some students would come to the ashram by nine in the morning and wait. Swamiji would finish His breakfast by 08.30 and interact with the students. If students were late, their punishment was to converse more in English in that day's class. Sixty children came to the ashram every Sunday, without fail.

Before the class began, all the students chanted 'Om' three times and the holy Gayatri Mantra seven times. After the class, biscuits and chocolates were distributed, and the students would say, 'Thank you, Swamiji' in a loud voice. It was so endearing to watch. Every month, the children would sit for a test and after correcting the test papers, Swamiji would gift them pens, pencils and notebooks.

For nearly two years, the children received English education from Swamiji. Soon, Swamiji would have to travel abroad for discourses. Due to the increasing demand on His time by devotees, ashram issues and His writings, He was unable to continue with the classes. Teaching was just one of the many things which Swamiji did without expecting anything in return. But while He gave freely and never took gifts of money and sweets from devotees as a strict matter of principle, it seemed that the Jaganmata Herself was providing for the ashram.

One morning, in the days when we were still living in the two-room mud cottage, I prepared a light breakfast of upma. We had run out of tomatoes and so the upma did not have its usual flavour. It was also particularly salty that day. I served the breakfast to Gurudev.

He ate two spoonsful and said to me 'How come it's tasting different today, Swamiji? It tastes like you forgot to add tomatoes and instead added more salt.'

I hesitantly told him that we didn't have any tomatoes. Swamiji said, 'Oh, had you mentioned earlier, we could have arranged for tomatoes.'

How? I thought. Just like me, even He doesn't really know anyone here. I wanted to say that the only way to source tomatoes was to send someone to town. And the return trip to town is the better part of a day's labour, much of which involves trekking and fording the river.

'Mother Divine arranges for everything, Swamiji,' He said to me lovingly, reading my thoughts.

'Sorry. I didn't know whom to tell,' I said. 'This place is still new to me, and I didn't want to bother you.'

He nodded in understanding and thanked me for the breakfast. He then washed His hands and continued to do His work. I felt bad about letting Swamiji down, and quietly returned to the kitchen area. A mere five minutes later there was a knock on the door.

I opened the door to find a villager holding a bag of tomatoes in his hand. He gave the bag to me and left. I was most pleased with this development. Now I could make a truly complete and flavoursome upma or curry. Just fifteen minutes later, someone knocked on the door again. It was another devotee with a bag. I took the bag from him to find he too had brought tomatoes. Our tomato problem was most definitely solved without our having told anyone, I thought. I was about to go back inside, and there came another person, who worked in the nearby field. To my surprise, he was also carrying a bag filled with tomatoes. There were easily five kilograms of tomatoes with me now.

It was divine grace. I had enough tomatoes to last me a week. I put them all in one place. But the tomato business was far from over. In the next one hour, three more people came bearing bags full of tomatoes. From not having one tomato to flavour Gurudev's upma, I was now inundated with somewhere in the order of twenty kilograms. And there was no place in the kitchen to keep them. I emptied an old cardboard carton to store them. That proved too small, so I had to tell the villagers that I needed their bags, and that I would return them a few days later. I was amused and astonished in equal measure. A veritable bounty of tomatoes had arrived, all within a period of one hour.

I was stacking the bags in one corner, trying to keep them from blocking the entrance, when Swamiji, who was working inside, came out and asked innocently, 'What is this, Swamiji? You said there were no tomatoes, and there are so many here!'

I could only smile at Gurudev's leela and hold my hands together in surrender. He had in no time filled our little room with enough tomatoes to last us a month, without telling a single person that we needed them.

The Siddha

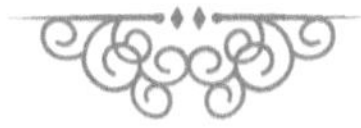

Swamiji's miracles are legion. So numerous are they that it is quite a challenge to decide on which of them I should recount here — and an accomplishment in itself just to remember them all. Having been in His service, I have witnessed unbelievable feats, startling even the believers into questioning who Swamiji really is. There are a few notable incidents from my initial days at the ashram.

Maryog is a small village on the way to the ashram. There was one young man from the village who was serving in the Indian army. He had been married for four years, but his wife had been unable to conceive. The couple began to visit Swamiji every week. The husband even showed his test reports to Swamiji. They had undergone all kinds of tests and treatments in the hospital. Their reports were all fine; there was nothing wrong with them physically.

On days when the river would overflow, making it impossible to cross, the young man would walk the five extra kilometres for one glimpse of Swamiji. Swamiji finally told him to bring ninety pieces of amla (Indian gooseberries).

'You'll be blessed with a child soon,' Swamiji said to him in His quiet manner. The man's elation knew no bounds. He touched his head to Swamiji's holy feet and left the room, his eyes moist with joy. I was no longer surprised by anything Gurudev did or said. His word was the truth. Anything He would say would come to pass, just as He had predicted it would. He could see anyone's past and future. He knew about their samskara (upbringing) and faith in God as if He was looking at a mirror. It was but a routine feat for Gurudev to grant a child to a childless couple.

The young man returned with his wife and as instructed brought ninety gooseberries with him. The husband and wife both bowed and offered their pranams to Swamiji. He looked at their expectant faces, which were filled with hope and just a hint of fear at being in the presence of such a saint.

With His eyes filled with kindness, He said to them, 'There's nothing to fear. You'll be proud parents soon enough.' Upon saying that, Swamiji immediately closed His eyes. A sudden calm fell upon the room as He prayed to Mother Divine. His radiant countenance glowed with the Jaganmata's grace. His fingers entwined in a mudra as He chanted a special mantra under His breath, turning the gooseberries into a medicine. He instructed the couple about the usage of the medicine. The instructions had to be followed, without fail, for ninety days.

Only six weeks or so had passed when the young man came to visit Swamiji. Happiness writ large on his face, he could barely wait to tell Him that his wife was pregnant -- after four long years of waiting. Tears of joy and gratitude flowed freely as he gave Swamiji the good news.

With word of His miracles reaching far across land and sea, it was perhaps inevitable that people would doubt Swamiji and come to see Him with the intention of testing Him. As soon as such individuals walked in, Swamiji would know their intent and say, 'You have a mole on your abdomen' or 'Your fields are in a place where three roads meet' or 'You are a drunkard' or 'you are a womanizer' or 'you have brought a red flower hidden in your bag to see if I know' or 'so and so is your Kuldevi (or Kuldevta) (family god)'. There have been hundreds of such instances. The very people who visited the ashram as sceptics would be rendered speechless by Gurudev's divine perception.

Once, a husband and wife sought an audience with Gurudev. They very humbly offered their pranams and sat before Swamiji, their palms pressed together in reverence. The wife spoke up, 'Swamiji, my husband comes home drunk every day. The children are scared of their father and it's affecting their studies. He doesn't do any work and there's neither any money nor peace at home.' Hiding her face in her dupatta, she began to cry softly. In the gentlest of tones, like a father speaks to his daughter, Swamiji assured her that He will counsel the husband and make it all go away.

He then addressed the husband with as much love and advised him to keep a forty day vrata (fast) and to stop beating his wife, because that would make Jaganmata angry. The man replied that he did not hit his wife. Gone was the soft countenance as the lines around Swamiji's mouth tightened. 'This is the abode of Jaganmata. You cannot lie here. Did you not hit her and swear at her just yesterday?'

The husband's face turned ashen as he tried to hide his shame at being caught in a lie. He fell at Swamiji's feet and begged for His forgiveness. Both husband and wife were truly in awe of Swamiji, as He had never met them before that day, and yet He had intimate knowledge of their affairs.

On one Tuesday morning, many locals from the nearby villages had come to see Swamiji. Among them was a particularly dejected soul, a woman whose husband had left her six months earlier. He had just dropped out of her life. The food vessels in the house were empty, there was no money to pay the children's school fees, and soon they would have no roof over their heads. Abject misery was etched in every line of her face.

'How am I going to look after my children, Swamiji?' she cried, her heart filled with the pain of desertion and helplessness. 'My husband has abandoned me. He refuses to even take my phone call, much less agree to take me home.'

When her tears subsided, He said to her in a firm but kind tone, 'Your husband will call you before the sun sets today.'

The lady immediately went quiet, and I felt butterflies in my stomach.

'And he'll take you back with honour,' He added. 'Here, take this flower and keep it with you.' Gurudev whispered a mantra on a flower.

Gurudev's word was enough. It would surely come to pass. But for her satisfaction, He gave her a flower, after energizing it with a special mantra. He told her to keep that flower with her always; it would bring her peace. The woman smiled as she took the flower, and did her pranams with the utmost reverence.

She left with a peaceful look on her face, hopeful that the flower she clutched in her palm would change her fortune. Swamiji continued to see other people. The queue was particularly long that day and one by one, they continued to come.

To my utter surprise, about an hour later, after Gurudev had just finished seeing people and was ready to get up and leave, the woman came rushing back toward the ashram. She urged me to let her meet with Swamiji one more time. Normally I would have asked her to wait her turn, but something about her excited manner told me that she had something important to share with Swamiji. She stepped inside, almost tripping on the mat in her excitement. Swamiji was quick to say, 'Steady.'

'Swamiji! I was walking back home when I got a phone call from my husband! He said he's coming to take me back home! How's that possible, Swamiji? I haven't heard from him in six months, not even once.'

'It's all Her grace,' Gurudev said, pointing an elegant finger heavenward.

Her eyes moistened as she continued, 'I don't know how to thank you.' Tears then ran down her cheeks freely. By now, I was used to seeing people walking in tearfully and walking out equally drenched in tears; but the latter were tears of joy and release.

Gurudev just spoke solemnly, 'Nothing is impossible with the grace of Mother Divine.'

People thronged to the ashram on visiting days. Many had serious troubles but there were also those present just to have His darshan, to speak to Him and rejoice in His presence. His smile never wavered, no matter how tired or ill He was or how hectic His schedule had been. The most endearing thing for me was the way He would address the village folk, 'Jai ho prabhu' (all glories to God) or 'Jai ho mataji' (all glories to Mother Divine) as soon as they stepped inside the discourse room. His beaming face would welcome each one with the same love and enthusiasm. He remembered their children's names, wives' names, husbands' names, cows' names -- even a young lamb's name that had been mentioned in His presence.

His care in words and gestures wasn't for show or for the little while that they were there. He remembered each one -- their troubles, their joys. Swamiji was everyone's Swamiji: everybody felt loved and cared for in His presence, just as an idol in a temple belongs to everyone and no one.

Gurudev and I would chant Lalita Sahasranama at least once a day, whenever we found time. Both of us chanted the dhyana shloka (opening verse), and then Swamiji would chant the first line and I would chant the second line. We would alternate and finish the entire Sahasranama. There were times when I would get stuck at some verse, but not once did Gurudev ever falter – He recalled verses effortlessly from His memory. Here I was, with the divine being who had seen Jaganmata: the one who would converse with her, and who was in the highest meditative state offering prayers to the Divine Mother at all times. And it was by Her grace alone that I was serving Gurudev.

Swamiji always began His discourses or bhajans by chanting the two shlokas Sri Vidyam Shiva vama bhaga and Sindhuraruna vigraham. Only then would he begin. When these two verses are chanted, their blessings resonate to the highest realms, then fall like parijat (jasmine) flowers from heaven, infusing the devotees' minds with happiness and peace.

Saving Lives

One time, I was cooking food for Gurudev. Those were the days when we didn't have a gas stove. We used to build a fire outside; Gurudev would set His table close by, and His meals were served to Him straight from the pot and the hotplate. Pradeep Brahmachariji (now Swami Raghavananda) had gone to Orissa, and I was the only one in Gurudev's service. I was making chapattis for him and serving them to Him hot off the griddle, one by one, when I saw two ladies running toward us.

I went to greet them and talk with them before they disturbed Swamiji's meal. They stopped abruptly before me, and breathlessly asked to see Swamiji. Gurudev was seated, eating quietly, His back facing them. Though they were obviously agitated, I told them that this was not the time and that He was having His meal. Gurudev eats very little, so I am always anxious that He eats His meals properly. If something is not right, He doesn't complain — He simply skips his meal. The ladies were insistent, however. One of them, her words tumbling out in strings punctuated by short, feverish breaths, told me the reason for their visit.

Her sixteen-year-old niece had consumed poison because a boy had yelled at her over the telephone, belittling her and swearing at her. Heartbroken, she had promptly gulped down a bottle of pesticide and fainted.

'Froth is coming out of her mouth. They are taking her to the hospital,' she said. 'We must speak to Swamiji right away,' the ladies demanded in unison.

The situation was quite surreal to me. These distraught ladies were almost beside themselves, telling me of a girl who was dying from intentionally drinking poison. And here was my Gurudev -- present, but far away, quietly savouring the nourishing, simple fare I had cooked for him.

When Gurudev eats His meal, He is almost in a meditative state. When He breaks the chapatti with His tender hands, puts some lentils on it and mindfully puts it in His mouth, it seems as if He is performing some divine ritual. Perhaps you need to enjoy the privilege of seeing Him eat to truly know what I mean. He eats as if every mouthful is a sacrament, and He is savouring God's grace as He chews. I didn't know what He would do upon hearing the ladies' news, but I decided that I must, at least, inform him without delay.

'Gurudev,' I said to Him, 'two ladies are here. A girl in the village has consumed poison and she's in a critical condition.'

Gurudev looked at me and kept silent for a few seconds.

'It's not her time yet,' He said matter-of-factly, and went back to eating His chapatti quietly. I signalled them to wait, because I had to prepare the next chapatti for Swamiji. Only momentarily was I surprised to see no reaction from Him when someone was dying, for I knew I was in no position to judge His response. Moreover, I was so engrossed in making sure His chapattis were cooked properly that I just didn't think of anything else.

After a few minutes, He finished eating. I offered Him one more chapatti, but He turned it down. He had only eaten three tiny chapattis. He took a few sips of water, arose, and went to the ladies. He asked me to get some water and put it in a bottle. The ladies started wailing as soon as He approached and began narrating the incident. Gurudev gestured them to stop talking. He whispered something into the water and said in His soft voice to them, 'Take this water and give two sips to the girl immediately. She'll be fine.'

'But, Swamiji,' one of them said, 'they are already rushing her to a hospital in Solan. A taxi was already called when we were about to leave for the ashram. She must already be in the taxi. We won't be able to get this water to her right away.'

Gurudev went quiet while they anxiously looked at His calming countenance. He murmured a mantra and blew in the air.

'Done,' He said, 'I've done what I needed to do. She'll be fine. I'll visit her in the hospital in a few hours. You have twenty-four hours now to get this water to her.'

'How do we contact you to tell you which hospital she's in if you plan on visiting her?' they asked.

Gurudev just smiled and said, 'Waste no time. Give her the water.'

'Are you really going to walk at this time and cross the river to see her, Gurudev?' I asked Him as soon as they left. It was a cold November evening, and the sun had already set. It would soon be dark.

Once again, He just smiled and said, 'Please have your meal, Swamiji.'

The next day, the girl's parents came in the evening and began crying.

'You saved her, Swamiji,' they said. 'Last night, she got up and started screaming that Swamiji is here. Swamiji has come to see me. She was talking to you.'

Gurudev took a flower from the ones they had brought and looked at it intently. 'Be patient.' He said. 'Let the storm pass first.'

'If you hadn't saved her, Swamiji,' the father said, 'she would be dead by now.'

'I haven't done anything. It's the divine grace.'

They left but returned two days later, saying that the girl was behaving weirdly and constantly murmuring to herself. According to the doctor, the poison had affected her brain. She was still in the hospital.

Gurudev took a flower, whispered a mantra on it, and gave it to them. 'Leave it in the water overnight and give it to her in the morning. She'll be fine.'

They came yet again a few days later and told Gurudev that their daughter was perfectly well again. She had been discharged from the hospital and was resting at home. They wanted to know when they could bring her for blessings.

An old lady was a regular visitor to the ashram. Her problem wasn't of the usual variety of health or wealth issues; it was of a more serious nature. Her son was in jail for a crime -- the murder of an old man. But where the world sees a monster or a criminal, a mother only sees her beloved child, and feels his pain. The old lady was devastated that her grown-up son was behind bars, and she was unable to eat or sleep at night. She just wanted him back home. Her daughter-in-law and her grandchildren too were suffering. With no proper means of taking care of themselves in his absence, they were destitute; and they languished without his support.

As many do, she shared her woes with Swamiji. 'I don't know if my son is innocent, but I am a mother and at my age, he is my only support. Please, Swamiji, help us. I need him by my side,' she implored Him. Hot tears ran down the creases of her face. Even while Swamiji gave a discourse to the villagers, she sat huddled in a corner, looking at Swamiji with pleading eyes.

He called her to Him as soon as the discourse was over. 'Your son will come back, Mataji. Everything happens with the will of the Jaganmata. No more than six more months, I assure you.' He said to her with a gentle smile.

The old lady had two sons. One son was in jail and the other worked as a mason in the ashram. One morning, the younger one came to us and said that he had to go to court, but since the harvest from the fields had not been good, they didn't have the money to pay the advocate presenting his brother's case. Immediately, Swamiji called me and asked me to get the sum the young mason needed.

From that day on, the old lady would simply come to have Swamiji darshan every Tuesday and Saturday. Her son was released from jail a few months later, when the case was dismissed on the basis of inconclusive evidence. Where there was no hope of his release, circumstances had changed and made him a free man.

Devotees would love to sit with Gurudev and talk with Him, and He was happy to take the opportunity to answer their queries and elucidate all kinds of spiritual topics when the occasion allowed. On one such occasion, a devotee said that it was frightening sometimes to be in His presence, because nothing was hidden. She said that since her mind had all sorts of thoughts and that nothing was out of Gurudev's view, she felt unsettled at times.

'You always seem to know our thoughts, Swamiji.' she said. 'Do you really read people's minds?'

'No, I don't read minds,' Gurudev said, 'and I don't think it's actually possible to read someone's mind thought-by-thought. If any so-called mind reader was subjected to a controlled test under laboratory conditions, he or she wouldn't pass it. Thoughts are less tangible, more like neurotransmitters firing in the brain. No one can claim to read them per se. There's nothing to read. What does happen, however, is just like when a moment of lightening illuminates the dark sky and you see everything, sometimes the person in front of me comes at a time when the lightening of the consciousness strikes. At that time, they become transparent. I can't explain it any other way. Besides, the same supreme consciousness connects all individuals, like the thread that holds various pearls to make a necklace.'

'Why don't we feel that connection with everyone?' one of the devotees asked. 'Why do we feel like individual pearls and not a part of the necklace? It makes me wonder if we really are connected so deeply.'

Gurudev asked for a notepad. He scribbled something on a piece of paper, folded it, and gave it to the questioner.

'I'm going to transfer a thought in Vidya Swami's head,' He said, momentarily looking at me. 'Him, because he's the most ready right now in this room. He already shares a deep connection with me by virtue of his devotion for me.'

He looked at me for a few seconds and then lowered his eyes before closing them completely. He kept his eyes closed for about thirty seconds (I couldn't say precisely, because I wasn't watching the clock). I felt extraordinary peace. Everything stopped for me.

'Say the word that comes to your mind, Swamiji,' He said as He looked at me.

'Any word?'

He laughed. 'No questions. Just say anything that comes to your mind. I want to see if I could successfully do thought transference.'

'Jala (water),' I said.

'Open your slip,' He said to the lady, 'and please read out what's written.'

She nearly jumped in disbelief and excitement. The word jala was written in Hindi on the slip.

Gurudev continued, 'I might have used the words thought transference, but in essence there was nothing to transfer. I merely allowed a momentary flow of consciousness.'

'Why can't most ordinary people do it?' The lady asked in wonderment.

'Concentration,' Gurudev replied. 'An average mind goes through 60,000 thoughts in a day across 21,600 breaths. That's roughly two thoughts every three seconds. I could hold my thought of water and connect with Vidya Swami and wait with that thought while the flow of consciousness was fully established. An untrained mind is unable to hold onto a thought with detachment. It's got nothing to do with one being ordinary or otherwise. It's simply a matter of training the mind.'

We sat there awestruck while Gurudev plainly stated everything, as if He was giving an informal college lecture. There was no pretence. He then asked me to sing a bhajan, and tears began rolling from his eyes. He had slipped into a bhava samadhi (in being one with the Divine), it seemed. He remained like that for the next thirty minutes. We sat there basking in His glory, feeling warm, devotional and sentimental.

Gurudev had many devotees from the surrounding villages, and He took a deep personal interest in their welfare, as He invariably did with His devotees. Perhaps His attention to their lives was most touching, because we could truly see the changes His ministrations brought to them. Many were underprivileged, and most would scarce have believed they could ever find such a powerful benefactor. One such devotee came to Swamiji with an issue that called for His intervention as both a spiritual and temporal leader.

The devotee's sixteen-year-old son had shoplifted a valuable item from a well-known store, and had been apprehended and handed over to the police. The case was before the court. He was the eldest of her children; the others were much younger, and the family hovered around the breadline at the best of times. The boy had fallen in with bad company. His friends had hatched the plan with him for the theft, but only this boy was caught red-handed. The other culprits had very cleverly escaped, leaving him to face justice for them all.

The boy's mother was distraught beyond measure; her son's whole life would be ruined. She was a widow and between tending to cattle and tilling land, she had neither the time nor the resources to keep visiting the courts and the police station. She pleaded with Swamiji to show her a way out of this situation. Swamiji told her not to lose heart and to bring the boy to him at once. She returned a day later with her son. Both of them did their pranams and sat down in front of Swamiji.

Swamiji spoke to the boy. 'Son, your mother is struggling to feed and clothe you, and instead of supporting her you are adding to her burdens. Right now there's work going on in the ashram. If you agree, I shall tell them to give you a job. In the ashram surroundings, your mind will slowly start to clear. So, tell me, are you willing to work?'

The boy replied, 'Yes, Swamiji,' without looking up. Swamiji promptly called the head mason and told him to engage the boy forthwith. He assured the head mason that the boy would come regularly. A few days later, the mother told Swamiji that there had been a marked change in the boy's behaviour and attitude. He had stopped mingling with the bad crowd and had become more responsible. But their problems were far from over. Twice every month, he had to go to the district court. It was a six-hour return journey from the village to the city, so he had to leave a day before the hearing.

'Swamiji, we are worried about the court case. I have small, school-going children at home. Every fifteen days, I have to travel to the district court with my son, leaving them on their own for three nights. Whatever money I make goes in travelling and paying the advocate's fees. Please help us.' She covered her face with her hands and started sobbing.

'The case will be over within the next three months. Everything will be all right,' He assured her.

Just as Swamiji said, the court case continued for another two months, and by the third month, the case was resolved and the boy was free of all charges. Today, he is working as a salesperson in a store in the city and takes care of his mother, younger brothers and sister.

A woman in the village nearest to the ashram had been mentally unstable for almost a decade. After fourteen years of marriage and three young children, her condition only seemed to worsen. The villagers openly called her a mad woman, and the community blamed her for not taking care of her children. Her husband, a hard-working man, would look after them all, including his wife.

We had been in the ashram for three months when a family from abroad came to see Swamiji. They had been long-time devotees of Swamiji, from His days before renunciation. We were still living in the mud cottage, and made room to welcome them. We were all sitting outside with Swamiji while the cottage was being cleaned. Swamiji was in His usual good mood and was singing bhajans in His deep, sonorous voice. Suddenly, we saw a woman running toward the ashram, screaming for help. Our guests looked alarmed, for the woman was in no ordinary state. Her waist-length hair was flying loose and she ran barefoot on the stones and thorns scattered on the ashram path, oblivious of the pain.

She began running faster upon seeing Gurudev, and as she got nearer she fell to the ground and started rolling in our direction, indifferent to the dust and pebbles under her. By now she was crying loudly. As soon as Swamiji saw the woman fall to the ground, He immediately left His seat to help her. 'What happened? Are you hurt?' He asked her gently, looking at all the dirt that now soiled her clothes. It only worsened her already dishevelled state. She raised her face to Him but didn't stop crying. The next moment, she began beating her hands on the ground and the glass bangles she was wearing broke, leaving bloody gashes on her wrists. Before we could make any sense of it all, she had fainted at Swamiji's feet.

Swamiji asked me to quickly get a glass of water. He sprinkled some water on her face and as soon as she regained consciousness, He helped her drink the water slowly. Her breathing was still ragged, and sobs shook her body.

She had a disconnected, lost look about her: her eyes appeared glassy, her hair was unkempt and her lips were dried and chapped. Gurudev calmed her down by speaking to her in a most gentle manner, encouraging her to breathe deeply. It took Him over thirty minutes to pacify her and help her to sit up. For the following one hour He sat next to her, asking her about herself, her family, etcetera. She answered His questions slowly, lapsing into silence between them.

She nodded each time Swamiji told her that she would be fine. In all probability, no one in her life had ever spoken to her with such love and care. An hour-and-a-half later, her husband came looking for her. He did his pranams to Swamiji and told us of their travails.

'Swamiji, everyday she fights with me. She doesn't cook any meals for the children or me. I work in the field the whole day and return home tired to find that the children have gone to sleep with empty stomachs, and there's no food in the house.' His voice was choked with emotion as he narrated her history of mental illness. Swamiji asked him to come on any Tuesday or Saturday. He assured him that with Jaganmata's grace, his wife would be healed. The woman rested for some time on a mat which we had laid out for her, and after a while, she seemed a little stronger and more collected. Once again, Swamiji began to sing in His sweet, melodious voice, making us all forget the ordeal we had just witnessed.

After a few days, the couple sat for a private audience in front of Gurudev. The husband related how his wife had seemed quite normal for the first couple of years after their marriage, but later began to show clear symptoms of mental illness. Gurudev chanted softly a mantra on a flower and asked them to immerse a petal in water and drink that water. This treatment continued for nearly a year, but the woman began showing signs of improvement from the very first month. She stopped shouting and shirking work at home, and began relating well to her children and husband.

Her mood swings and episodes where she would lose her grasp on reality became few and far between, till her behaviour became completely normal. She had been suffering from this condition for some twelve years, but with Gurudev's patience and care, she could now lead a happy, productive life.

Her illness wasn't merely a case of moodiness: she suffered a real affliction of the mind. Sometimes if Swamiji was busy speaking to other devotees when the couple came to the ashram, the woman would create a serious commotion. Like a one-woman riot, she would bang her head against the wall and break her bangles, screaming, demanding to meet with Swamiji. At such times, Swamiji would treat her with even more kindness and care. She created such scenes countless times, but Swamiji, the form of grace and patience that He was, would not be the least perturbed. He even began to teach English to her children, and gave her husband a job at the ashram.

The whole family of the woman and the child whom Gurudev had saved after they were attacked by a swarm of deadly wasps became great devotees. One day, they approached Gurudev and expressed their deep sadness that they only had one son. They longed for another child, be it a girl or a boy — a sibling for their son, who was already about eight years old. All the pandits and tantrics had told them that they could not have another child.

Gurudev said that it was best to leave it to Nature. But when they continued to plead for His help, He said, 'Okay, you'll have another child; but make no attempt to conceive at the moment. I'll tell you when the right time comes.'

A month later, Gurudev was travelling overseas and when He returned to the ashram, the family visited Him in great eagerness.

'My wife is expecting,' the man said both happily and shyly. His wife sat next to him with her head lowered.

Gurudev's face turned grave. He said, 'I'd told you to not conceive until I said so.'

They went quiet.

'It's not looking good,' Gurudev added.

They begged His pardon, but He didn't give them a flower or any special blessings. A few months passed, and complications developed with the pregnancy. The doctors advised that a caesarean be performed. The couple came running to Swamiji and talked about what the doctor had said.

'You have a bigger problem to worry about,' Gurudev said softly.

'Why, Swamiji,' they asked, 'what problem?'

'I would rather not say anything negative,' He replied.

They went to astrologers and tantrics who told them that both the mother and the child would die, and that they just didn't have another child in their fate.

Once again, they came to Gurudev and cried their hearts out.

'Don't worry,' Gurudev said in his usual compassionate voice. 'No harm will come to the mother; but the child ...' He stopped there.

'What will happen to the child?' they asked anxiously.

Gurudev shook his head slightly. 'Leave it to Mother Divine.'

As the time of her delivery drew closer, Gurudev was travelling again. While he was away, the lady gave birth to a baby boy -- stillborn. Despite their loss, their faith in Swamiji grew immensely. They came to see Him again and told Him the sad news.

'Don't worry,' Gurudev said. 'It was the will of Mother. You'll have another child, a healthy child.'

Their eyes lit up, and He gave them a flower in blessing. A few months later, the woman was pregnant again. They came to Gurudev for another private audience.

'Yes,' He said, 'all will work out this time.'

In the fifth month of the pregnancy, the woman fell down three times in four days, falling flat on her belly twice, and experienced great pain in her abdomen. Gurudev told the couple not to worry, but they couldn't resist consulting other astrologers. This only added to their woes, for every one of them said that this time, surely both the mother and the child would die.

The couple's elders were deeply troubled. The whole family came to see Swamiji. The woman's mother-in-law begged Swamiji to save her daughter-in-law's life.

'Nothing will happen to either,' Swamiji said. 'Both the child and mother will be just fine.'

Gurudev asked them to come at the same time the next day. The next day, after they had offered their pranams to Swamiji, He took some water from his kamandal (water pot), a beautiful black one made of wood, and sprinkled the water on the pregnant lady's abdomen while He chanted a mantra.

'It's done,' He said to them. 'No harm will touch them.' Both the women, young and old, began crying softly in relief and joy.

This time too, the doctor advised a caesarean delivery, but Gurudev told them that the baby would be born of a normal delivery at home. About three months later, the young woman gave birth to a healthy child, a baby boy, in the comfort of her home. Once again, Gurudev was away at the time of the delivery, but they waited for him to return to the ashram to name the child.

On the evening of 31 December 2011, a group of three devotees were due to arrive at the ashram. These devotees knew Swamiji long before His renunciation. Since it was winter, the sun descended behind the hills by 3.40 p.m. The devotees had not yet reached the ashram, and by 5.30 p.m., dusk had all but extinguished light in the sky. Swamiji looked a little introspective. It wasn't wise to cross the river after dark. Swamiji would normally have His dinner at this time, but He asked me to delay our meal till the devotees arrived. He said, 'They have travelled a long distance to come and see me, and it would make them happy for us to have the prasadam together, Swamiji. Let's wait for them.'

While we waited, Swamiji wrote on two pieces of paper and placed them inside two separate books. He then handed me the books and asked me to put them away.

Swamiji and had spread thick quilts and rugs in the room and kept it ready for the visitors. The group arrived by 7 p.m. Swamiji asked them in a kind voice why they were late. It was dark and He was worried. They apologized, offered their pranams and expressed their happiness at spending New Year's Eve with Swamiji. They were especially touched by Swamiji's concern for them when they saw their bedding had already been prepared.

Gurudev then gently asked me like a mother asks a child, 'What shall we make for dinner?'

'Swamiji, tell me what you'd like and I'll start the preparations right away.'

'Khichdi! Let's all have hot khichdi in this cold weather.' Within forty-five minutes, the khichdi was ready. All of us sat together in Gurudev's room and ate prasadam in His divine presence.

'It's truly delicious, the khichdi, Swamiji.' Gurudev complimented me on the simple meal throughout dinner, as if it wasn't khichdi but food from a five-star restaurant. One of His greatest qualities is His sincere appreciation of the smallest of gestures and things, which encourages us to better ourselves and strive for excellence in our lives.

After dinner, it was satsang time with Swamiji. A sublime evening, the last of that year, was spent singing the Divine Mother's glories. After sometime, Swamiji asked me to bring one of the books He had given me earlier and hand it to the devotees.

'There's a small slip in it. Could you please read it?' Eagerly, they pulled out the slip. I was equally curious, as I had no clue what was written on the slip. When they read it, they were speechless. They looked at each other, utterly astonished, disbelief giving way to smiles on their faces. They all spoke together, 'How did you know, Swamiji?'

Gurudev just smiled and looked at me. I still didn't know what was written on the slip. I said to them, 'Swamiji wrote this about thirty minutes before you people arrived. Now please tell me what's on the slip.'

They explained that they had brought three extra blankets for us to use in the ashram. They had left the package containing the blankets, still neatly wrapped, on the veranda outside. And on the slip their names were written, along with the message that they would bring three blankets to the ashram.

'What about the second slip, Swamiji?' I murmured to Gurudev.

'I was going to show it in the morning, but why not, bring it too.' He said playfully.

He told me to hand the book to the devotees and asked them to open it and read the slip, just as before.

'Oh my God, Swamiji!' they exclaimed. 'This is baffling. We were going to offer it to you tomorrow morning during the morning pranams.'

'What!' I exclaimed.

They told me that on the slip it was written that they would bring charan padukas (wooden sandals).

I wasn't surprised. I had seen enough in the preceding three months to know that He could tell about a person just by hearing his name. Knowing these small details was mere child's play for Gurudev.

A New Vidya

My sadhana was to begin in January 2012. At the same time, in the new hut overlooking the river, Swamiji had decided to commence His special sadhana. Another hut was constructed for my sadhana, above the existing main ashram building. Gurudev decided that we would both start our respective sadhanas on 8 January 2012. The workers finished the construction work on 7 January. Torrential rains fell throughout that night, and the cottage which was built for my sadhana collapsed. When Swamiji heard the news, He didn't show any emotion.

Instead, He said, 'Everything is as per the Jaganmata's wish. That room was not constructed properly, and that's why it collapsed. It's good that this happened before you went in there. Had it collapsed a few days or months later, it would have endangered your life. Mother Divine has taken care of you like her child.' Swamiji's words consoled me and warmed my heart.

We carried on with our sadhana regardless. During this period, Swamiji would take even less food than He normally did. My limited culinary skills didn't help, either. I hailed from south India, and had little knowledge of how to prepare north Indian food. It was sometimes difficult for me to prepare meals to Gurudev's taste. He never uttered a word, let alone created a fuss, about the tasteless meals I would place before Him. Sometimes when the meals were just too unpalatable for Him, He would simply go hungry.

I was unable to sleep on those nights that Gurudev went to bed with an empty stomach. I would sit for my sadhana, my mind disturbed; plagued by the thought that despite the good fortune of being in such a divine master's presence, I was unable to serve Him properly. It weighed on me heavily. Swamiji was not in the habit of drinking tea, coffee or cold drinks or eating any snacks in between His meals. He just liked to eat completely satvic food — without any onion, garlic, chilli or any other strong spices. The only spices I could use were cumin, black pepper and ginger.

Before His renunciation, Gurudev was accustomed to having meals prepared by five-star hotel chefs. He had lived abroad for much of His young life, savouring some of the best cuisines of the world; and here I was serving Him half-cooked, tasteless food. Sometimes when Gurudev wouldn't eat, I would cry and ask Jaganmata to give me strength, give me one more chance to serve my Gurudev, just as He would like. I prayed with all my heart. My prayer wasn't answered overnight, but slowly I gained the confidence to prepare better, healthier and tastier meals.

After about eight months, during another sadhana, He took only light food. This was my Agni pareeksha (trial by fire), for He was especially discerning of the purity of His food during His sadhanas. It is, I would conclude during Gurudev's sadhana, never easy being in the company of great souls such as Swamiji and serving them. They know our every move, our every spoken word and gesture. The purity of our thoughts and the sentiment behind our service is as clear to them as the holy water of the Ganga. But being of generous heart, they continue to indulge us, forgiving and overlooking our mistakes.

Swamiji's generous nature was to love everyone. With the villagers, He always spoke in a straightforward manner, using accessible language to help and comfort them. To the modern world, He would reach out through the Internet, writing detailed posts on spirituality – life, dharma (correct way of living in harmony with the universe), karma, moksha (release from the cycle of rebirth) and sadhana. He would touch the lives of countless devotees through emails, answering their questions thoughtfully and easing their grief and troubles. For each of them, Swamiji was as close as the most intimate confidante – guiding them, protecting them.

'Every person should design his own life – in line with his character, his samskara and interests.' Swamiji often says. Ever smiling, Gurudev addresses everyone respectfully, at all times. I have not heard Him address even a small child in the singular, or with informal lexicon. This gentleness of temperament is His power. He often advises me that Vaagdevi (Goddess Saraswati) resides on our tongues, and so we must always think first and talk later.

Though He would unceasingly talk of God, Swamiji seemed to be under no illusions regarding the limited spiritual interests of most people. One day He asked me to get the notes of His Himalayan sadhana. This was the intense, rigorous sadhana that had led Him straight to Mother Divine, or should I say, had drawn Mother Divine to Gurudev. After He went through His notes, He declared that the world was not yet ready for what He had written.

'Since I've come back from the Himalayas, Swamiji, I have not met one person – not even a single person – who has the same desperation to see God as I had. People are happy with reading the blog, listening to my discourses and getting answers to their life's problems. No one in this busy world has time for God.'

Saying this, He tore the notes into pieces. He had shown me these notes. Every detail of His meditative practises, of every hour spent in calling the Divine, had been documented in them meticulously. This was no mean feat: His meditations lasted between twelve hours and twenty-two hours daily over a period of thirteen months.

Gurudev had most scrupulously chronicled His every hour spent in meditation, expanding on certain parameters such as mindfulness, stillness of the body and awareness. His intent, as much as anything else, is to teach – at least, in the broadest sense of the word. It seemed He felt that the most profound of His lessons were not so much beyond the capacity of people: they were beyond their interest.

I was an eager student for His tutelage, however, for the spiritual path was my life's work. A good many years I had spent waiting for such an opportunity, and I would not let it go to waste. I followed His guidance assiduously. Mother Divine had answered my prayers for a guru, and I was thus happily obligated to make the most of Her blessings.

On the auspicious day of 12 August 2012, Gurudev taught me the first vidya, among the many that He knows. He showed me the particular way to sit for this meditation and the exact method to practise it. I practised it for ten days, and on 22 August I showed it to him. He sat in siddhasana, His eyes closed and hands posed in a special mudra. I sat quietly by His feet.

After a little while, He instructed me to shut all the windows and doors, and asked me to hold his hand and press it for two minutes. He then began the kriya (practice).

I came and stood by His side and pressed His fair and delicate hands. Ten seconds must have passed, when I felt a jolt of indescribable energy passing from His hand to mine. My hand began to tremble uncontrollably, and despite my attempts to keep it steady, it continued to shake. It felt as if I had lost all control of my own hand.

But it wasn't just my hand that was shaking. Gurudev's body was quivering with the energy that seemed to expand in front of me, filling the space around us and within me. My consciousness seemed to be suddenly yoked to His. How was this possible? It felt like He was everywhere at once and not merely seated in His asana. Could this be the shakti avahan (invocation of the Divine Mother) that I had read about in the scriptures?

Soon, my mind was completely without thought. I was one with the energy current that flowed from Gurudev to me. My mind had lost sense of my body, and overflowing with pure bliss and joy, I wanted to cry out. I was no longer whom I perceived myself to be: my body, my mind all ceased to exist in the divine ecstasy. I was no more than a dot travelling in space. Where was this place where there was no beginning, no end? Gradually the sensation became less intense, and then this flow of energy ceased completely.

It felt like more than four hours had elapsed, though in reality it was only around five minutes. I was still far away, and it was a little while before I would regain consciousness. I opened my eyes to find Gurudev's eyes fixed in space. I was too moved to speak. I, a mere devotee, had just experienced my master's power, a glimpse of divinity that is ineffable -- the glorious quintessence of all scripture.

I immediately raised my hands, pressing my palms together in namaskara, my heart so filled with His grace and overcome with gratitude that I had no words to thank Him. I bowed down to him again and again. There are hundreds of disciples who cling to and serve their masters all their lives, but never experience what I just did -- the other dimension, the existence of a reality that I had only thus far read of in scriptures. For a long time afterward, I was in no state to speak or even try and encapsulate what had transpired in that tiny discourse room.

The Karmic Debt

'Fear is more powerful than kama (desire) for humans. See how during daylight a man is fearless. But once night descends, he loses some of his bravery and is afraid of what the darkness holds.' Swamiji was looking at the dark sky, the twinkling stars bright like the many eyes of the Lord.

His delight at beholding the beauty of the sky was apparent in the tilt of His head, and the captivating smile that was even more radiant than the stars themselves. Away from the hustle and bustle of the city, with its beguiling, earthly promises of light, one could see the clusters of stars like distant bunches of grapes filling the quiet sky.

Ever keen on learning, I would request Him to share His sadhana experience. Swamiji had been meditating since He was a child. It seemed there was nothing He didn't know or couldn't answer. Whether it lay in the purview of the scriptures or outside it, He always managed to satisfy my curiosity. Our discussions ranged from intense meditation to Ma's darshan, the secret of ekaant or solitude, mantra rahasya, secret mantras that are passed in strict oral tradition from the guru to the disciple, asan rahasya, how to tame the wayward mind -- and the most intriguing of all: antra sadhana (Tantra practise). Sometimes while clearing my doubts, Swamiji would hold my hand and explain a matter to me as one might explain it to a child.

On that particular evening, as we savoured the celestial delights above the ashram, He began to talk about the first goddess of the Dasha Mahavidya, the Goddess Kali, the fiercest and most fearsome aspect of the Goddess Durga. Swamiji began to describe the Goddess as if she stood right in front of Him. His eyes, unblinking and focused in the dark, glowed like embers. His voice became as deep as the night itself, powerful and mystical. In a matter of seconds, goose bumps were creeping up my arms as he spoke:

'A ferocious sword in one hand, a head dripping blood in another, Her tresses, dark as an abyss, flow past her knees. A garland of skulls adorns her neck, eyes like bright bundles of light glow in Her dark face. Her tongue pink and pointed as a lotus petal is poking out of Her mouth, dripping blood. Another pair of hands are gracefully still in the abhaya and vara mudras. The Goddess stands nude; her pointed and full breasts like twin mountains stand proud. Her nudity evokes not a trace of kama or lust. The fragrance of a rose, heady and all powerful fills the nostrils. Her teeth, white as snow, shine bright in her moonlike face. She's the fierce, fearsome force that roots out evil.'

The night had fallen silent, as if it was listening to Swamiji's description of the Goddess. I was so immersed in the magical form He had evoked, that it took me some time before I could speak again. Swamiji had brought the divine form to life. By His words, His vision of the Goddess Kali had become my vision, as well.

'I feel like I've seen the Goddess too,' I said most excitedly.

'Mere words cannot capture that divine form. You must do sadhana and see her real form.' Swamiji's words fell mellifluously on my ears.

I quickly bent down to touch His feet. 'Swamiji, may I have your blessings for my sadhana?' He touched my head lightly, and smiling, turned around with His usual alacrity, His robe giving a short swish as if it was trying to keep up with Him, and headed back to the cottage.

Many such evenings followed when Swamiji unveiled the secret of Tantra sadhana to me. I had heard of such feats but didn't believe that such vidyas actually existed in our day and age, leave alone that it was possible for me to attain them. The more time I spent with Him, the more I began to realize that there isn't a Tantravidya or Tantrasadhana that Swamiji doesn't know.

Day by day, my desire to learn sadhana from Him grew, to experience for myself the divinity my master carried within Him. Ten wonderful months had passed since I had come to the ashram. I longed for Him to bestow His grace upon me.

The third day of April 2012 was a blessed day, the ninth day of Vasant Navaratri, Sri Rama Navami — and the most important day of my life. I received diksha (initiation) from Gurudev on this auspicious day. As was the morning routine, I prepared breakfast for Swamiji and went to serve it to him. I received the kashaya-vastra (saffron robe) from His divine hands and two important steps of Sri Vidya. He asked me to hold a small bowl of water in my hands, and instructed me to repeat after Him:

'I hereby give you all my karma: the karma of this life and all my purva janma karma (karma of previous births). Everything is offered to you.' Then He received the water bowl from my hands. My Gurudev had just taken all my karma and sins, just as Lord Shiva willingly consumed the poison from the churning ocean, so that it would not affect the world. I do not have words to describe my feelings towards Gurudev at that time. He had accepted me as I was, and accepted all my karmain in a moment.

A verse from the Shiva Mahimna Stotram came to my mind.

asita-giri-samam syāt kajjalam sindhu-pātre
sura-taruvara-shākhā lekhanī patra-murvī,
likhati yadi grhītvā shāradā sarva-kālam
tadapi tava gunānām īsha pāram na yāti.

This verse relates how the Goddess Saraswati made the whole earth a sheet of paper -- a tree her pen, the oceans her ink -- and began to write of the greatness of Lord Mahadev. And she could not do it. How can I, a mortal with all the attending limitations and frailties, try to describe my Gurudev's virtues?

After the ritual, I placed over His head a garland of marigolds in full bloom. I smoothed sandalwood paste on His feet and sprinkled flowers over them. I eulogized Him and offered my life to His lotus feet and did sashtanga pranam (reverential bowing). I prayed that He let me serve Him all through my life. I was the first to receive diksha from Swamiji. By the unbounded mercy and grace of Jaganmata, I was fortunate to be initiated by Swamiji. Thousands of pranams I offer to the feet of Gurudev. I am indeed blessed.

Soon it was Saturday again, and the hour in which the villagers seek Swamiji's audience. He was there at eleven and had met the five or six families who had come to seek His blessings. The time was 11.35 a.m., and it seemed that everyone had taken Gurudev's darshan. I went inside to Him.

'Swamiji, no more visitors are here. I shall go and prepare your prasadam. It is nearly noon.'

Swamiji looked at me, smiled and said, 'Swamiji, three more people are yet to come.'

I was quick to reply, 'No, Swamiji, no one is around. I cannot see anyone coming down the ashram road.' The ashram is nestled in a valley on a plain flanking the river Giri, and from its vantage point, one can clearly see the distant figures of anyone either proceeding from the riverside or descending from the villages in the hills above. I had looked carefully in all directions before going inside to tell Swamiji that the last of the villagers had been granted an audience. I was certain that I wasn't mistaken.

'I assure you three more people are coming – within the next five minutes they'll be here,' He said, reaching for a pretty white flower a devotee had placed at His feet. I sat outside and waited. It was Gurudev's command, so I didn't question it openly; but in my mind a niggling doubt persisted nonetheless.

Not even five minutes had passed when I saw three people walking toward me, just a short distance away. It was as if they had materialized out of thin air. I sent them in one by one, eagerly waiting for them to finish. As soon as the last one emerged from his audience with Swamiji, I barged in.

'Gurudev, I looked outside, and there was absolutely no one in sight. How did you know, sitting inside the room that three more people were on their way?'

Gurudev just smiled and said, 'Will you feed me now?' I couldn't help but chuckle. He was always making everyone laugh; there wasn't a dull moment around Him. An embodiment of love and happiness, His face wore an almost perennial smile. But my curiosity was not satisfied.

'Who are you?' It was more a plea than a question that rose to my lips, out of sheer awe and bewilderment. He knew about things that my eyes couldn't see and my mind didn't or couldn't understand; and yet, in some sense I knew so little about Him. I never doubted His word again, though.

———

One afternoon, three villagers came to visit. They said they had been suffering from piles for many months. They asked if they would be cured. They just wanted some relief from their pain. Swamiji listened to them patiently and then called for me. In front of them, Swamiji asked me, 'Swamiji, these three men have this problem. Please tell them if they will be cured or not.' I stood there, not knowing what to do, wondering why suddenly Swamiji was asking me for an answer.

I began to sweat. Swamiji understood my state of mind.

'Please don't worry. Tell the answer from your heart.'

I was still not sure what to say. I asked His permission and went back to my room. There I bowed down to Jaganmata and asked for guidance. I went back and told Swamiji that their conditions will be cured.

He then turned to the villagers, 'This Swamiji has told that you will be cured. I will now give you a flower, energized with a mantra.'

Later, He called me and said, 'Swamiji, do not get anxious or worried. I'm trying to train you to read the future. Do not tell anyone blindly that they will be cured completely. If you say so, then Jaganmata will have to keep your word. Just listen to your inner voice before you answer, and the rest will take care of itself.'

'I only want to do and be in your seva, Gurudev; and I don't want this responsibility of answering people. I'm not capable of handling this.'

Swamiji gently told me that one must do loka kalyana (work for world welfare), and strive for the betterment of society.

Otherwise, what was the use of doing sadhana? He said to me, 'If someone comes to us with their problems and difficulties, it becomes our responsibility to give them some solution or remedy. I am with you. What's there to worry about?'

I humbly bowed and accepted this new responsibility, as it was given by Gurudev.

It was my first special Guru Purnima with Gurudev. As usual, He had His breakfast in the morning. Before breakfast, I had offered my pranams and prayers to him, and lovingly, He had kept His palm on my head and blessed me. A few devotees were staying on in the ashram for a couple of days. There was a simple celebration at the ashram that evening. I served dinner to Swamiji by 5 p.m. and thereafter left for my room, as my sadhana was in progress at that time. Around 7 p.m., Swamiji's throat began to itch, probably due to some kind of allergy. During satsang, the devotees noticed His discomfort and made a herbal tea of tulsi, ginger, black pepper and jaggery. It proved to be too hot and peppery, and Swamiji began to hiccup.

Swamiji had mentioned to me long before this that once His hiccups start, it could take as long as three days for them to subside, however hard He might try to stop them. It had been like this since His childhood. Swamiji continued satsang till 9 p.m. and then went to his room. His sadhana time was early in the morning. During His morning sadhana, He didn't have any hiccups. But just as He finished, they started again with a vengeance. It was very disturbing for Him, as the frequency of the hiccups didn't allow Swamiji to speak, eat or drink properly. For breakfast, I had made tomato soup, since He didn't take any grains, beans, pulses or solid meals during the sadhana period. I urged Him to have some soup.

'I've been hiccupping since last night. I wasn't able to sleep at all. Only during the sadhana time did they subside. I'm not sure I can have the soup, but I'll try.'

He began to drink the soup I had prepared while He spoke with me. Halfway through, His hiccups worsened.

He jokingly said to me, 'What Swamiji, you are doing so much of sadhana and penance, can't you cure these hiccups?'

He was laughing in between the hiccups when He said this to me. I joined Him in laughter because Gurudev was in His playful mood, but I was concerned by His obvious discomfort.

'Please Swamiji,' I requested, 'Please ask Mother Divine to stop these hiccups.'

Gurudev laughed again. 'Call upon Mother Divine for hiccups?'

'Yes, Gurudev,' I reiterated. 'If I'm your son then please ask Mother Divine to stop the hiccups. I can't see you like this.'

On hearing my words, the innocent, pure hearted Gurudev said, 'Jaganmata, please stop this.' Swamiji uttered those words, and that very moment the hiccups stopped. I was stunned.

The Goddess, whom I thought to be sitting far above, was indeed listening to Swamiji's every word. But the very next moment, tears began rolling down Swamiji's cheeks. 'O Mother, for such a trivial issue I bothered you. Forgive me.' He cried. He pushed the soup bowl away and said to me, 'We should not have done this.'

Swamiji asked me to leave immediately, His face quiet and drawn. I felt terrible seeing Gurudev so distraught -- and even more so for my part in His grief. I came to the kitchen and shared the incident with the devotees there. I blamed myself for the foolish thing I had done. I didn't know that the Jaganmata would respond so quickly to Swamiji's request.

I realized that even though I had been with Him for months now, I still had only a vague comprehension of the level at which Gurudev operated. Every incident only reminded me that without His grace, there was no way of even knowing Him.

The Sacred Kamandal

Gurudev's kamandal is kept in the discourse room, on a side table by His cot. There is an aura of intrigue about it. No one dare touch the kamandal or its contents, though it is kept in plain sight. Swamiji had instructed me that the water in the kamandal was to be used in extremely rare circumstances, for the essence of His tapas was in the sacred water in the kamandal.

One man staying near the ashram with his family was addicted to bhang (marijuana leaves). The addiction had become unmanageable, making him severely ill, causing headaches and a general malaise that rendered him useless for any kind of work.

He sought medical help and underwent numerous tests in the hospital, but the results were all normal. According to the reports, there was nothing wrong with him. The man, however, was anything but healthy. He had lost his appetite and felt dizzy if he went out in the sun for just a short time. He was far too weak to even make his way to the ashram. His was a poor family with four little children -- and he was the breadwinner.

It was a new moon night, around 11.30 p.m., when a villager called me and apprised me of the situation. Gurudev was not in the ashram at the time; he was away on His ekanta sadhana, solitude.

The man was completely bedridden and moaning in pain. He had not eaten anything solid for the preceding fifteen days, and was passing in and out of consciousness. I asked the family to come to the ashram. Before leaving, Swamiji had taught me a few vidyas, and instructed me what to do if any dire emergency arose. He had strictly warned me that the water in the kamandal was only to be used in the rarest of rare situations. I believed this to be one such situation. Two members of the man's family came and pleaded with me to help him. They told me that his condition was very serious; he may well be on his death bed, they said. I went inside the visitors' room and did my pranam to Swamiji's photo and his paduka. In a bottle half filled with water, I mixed a little water from the kamandal. After seeking Gurudev's blessings, I gave that water to the late-night visitors and issued them with appropriate instructions.

The family followed my instructions with great faith for the next nine days. On the tenth day, the once bedridden man walked to the ashram to tell me that he was now much better. His symptoms were more manageable. He promised that he would not use any intoxicating substance in the future, and begged me to heal him completely. I prayed to Gurudev and gave him the flower that I had offered to Gurudev's paduka that morning. Day by day, his health improved and within a month, he was back to normal. He is now a devotee of the ashram, actively helping out here.

Another family stayed near the ashram. They had been Swamiji's devotees from the very beginning. The couple had a ten-year-old boy, and then they had another child. The new-born baby boy was born hale and hearty, but the mother had no milk to feed the child. Even after seven days, the mother was unable to breastfeed the child. There was simply no milk.

The new parents came crying to Swamiji, who with His usual kindness and love, prayed to Jaganmata and gave them a flower. The man returned the next day to tell us that milk had started flowing from the mother's breasts the previous night, and that the child was now nourished. He offered his pranam to Swamiji and thanked him profusely.

Three months later, the man returned. This time the problem had reversed: the mother had plenty of milk for her infant son, but he was unable to drink it. It was the peak of summer, and the little one's eyes and mouth had been watering day and night for the preceding three or four days. I quickly finished my dinner and went to the discourse room. Swamiji was travelling abroad at that time. After I offered my pranams to His photograph and paduka, I filled a small bottle with water, mixed some from the kamandal and gave it to the father.

'Wherever Swamiji is now, He's protecting us. Pray to Swamiji and give the water to the baby.' The very next morning, the father was back to tell me that his baby's condition had improved dramatically, even miraculously. The infant had been completely cured, and was once again feeding like a healthy child. The father's happiness knew no bounds. He was ecstatic, and so was his wife. They had been worried sick, afraid that they would lose their child. The happiness on his face was a delight to behold. I truly felt grateful to Gurudev for making me an instrument of His grace.

I am specially mentioning this incident because for the most part, the villagers around the ashram do not seek mukti or moksha (liberation from the cycle of rebirth). It is solutions to everyday issues and struggles that they need. Their cattle, children, food – these are their concerns, and if their welfare is assured, that is all they need to be happy. Their lives are untrammelled by dreams of acquiring great wealth, luxury cars, mansions or businesses. Numerous incidents such as this – indeed, there have been too many to recall – have happened before my eyes. They happen every day, each as moving to witness as the one before.

Sri Hari

Gurudev spoke of building a temple. We already knew about Swamiji's Himalayan penance, His darshan of Jaganmata and Chakradhari Lord Vishnu. It was decided that the temple would be built in commemoration of that event. It was Swamiji's desire that we have a sculpture of Lord Vishnu with Goddess Lakshmi's bhava (being) in the same idol.

Like the expression in Sri Lalita Sahasranama, kantardha vigraha (She has half the body of Her husband Shiva), Swamiji did not see any difference between Shiva-Shakti and Vishnu-Lakshmi. He said that we all will perceive them in the idol as per our bhakti and shradha, devotion and faith. So it was decided to have a vigraha (idol) of Lord Vishnu idol with devi bhavam at the ashram temple.

One morning during breakfast, I mentioned to Swamiji that I had once been to Kanchipuram near Chennai and visited the Varadharaja Perumal Temple. The temple deity there is a beautiful big chaturbhuj (four-armed) idol, made of black stone. Gurudev looked at me happily and told me that He had such an image in His mind – an idol of black stone, and not white marble. He searched the Internet for images of Varadharaja Swami.

The usually poor Internet connection was unusually fast that day, and it was no less of a miracle than many of the others I had seen at the ashram, for the images to display almost immediately. Upon seeing the idol, Swamiji expressed His wish that we should have a similar idol. I suggested that we enquire from someone in south India, since black stone idols are made there; north India has nearly all white marble idols.

Swamiji had many devotees in Chennai and Bangalore.

'Please ask someone, Swamiji,' I said. 'They'll jump at the opportunity to serve you.'

Gurudev just smiled and said, 'Swami does not ask or appeal. We want this idol and this idol will come. Just wait. T.R. Ramachandran from Chennai will email us. The thought is already there in the universe.'

In the evening when I went to Him with His dinner, Ramachandran from Chennai had already emailed him out of the blue, seeking his blessings.

'Wow, Swamiji,' I exclaimed. 'Please ask him now!'

'Not yet, Swamiji,' He replied. 'Transference of thought from universal consciousness is happening as we speak. He'll email us again. Let everything align.'

The next day, Ramachandran wrote again, saying he really wanted to do some service.

Swamiji decided that now was the suitable time to ask for the information. He wrote back, explaining our purpose and what information we needed. We needed an idol similar to the one in Kanchipuram – a smiling-faced, four-armed deity in black stone, adorned with a lotus, shanka, chakra and gada (conch, discus and mace).

Swamiji sent this email in the morning. In the evening, Ramachandran wrote back telling Swamiji that unexpectedly, after many months without contact, one of his friends travelled 200 kilometres to see him that very day. While talking with his friend, Ramachandran casually mentioned the idol. His friend, by sheer chance, knew the chief sculptor of Sripuram temple at Vellore. This sculptor had carved the idol at the Vellore golden temple, and he agreed to sculpt the idol for us. Everything seemed to be falling into place.

Swamiji was adamant that while performing the arti to Sri Hari, our minds be pure and free of any selfish thoughts. There was to be no asking for remission of our sins, or seeking monetary or any other material benefit. We were to simply behold the divine form, feel the bliss and sing the Lord's glory. Arti was to be done twice a day -- morning and evening.

One morning when I took Swamiji's tomato soup to Him for breakfast, He mentioned the arti of Sri Hari.

'What should we do, Swamiji?' I said. 'Should we take one of the standard artis?'

Gurudev asked for His notepad and started scribbling. In a mere five minutes, He had composed a beautiful temple arti. There was to be no going back and changing it. He wrote it, and it was final.

I offered my pranams to His lotus feet. My heart was so filled with His love and grace.

Jaya jaya arti hari tumhari
Vishnu prabhu srinath murari||

All glories and a million obesiance to Bhagwan
The one who is Vishnu, almighty, consort of Sri, all encompassing

Sri Hari's idol is Prakruti-Purusha, Shiva-Shakti, Vishnu-Lakshmi; and in accordance with their devotional bhava or sentiment, the devotees would experience the Lord's and the Goddesses' magnificence. The arti encapsulates the glory, the greatness of the two divine principles of creation.

When the idol was in the final stage of its sculpting down south, there still was no approach road to the ashram. Swamiji didn't want the Lord to be carried all the way by river: He wanted Sri Hari to arrive most comfortably, right to the ashram doorstep. There would be no other option then, than for a road to be constructed through the mountains above the ashram; an arduous task and momentous undertaking at best.

Soon after Swamiji expressed this desire, though, the universe rushed to fulfil His wish. Some village elders and devotees came to Swamiji and said that they needed His ashirwad (blessing), and they would work day and night to build a road to the ashram.

The villagers decided that the road was going to be a token of their devotion and love for Swamiji. They came together under an oath that they would put aside their personal work and turn all their energies toward this goal, until it was realized. They worked tirelessly – uncaring of the cold weather – throughout the days and into the early evenings, until darkness forced them to stop. Despite the challenging terrain and weather, the fruits of their dedication would be enjoyed remarkably quickly. They finished laying the road in time.

In February, Sri Hari's idol travelled along the road and reached the ashram. The Lord had come to establish peace and faith on earth; to guide many sadhakas (seekers); to show the path of mukti. In a mere fifteen days, an eight-kilometre road that connected the ashram to another road had been laid in the mountains.

Throughout the last stretch of five kilometres, villagers stood beside the road, crying out loudly, *'Sri Hari ki jai'*, as the truck carrying the idol descended from the mountains to the ashram. The whole village had assembled near the ashram compound to welcome the Lord's idol. It rained then, as if the Gods from above were showering their blessings, welcoming the Lord to His new abode. Swamiji, in His usual cheerful manner, said it was a good sign. Sri Hari had indeed arrived.

Everyone was curious about the day of the idol's pratishthapana (ceremonial placement). Just a glimpse of the idol would bring great peace and bliss. Swamiji had addressed the people gathered there, 'The Lord is ever merciful. He will be here, giving darshan for many yugas (ages) to come.'

Gurudev distributed sweets to everyone in celebration. Afterwards, He looked at me and said, 'Swamiji, this day is full of pleasant surprises. This road finally got made, the Lord's idol was the first one to travel on the road, and we had an auspicious shower too! What more can we ask for?' I was thrilled to see Gurudev smiling like a little child who is pleased with His handiwork.

And it was true indeed that the building of the road was a miracle. As much as anything else, the miracle was of bringing together the villagers, who put aside age-old feuds and grievances in working together for a shared vision. Moreover, that the road had been completed in such a short time, given the limited resources and the remoteness of our location, was astounding.

I was reminded of a verse from Bhagavadgita that Gurudev cited often:

īśvaraḥ sarva-bhūtānāṁ
hṛd-deśe 'rjuna tiṣṭhati
bhrāmayan sarva-bhūtāni
yantrārūḍhāni māyayā

It means that the Supreme Lord is situated in everyone's heart, directing the wanderings of all living entities, like a charioteer riding a chariot. Now, the Lord himself was residing in everyone's heart here. He was the inspiring force behind the road.

In the future, this place would be known as Muktikshetra Sri Badrika Ashram. The Lord himself had made the stage ready for his leela.

16 March 2014 was the date fixed for pratishthapana. The day when we would begin the Vedic rituals was 2 April 2014, though. The idol weighed about 850 kilograms, making it difficult to have both the pratishthapana and the ritual on the same day, so the process would be completed on 4 April 2014.

Under Swamiji's watchful eye, a few villagers, Swami Paramananda, Swami Raghavananda and I teamed up and set about moving the idol to its base inside the inner sanctum. At first, we could not even move the idol; it was far heavier than I could have imagined, and it wouldn't budge with just our muscle power. We used a rope and two big wooden logs as levers and slowly heaved the idol toward the sanctum. Ismita hovered around, offering us encouraging words as we puffed and panted, and Swamiji kept us all in good humour as we sweated and manoeuvred the idol. He even helped us as we strained at this literally burdensome task.

Ever one to see the humour in a situation, Swamiji asked us if the rope was two inches short. The handful gathered there started laughing as Swamiji explained that when Sri Krishna was a young boy, each time Ma Yashoda tried to tie him up for his naughtiness, the rope would fall two inches short. After teasing her a little, the Lord would finally let Ma Yashoda tie him. Similarly, I felt that Sri Hari had reduced the weight of the idol when he saw us trying so hard to move it. After that, it was just a matter of time and the idol was in its rightful place -- the place where Lord Narayana would stand and bless the universe.

All of us present there were filled with joy. Gurudev loudly intoned, '*bolo Sri Hari bhagwan ki jai, govinda govinda govinda, bolo Jaganmata ki jai, namah parvati pati har har mahadev.*'

(All glories to Sri Hari, Govinda, Govinda, Govinda, All glories to Mother Goddess, Humble obesiances to Mahadev, consort of the Goddess.)

Gurudev was helping us with the wooden logs. How lucky we all were to be with Him in such special moment.

We had hot prasadam prepared in the ashram's Annapoornagriha. Everyone's heart and mind was full.

The next day after I served Swamiji His breakfast, I was singing to myself the song written by Tulsidas, '*Raghuvar Tumko Meri Laaj*'. Swamiji said, 'Oh, I did not know that you knew this song. Please sing loudly, it's a beautiful song.' Swamiji liked it very much, and decided that we would both sing it during the pratishthapana ceremony. Swamiji's grasp of music is unearthly; He can catch the nuances of any song within a few seconds. Some days later, I had the good fortune to learn another Shiva song with Swamiji:

Gowranga ardhanga ganga tarange
Yogi maahiya kouroopa raaje||

The beautiful fair-coloured form of Shiva, the greatest yogi, consort of Ma, is accentuated with the wildly flowing ganga from his matted locks.

We would enjoy every moment of singing together. Gurudev would talk about the swara (notes of the scale) and lyrics, where to sing in a higher key, where to place a restand when to bring the song to a close. His knowledge of music was astounding, especially since He had never undertaken any formal training. Our conversations would be as enthusiastic as those of young boys. I had never seen such a life force pulsating in a human form like this before. He was my Guru, parent, guiding force. Truly, my life was graced just being with Him.

A few days later, a couple came to Swamiji. They had two small daughters. One of the daughters, a sweet-looking ten-year-old child, had a clot in her brain. Her right arm would move up and down like a spring, a movement she couldn't control. Only if two adults held her arm would it stop moving. The child's health was failing, deteriorating by the day, and at a rate where she would soon be reduced to a mere bag of bones. The couple had taken their child to Solan, Shimla and Chandigarh for consultations and tests. They came to Swamiji with the MRI scan report and showed it to Him.

They were uneducated people and had no clue how to read the report, nor could they properly comprehend the problem with their child. But they well understood, of course, the gravity of her situation. Both the mother and the father began crying, urging Swamiji to cure their daughter. Swamiji went through the report in detail. He was quiet for some time.

The girl's parents were beyond desperate. Her mother implored Swamiji to save her daughter. She was willing to do anyupavasa vrata (fasting penance) to heal her child. She begged Swamiji, alternately crying and speaking, her sentences punctuated by sobs. Swamiji asked her to be quiet for some time, but she was beyond reasoning with, and just went on wailing and pleading with Him. Swamiji pulled out a rudraksha, energized it with a mantra and mudra and gave it to her. It had to be used for the next three months, He told her.

The child, too, was present. She just stared at Swamiji with her big quiet eyes in her small and tired face -- she had no idea that Swamiji had just given her the gift of life. The same little girl comes to the ashram now, and she laughs, plays and jumps about like any other normal child. I still remember her face, though -- the resignation to her fate, and the complete openness to Swamiji's intercession that her young features evinced -- when she had not long to live.

One time, Gurudev was sitting outside with a few devotees. It was Saturday, so He said He would meet the villagers outside. A couple visited Him for the first time from a distant village.

'Please bless us with a son, Swamiji,' they pleaded. 'We have no child.'

'What do you mean you have no child?' Gurudev asked. 'You have daughters.'

They folded their hands immediately. 'Yes, Swamiji, by child we meant a son.'

'Why,' Gurudev persisted, 'is there a difference between a son and a daughter?'

The woman started crying and said there was immense pressure at home from the elders and other relatives. She had already given birth to seven daughters and all she wanted was a son. The man questioned who would look after his fields and carry on his bloodline if he didn't have a son.

Gurudev just chuckled and looked at me smilingly.

Suddenly, the couple fell at his feet and began wailing loudly. Gurudev had been in a light mood until now.

'Get up,' He commanded softly.

'Please, just bless us with a son, Swamiji,' they repeated.

'Do you still want a son, even if he'll trouble you?' He asked.

'Yes, Swamiji,' they replied without any hesitation. 'That's all we want. We have come to you with great hope.'

'So be it,' Gurudev said and looked each of them in the eye. He whispered on a small rudraksha bead.

Elated, they tried to offer Him money but of course, as always, Gurudev refused. For the first three years, there wasn't even a donation box at the ashram. Gurudev simply hosted the devotees Himself, paying the costs from His small monthly stipend.

Ten months after the couple's audience with Swamiji, the woman gave birth to a baby boy and the couple came, in due course, to thank Gurudev. They again brought fruits, flowers and offered money. Gurudev only kept one flower, refused the money, and returned the fruits.

'But we are really giving it out of happiness,' they said. 'Please accept it.'

'Distribute the fruits among the devotees outside,' Gurudev said. 'And use this money to help someone. I don't require it. I've kept one flower.'

The Storytellers

The ashram temple inauguration and pratishthapana ceremony preparations were in full swing. Devotees began arriving a week before the scheduled date of 4 April 2014, and the kathavachak (orrator) team that would recite the epic of Srimad Bhagavata Purana arrived from Benaras.

On 1 April at around 4 p.m., Swamiji was having a satsang with devotees on the wide terrace outside. He told a thought-provoking story of how a mumukshu, a monk, came to Buddha and asked him how long it would take for him to attain atma sakshatkara, (self-realization). Buddha replied, 'The huge mountain that you see in front of you is tall and wide, towering over the sky; by the time you finish cleaning it with a silk cloth, you will get sakshatkara.' This story exemplifies the seeming eternity and Herculean effort it takes to master the less evolved tendencies of the mind and completely purify oneself.

Gurudev then asked Swami Paramananda to call the kathavachak team's leader. He wanted to introduce him to the devotees. The leader told Swami Paramananda that they were doing arti, and he would come after they had finished. Some time passed, and Swamiji sent for him once more. Again he didn't come. Thrice Swami Paramananda went to call the leader, but he still did not come.

Gurudev finally sent a word asking if they were all right and if they had any problem. The team leader sent back a message saying they were not happy with their accommodation, and that they wanted better rooms for their stay. We had made arrangements for them to be lodged in the room where Gurudev normally took pravachan. A new cot, new sheets and new mattress had been laid out so they might be comfortable.

Swami Paramananda and I had overseen all the arrangements. We had to walk for kilometres simply to get a small item like a packet of salt, so one can imagine the logistical undertaking, the work and the resources required to cater for and accommodate 180 people at once; especially given the rudimentary infrastructure at the ashram. Each of the four newly built guest rooms was filled with eight–ten devotees, and some eighty devotees slept in the hall. In fact, there was no room left for Gurudev to give a private audience to devotees.

On hearing the team leader's disgruntled response, Gurudev did not think twice before giving up His room for them. He said that they were our guests, and respected Brahmins, and we had to take good care of them. Swamiji decided to meet the devotees in the kitchen or under a tree. It was very important that the Kathavachak team was comfortable, he said. But still, they were far from mollified and continued to bluntly express their dissatisfaction.

Gurudev, Swami Paramananda and I went to meet them. Swamiji asked them in a kind and concerned voice, 'Prabhu, Namaste. I sent for you because I wanted to introduce you to everyone. Please tell us how we can make you comfortable.'

Gurudev then quoted a verse from Bhagavadgita.

deva-dvija-guru-prājña-
pūjanaṁ śaucam ārjavam
brahmacaryam ahiṁsā ca
śārīraṁ tapa ucyate

'To offer puja to Gods, jnani, mahatma, guru and Brahmins and to follow simplicity, brahmacharya and ahimsa are considered to be penance related to the body,' said Swamiji and folded his hands. 'It is our duty to take care of you.'

The kathavachak did not rise to greet Gurudev or reciprocate. He stayed seated, obviously disgruntled. The team of pandits with him also seemed to think that Gurudev was just another baba in robes. None of them paid their respects. Still, Gurudev kept smiling. Then the kathavachak said that he had an elite team of Brahmins and they wanted some other accommodation. But there was no other accommodation. They had been given the best room — Gurudev's own room.

The kathavachak embarked on a short tirade, saying that he was in popular demand, that his team of pandits did the best pujas and that he had seen enough swamis and babas. All the swamis are just talkers, he said, while he was a true devotee of Krishna, singing his glories through the Bhagavad Purana.

Gurudev's expression turned serious. 'Talker, huh?'

He summoned two Brahmins from the team and asked them to put their fingers on His pulse. Swamiji took a deep breath and focused his drishti (point of attention) on the brahma randhra (crown point). His heartbeat began to slow, and after a couple of minutes, it stopped completely. Swamiji looked like Mahadev as He sat in dhyana mudra (one hand within the other). He was very much there in the body; but the vessel had stopped breathing; its heart was still – and the two Brahmins could discern no pulse. Never in their lives had they, or indeed I, witnessed a feat like this. Gurudev sat immovable as a rock, alive and radiant.

Immediately, both pandits pressed their palms together in utmost respect and fell at Swamiji's feet. After some moments, Gurudev brought himself back from His dhyana, and continued to astound the team. He went on to narrate incidents from the kathavachak's past as if he was seeing the incidents unfold before Him. To say that the kathavachak was shocked would be an understatement. He immediately rose from his seat like a man haunted by an apparition. The blood drained from his face, and with a bewildered expression on his ashen features, he struggled to come to terms with the power he was witnessing from Swamiji, whom he had, just minutes earlier, challenged in quite an uncouth manner.

'Among all the pandits here, only two have swara shuddhi (refined notes). But even their minds are polluted, including yours. You all are full of lust.'

I had never seen Gurudev speak like that, in such a forthright manner, to anyone. His voice wasn't loud or harsh, but the power and conviction behind His soft words was almost too much to bear.

He then chanted a few verses from Sri Rudram Chamakam (a hymn to Shiva) in His sweet voice to show them the correct pronunciation. The pundits were dazed by Gurudev's persona and the miracle He had just performed. All of them stood up, bowed down respectfully, stood again and assumed the namaskara posture. As Swamiji was walking out of the room, the leader too bowed down. He was most perturbed by the turn of events. He had disrespected the word of a saint he now believed to be a siddha. He had just witnessed a divine being walking in human form, unbound by the laws of nature.

The kathavachak team were gracious, at any rate, and behaved impeccably for the rest of their stay at the ashram. Every member of the team sought a private audience with Swamiji, too, and had his blessings.

Bhagwan

'This is going to be one of the holiest places, just like Puri and Badrinath. The ever merciful Lord will be giving darshan here for many yugas to come. Nature is joyous. Gods will shower their grace here with rain tonight.'

The day of the consecration ceremony was 4 April 2014. It was a sunny day, and yet just as Gurudev had said, it rained that night.

Swamiji gave His opening address at the temple hall, which was packed with devotees, sitting with rapt attention. They waited with as much awe as expectation. The majestic wooden doors to the garbhagriha had been closed for three days and two nights, and behind them the vigraha (idol) stood blindfolded by a red cloth of the finest silk. Before the blindfold could be removed, the rite of Prana pratishtha, where Swamiji would infuse the deity with life, had to be performed. It is only after this rite that worship may be offered to the vigraha in any Hindu temple, so it is thus a routine Vedic ceremony. But there was nothing routine about this day or the manner in which the Divine was brought to dwell in stone.

Everyone was curious about the Lord's appearance; and everyone was captivated, for a mere glimpse of Him held the promise of great blessings. All attention fell upon the doors guarding the idol that would soon be thrown open. The kathavachak team of eleven pandits (ritwiks) recited the Bhagavata Purana. The chant of these holy verses imbued the pristine temple walls with the Divine's name. Like a new bride, the temple was adorned with flowers and garlands of marigolds, sunflowers and roses. A solemn, sacred energy pervaded the ashram like the soothing coolness in the moments after a sudden rain shower.

In the past, I had witnessed countless miracles in Gurudev's presence, but this day was unlike any other. Behind closed doors, the mystical was coming to life from stone and flesh. One was the dark vigraha, sculpted of black granite -- silent, watchful, still -- the Lord immanent awaiting. And the other: the living, moving, breathing one performing the dashamaha mudra (ten great mudras) with swift, graceful movements of His fingers. This is a set of special mudras performed by the practitioners of Sri Vidya to invoke the Para Shakti, the supreme Goddess. Its significance is such that it can scarce be explained in a book. A myriad things defy explanation with Gurudev, anyway.

The garbhagriha was alive with Swamiji's radiance. Just as the ascending sun dazzles, His tejas were now shining such that the idol and its worshipper seemed one. It was as if Swamiji was eulogizing Himself. His voice, like thunderclaps that tear apart the sky, began to bring the vigraha to life.

May Sri Hari give me the words to recall the glory of that celebrated day.

Govinda! Govinda! Govinda!

Swamiji's invocation rang out to the valley as He flung open the doors to the garbhagriha. The Divine was set to meet the world. A sea of eyes moved past us Swamis for a glimpse of their Lord. Hundreds of devotees moved forward, their hands pressed together in namaskara. Some tiptoed and peered over those in front of them to get a closer look, while others nudged even closer to pay their respects.

The festivity, the elation, the wonderment in the air was reminiscent of ancient accounts of Lord Rama's welcome to Ayodhya after His years in the forest. Emotion reigned at the Lord's arrival, deep affection and gratitude thick within the holy air. Faces softened by prayer, tears and love proceeded, one by one, to offer their obeisance, jala (water), and flowers at the Lord's feet. It was a divine moment, adbhut (magnificent) – one never to be seen again.

Some felt that the dark vigraha was smiling with benevolence; some saw a tear-stained cheek of the ever compassionate Lord. Others saw their love mirrored in His eyes. But those like me who sought Swamiji before Narayana, and now saw the Lord with Him, also saw that one comprised the other. Tantra says that the one who realizes God becomes one with the supreme soul. He becomes God.

What I saw that day reaffirmed my belief and the belief of many, for Swamiji had only just begun. After everyone had offered abhishekam to the Lord – villagers, devotees from the city, children, women and men – Swamiji and I once again entered the garbhagriha. Quietly and swiftly I shut out the outside world, as Swamiji settled down in dhyana and chanted the ancient, mysterious Vishnu Sahasranama. This was not the ordinary Vishnu Sahasranama found in handbooks and booklets but the secretive, tantric chant given by Lord Shiva to Ma

Parvati. I didn't recognize the verses, despite having recited the Sahasranama since I was twelve, when I first learnt it at the Sri Ramakrishna Ashram in Bangalore.

Gurudev had explained that in the standard Vishnu Sahasranama, some of the names of the Lord are repeated. What He would chant today was a special sahasranama. The Lord's name is not repeated even once in the thousand names by which He is called upon in this original chant. It remains all but unknown to the world. Swamiji had firmly stated that this was to be the first and the last time He was going to recite the original Vishnu Sahasranama in the temple. Any kind of recording of this was forbidden, its energy being too sacred for one to hear merely for leisure.

Swamiji's powerful, hypnotic voice issued forth, filling the temple hall and reverberating out to the stoic mountains, lush valley, flowing river Giri and vast blue sky. The verdant environs of the ashram that looked virginal green were yellowed and barren not two years earlier. Gurudev had foretold they would spring to life. They were now not only green with foliage and grass, but vibrant with heavenly benedictions of the Lord's coming.

Later, many devotees would ask me if there was a woman singing in the garbhagriha. I was at first amused by the question. But when many swore that they had heard two voices -- a male and a female, alternating with the verses -- I realized that being too close to Gurudev at that time, I may have overlooked some blessed phenomenon. They told me that one line was in a female voice and the next one was in a male voice. I wasn't exactly surprised, because anything was possible with Him.

Hands pressed together in reverence, I listened to the Sanskrit verses, my heart overflowing with love for my Gurudev.

He was in the bhava (character) of Jaganmata, the Adya Shakti, worshipping Her consort. The chants came to an end, and with it my trance-like state; but my entire body still tingled with the ancient power that had befallen my ears.

Soon I handed a flawless mirror to Swamiji. He held it up to the vigraha, the effulgent Lord. The mirror could not contain His glorious reflection. With a loud, piercing sound, the mirror shattered into pieces. It had cracked instantaneously, just as the first light of the sun extinguishes the inky darkness of dawn. The mirror, like the world, was incapable of containing God's immense power.

I had only heard about the mirror being shown to the vigraha at the time of Prana pratishtha, but I never expected that it would actually crack. It was not so much a question of doubting Gurudev, who had foretold the cracking of the mirror, as much as it was simply inexplicable to me. I was just as intrigued as everyone else at this occurrence.

We showed the shards of the mirror to the devotees, so they could see their reflection in the very mirror that had beheld their Lord not moments earlier. The pieces were later immersed in the river. Devotees closer to the garbhagriha caught glimpses of Swamiji clad in a black robe as I opened the doors to step out. Fresh whispers and murmurs abounded, as everyone had seen Swamiji enter the sanctum sanctorum in an ochre robe. His robe had changed colour, they whispered in amazement. It was a day full of surprises. And the best was yet to be experienced.

As we went about showing the mirror's shattered pieces to the hundreds assembled, Gurudev was inside the garbhagriha, alone with the vigraha. Once again the door was closed. Finally the sacred hour was upon us, a time that would mark the beginning of the well-being of mankind for thousands of years to come. Swamiji would now transfer his jagrata vidyas (awakened knowledge) to the idol. I didn't know what was transpiring in the garbhagriha at that time, except that soft whispers in various pitches and tones -- male, female and unearthly voices -- were heard by everyone who was close by.

The idol, He had promised, would be the guardian of His many tantric vidyas, His graces, and would bestow them upon the rightful seekers when the time came. The living Gurudev's potent energy suffused the hall as He summoned His latent powers. The first row of devotees later insisted that they sensed Gurudev's moving about with swift, fluent motions inside the garbhagriha. They could see the shadow movement of His feet, too, from under the tall sheesham (Indian Rosewood) doors, as He moved about like Lord Shiva performing the eternal cosmic dance.

Occult syllables permeated the air, their primitive utterings inspiring awe and fear. He seemed to be moving about in graceful circular movements, all about the garbhagriha. As the minutes passed, the shadows of His feet still shifted under the doors, and then a most peculiar sound tore through the festive ambience. It was a celestial battle cry: a hair-raising, fear-invoking ululation. The scriptures tell of Ma Kali issuing such a sound as she enters the battlefield to slay the demons. It was the most unearthly sound I had ever heard.

Only, I had heard it before. It was nearly two years earlier when I had been in Swamiji's service for only a couple of months. I had come to love my Gurudev dearly, but a part of me was also afraid of the things I didn't understand about Him. Despite His youthful appearance and joyful disposition, I could plainly see He was no ordinary monk.

It was a nightly ritual in the small mud cottage for me to cover Him with a blanket, do my pranams, switch off the light and gently close the door. That night, I was about to shut the door and leave, when he called out, 'Swamiji, sing a bhajan before you leave, please'.

I sang *'Sarda Rupa Tali'*, a Kannada bhajan to the Divine Mother. I opened my eyes a few minutes later to find Gurudev deep in samadhi. It was not unusual for Gurudev to become oblivious to the world and slip into samadhi at hearing the glories of Mother Divine; and it was especially common in those times, for it was only a few months since He had received the darshan of Her divine form. Gurudev's face was ever more radiant, and quietude surrounded Him. The smiling, compassionate face now wore a serenity that was not of this world; a stillness and strength, a power that I am in no way fit for or capable of expressing.

I slipped out quietly and went to the other room. In the middle of the night, I woke to the sound of a mellifluous voice. Gurudev was speaking to someone in the most loving manner. The inflection in His tone told me that He was not only familiar with His companion; He obviously held whomever He was addressing in the highest regard.

To whom is He speaking? I wondered, for there were pauses between His words, as if He was listening to responses. There was no one in the cottage except us; in fact, there was no one else in the whole ashram. At least, the cottage was the ashram back then. A few minutes went by, and He began chanting a stotram (hymn addressed to a divinity). At first, I couldn't tell what he was chanting, but soon it became clear that He was singing the Mahishasura Mardini Stotram — a devotional verse addressed to the Goddess Durga, where Ma is depicted with eighteen arms, riding on a lion or tiger, carrying weapons and assuming symbolic mudras as she slays the Demon Mahishasura.

Was Swamiji conversing with Jaganmata?

Even after the stotram finished, the conversation went on for a good twenty minutes. I couldn't really hear what was being said, but I knew without doubt that there was more than one person in Swamiji's room. Suddenly I heard a loud, blood-curdling cry, the kind that sends goose bumps up your arms. The sound was in Gurudev's voice. It penetrated the mud wall that separated us and brought a chill to my soul.

I felt terrified, for I had heard that it was Ma Kali who uttered such a sound. And then immediately all sound ceased; pin-drop silence with the quiet eeriness of the night descended upon us. Even the ever-cheerful river Giri seemed to fall silent that night. If my mind had no answers, it had no questions either.

I watched the door carefully, hoping I might catch a glimpse of the Divine Mother, but other than a heady fragrance and a sudden flash of light, I noticed nothing.

What is surprising about this is that in the way of toiletries, all Gurudev had was one soap. We even shared the same washroom, which was no more than a small box of mud walls. Yet Gurudev would emit a fragrance that was not of this world. This sweet, heady fragrance seemed to follow Him at all times.

The following morning, I somewhat hesitantly asked Swamiji about the previous night. He smiled enigmatically, and said, 'Divine grace.'

Today, at the consecration, the cry was no different from that night – once again, Ma was here in our midst. Replete with Swamiji's divine power, the vigraha shone anew, the dark stone now gleaming as if bathed in mystery. The mystical Lord's grace flowed in four directions.

Gurudev flung open the garbhagriha doors, intoning loudly,
'Bolo Sri Hari bhagwan ki jai!
Govinda! Govinda! Govinda!
Bolo Jaganmata ki jai!
Namaha Parvathi – Pataye Hara Mahadev.'

The devotees joined in with a resounding 'jai', the physical vibrations of their affirmation as palpable as the spiritual. The joy, the celebration they gave voice to was uplifting and heart-warming in equal measure. It was as if the Divine had chosen us to partake of this holy moment, the beginning of a resurgence of our Sanatana Dharma (Hinduism).

To say I felt blessed being a part this holy day, to be standing beside my Gurudev, would barely do justice to my feelings. I felt as if I was born just to serve my Gurudev, the charismatic soul who only spoke the truth and was now ushering in an era of spirituality.

I looked around and saw devotees awash with waves of ecstasy. Did they even know who was among them? I won't say that I did entirely. But I felt like falling at Gurudev's feet, because what I was seeing now in and around Him was only a fraction of what he had shown me in the preceding year.

But the question remained: who was Gurudev, really? This had perplexed me throughout my time with Him. I had only to become accustomed to one aspect of His being, when another would be revealed to me.

One morning, I had gone to Gurudev with his breakfast. I was doing a Devi sadhana He had taught me. When I had entered His hut that morning, something was quite unusual about Gurudev. His soft face was especially radiant, and the room seemed to shine with His presence. Spontaneously, I knelt and clasped his feet.

'Who are you, Gurudev? Please tell me.'

He laughed and said, 'I'm a simple sadhu in a complex world.'

Tears formed in the corners of my eyes, and I persisted in earnest, 'No, Gurudev, please tell me: who are you?'

Gurudev's expression became reflective. 'Telling won't accomplish anything, Swamiji,' He replied solemnly. 'Why not see it for yourself?'

'When will I see it, Gurudev?'

'Why?' He asked, 'the energy experience the other day wasn't enough?'

I lowered my head. It was true. The day I had touched Him and felt a massive surge of energy pass through my body had given me a glimpse of Him; but greedy as I was, I still wished for more. I was no longer doing any sadhana for a vision of any deity. I was merely doing it because I wanted to see more of my Gurudev.

'It'll happen when Devi wants,' He said.

I raised my head to look into His gracious countenance, and He was smiling. When you spend time with Gurudev, you begin to see that His smile often tells more than His words. I felt butterflies within me -- those of a happy kind -- because He had a playful smile on His face. I served him breakfast and went back to my hut. That night, the same night when I sat down for my sadhana, a strange thing happened.

In the middle of the night, as I focused on my japa, I felt a lotus in my heart unfurl. I kept my eyes closed to behold the most exquisite vision. Red light radiated from that lotus, and in it was seated the Goddess Mother. What a magnificent form it was! But to my dismay, I could only see half of Her form. I had beheld this for just a little while when it began to expand: the other half was emerging. Not Shiva, not Vishnu, but Gurudev was standing in the other half. I was startled at first, and then I kept staring at Gurudev and Devi, together in one form. I opened my eyes to prostrate myself before Gurudev, but the form disappeared.

I somehow finished my japa after one hour, but I couldn't sleep for another two. It was as if my whole being had been electrified, and my body, my emotion and my spirit -- my very being -- was charged with a divine current. I was ecstatic. I felt a consuming urge to run out of my hut and call out Gurudev's name with all my strength; but I held it back for fear of waking Him. I finally settled myself and went to bed in the early hours of the morning, and woke up another couple of hours later to make breakfast for Gurudev -- tomato soup. That's what Gurudev has in the morning -- tomato soup blended with a bit of paneer, a pinch of salt and a dash of black pepper. No ghee, no masala -- nothing else.

Eagerly, I reached His hut with His breakfast. He was working on his laptop, so I asked him to have his soup before He continued. He offered it to Mother Divine and had a sip. Normally, He would say that the soup was very nice. Today, He just said, 'So, Swamiji. Happy now?'

'Ji, Gurudev?' I asked.

'Happy, now that you have seen a bit more?'

Today, I couldn't hold back my tears. And they were tears of joy. 'Thank you, Gurudev,' I said. 'Please always keep me in your service.'

My vision of Him right in the middle of my sadhana had been a transformational moment for me. As Gurudev says, once you become butter from milk and then ghee from butter, there is no going back to milk or butter. My faith in Him went through that irreversible transformation.

'Gurudev,' I said, 'I no longer wish to see any Devi or pray to any God. I've found you.'

Gurudev smiled and said, 'And yet, you must discover yourself.'

'You are my discovery, Gurudev.'

'Nice soup, Swamiji.' He said in response. Smiling. Playfully.

———

Namastē namastē vibhō viśvamūrtē
namastē namastē cidānandamūrtē.
Namastē namastē tapōyōgagamya
namastē namastē śrutijñānagamya

Salutations and prostrations to the supreme scholar,
the chief of all,
Obeisance to the One who is an embodiment of
existence and bliss,
All glories to the One knowable through penance and yoga,
All glories to the One unknowable through the inner knowledge
of the Vedas. Forgive me for my mistakes in rendering His glories.

Acknowledgements

It is with a deep sense of tranquillity and peace that I sit down to express my gratitude to all the wonderful people who have helped shape my voice.

I sincerely thank the lovely Ajitha Ganeshan, Commissioning Editor, HarperCollins *Publishers* India, with all my heart for placing her faith in me yet again. A big thank you to Carl Hart, for his invaluable suggestions while editing the book. Thank you, Rea Mukherjee, for flawlessly carrying out the task of getting the book to print from start to finish.

This thank you note would not be complete without mentioning, Sameer Mahale, Sales Head, at HarperCollins. Sameer's drive to make all of Swami's books a success is truly remarkable. A special thanks to Bonita Shimray for the wonderful cover design.

I would also like to thank Prasad Parsuraman, a wonderful soul and an ardent devotee of Swami, who helped us translate Swami Vidyananda ji's original writing from Kannada to English.

Closer to home I am very grateful to Navjot Gautam for being a good friend and confidant, for always inspiring me with her utter devotion to Swami. To Swami Vidyananda, for the care and protection he bestows on me in his childlike ways.

My deepest gratitude to Mani and Manik for helping me settle in a new city, in my new home, every step of the way. It just wouldn't be possible without the brother-sister duo. They were a godsend.

I thank Gunjan Sharma for being friends with me for over a decade now. A beautiful person, she is full of love, care and laughter.

I fondly thank Dr Renu Madan, an extremely warm-hearted person, always prompt to give me a hug at the most opportune moment. My deepest gratitude to Ma Shamta, for the extraordinary drive and zeal with which she runs our little ashram splendidly, caring little for her own health or welfare. She is a rare gem in a bed of pebbles.

To Benoo, my heart, my black lab, the apple of my eye. It is her unconditional love that has seen me through some of the darkest nights of my life. I thank my awesomely talented brother, Om Tandon, and his darling and equally gifted wife, Pavitra, for their love and support in my every endeavour.

To Deepa, Bhupendra and the children, their arrival in my life is nothing short of a miracle. My heart fills with immense gratitude at the mere thought of Mata Rani and Didi, their love and care is beyond compare.

Finally, to Swami, thank you for watching over me, for standing by me. For being the epitome of truthfulness, love and humility. Above all, for absolutely everything.